The Fuzzy Logic of Encc
New Perspectives on Cultura

GW01402605

Cultural Encounters and the Discourses of Scholarship

Edited by
Gesa Mackenthun

Volume 1

This series seeks to stimulate fresh and critical perspectives on the interpretation of phenomena of cultural contact in both transhistorical and transdisciplinary ways. It brings together the research results of the graduate school „Cultural Encounters and the Discourses of Scholarship," located at Rostock University and sponsored by the German Research Foundation (DFG). One of the concerns of the volumes published in this series is to test and explore contemporary theoretical concepts and analytical tools used for the study of intercultural relations, from antiquity to the present. Aware of significant recent changes in the ways in which other cultures are represented, and „culture" as such is defined and described, the series seeks to promote a dialogical over a monological theoretical paradigm and advocates approaches to the study of cultural alterity that are conscious of the representational character of our knowledge about other cultures. It wants to strengthen a recognition of the interdependencies between the production of knowledge about unfamiliar peoples and societies in various scholarly disciplines and ideologies of nationality, empire, and globalization. In critically investigating the analytical potential of postcolonial key terms such as „hybridity," „contact zone," and „transculturation," the series contributes to international scholarly debates in various fields oriented at finding more balanced and reciprocal ways of studying and writing about intercultural relations both past and present.

Forthcoming volumes:
Bonded Labor in the Cultural Contact Zone. Slavery and Its Discourses from Antiquity to the Present (2009)
Embodiments of Cultural Contact (2010)

Sünne Juterczenka
Gesa Mackenthun (eds.)

The Fuzzy Logic of Encounter

New Perspectives on Cultural Contact

Waxmann 2009
Münster / New York / München / Berlin

Bibliographic information published by the Deutsche Nationalbibliothek
The Deutsche Nationalbibliothek lists this publication in
the Deutsche Nationalbibliografie; detailed bibliographic data
are available in the Internet at http://dnb.d-nb.de

The publication of this volume was sponsored
by the German Research Foundation
(Deutsche Forschungsgemeinschaft).

Cultural Encounters and the
Discourses of Scholarship, volume 1

ISSN 1868-1395
ISBN 978-3-8309-2124-0

© Waxmann Verlag GmbH, 2009
Postfach 8603, 48046 Münster

www.waxmann.com
info@waxmann.com

Copy-edited: Paula Ross, WordsByDesign
Cover design: Pleßmann Kommunikationsdesign, Ascheberg
Cover image: Jan Vermeer, *The Geographer* (1668)
Städelsches Kunstinstitut, Frankfurt a.M.
Typesetting: Stoddart Satz- und Layoutservice, Münster
Print: Hubert & Co., Göttingen

Printed on age-resistant paper,
acid-free as per ISO 9706

Contents

Introduction

GESA MACKENTHUN, SÜNNE JUTERCZENKA

This volume seeks to add a new dimension to the study of cultural encounters – one of the best studied topics within the humanities in recent years.[1] While phenomena of cultural contact and conflict rate high on the agenda of scholarship conducted in the light of postcolonial studies, new historicism, cultural materialism, historical anthropology, and other approaches influenced by the postcolonial turn in the humanities, the reflection about the implicit vantage points from which the meeting of different cultures is analyzed often remains underresearched.

The Fuzzy Logic of Encounter is an attempt to move that reflection on the imbrications of cultural contact and the discourses of scholarship to the foreground. The group of scholars brought together here seems to be particularly well equipped for such a project, having been trained within seven different disciplines: literature, archaeology, history, religious studies, anthropology, musicology, and linguistics. Each of these disciplines has developed its own terminology and concepts for the analysis of cultural alterity, and although today's discussions are dominated by the critical languages developed within anthropology – especially since the linguistic turn caught hold of that discipline (see Clifford/Marcus) – and postcolonial literary studies, many areas of terminological ambivalence and potential misunderstanding remain. The purpose of this volume is to offer a platform for bringing these different critical registers into contact with each other and to encourage interdisciplinary dialogues about the ways in which scholars talk about intercultural relations.

The Geographer and the Warrior

The intention and program of this book are well illustrated by the title image – a montage of Johan Vermeer's famous painting *The Geographer* (1668) and a much less known drawing of a native of the Marquesas Islands produced by the American navy captain David Porter in 1813. Vermeer's *Geographer* and its companion piece, a painting called *The Astronomer* (of the same year, and featuring the same human model and location), have frequently been used as pictorial articulations of

---

1   The essays collected here are extended versions of papers given at the two-day symposium "Cultural Encounters and the Discourses of Scholarship," organized by the graduate school of the same name at Rostock University in November, 2007.

the Western idea of scientific exploration, most recently in a book on early modern British cartography by Bernhard Klein and an essay collection on the emergence of the modern 'community of knowledge' (*Wissensgesellschaft*) edited by Richard van Dülmen and Sina Rauschenbach. Our choice of *The Geographer* was informed by the idea that, unlike many other early modern representations of scientists, Vermeer's painting contains an ambivalence which we accept as a ground for critical intervention by adding the Polynesian warrior, who seems to grow out of the geographer's map and faces him defensively and defiantly.

We agree with Bernhard Klein in regarding *The Geographer* as a metaphor for the mutual interferences of scientific work, territorial expansion, and its aestheticization in the early modern period (Klein 1-5). Klein emphasizes the opposition between the enclosed space of the study, readily furnished with the paraphernalia of the man's occupation (a globe, a map of the Mediterranean on the wall, another map in front of him, and the compasses in his hand), and the space outside the window, which remains as mysterious to the viewer as the contents of the map under construction. What distinguishes this painting from others with a similar theme is the thoughtful gaze of the geographer, which seems to be oriented to a point between window and map, as well as the gesture of the hand holding the compasses. Taken together, these body positions may indicate a moment of repose and reflection, maybe of a passing recognition that the representation on the map – due to its subjection to the discourses of geometry and mathematics – excludes the plenitude of life that the geographer can observe through the window: the reality of people meeting and talking in the street, perhaps swapping goods in the market square. The image suggests that the geographer sees more than we see but by excluding the objects of his gaze it alerts us to the very selectivity of representation, whether aesthetic or scientific. It also confronts us with the problematic fact that Western scientific discourse traditionally gives priority to the observing subject, "which places its own point of view at the origin of all historicity," and not to an analysis of what Foucault called "discursive practices" (xiv).

There is hardly a profession as involved with the project of European expansion as that of the geographer, whose precisely drawn maps of foreign lands allow explorers, missionaries, and traders to reach their destinations. However, they do not prepare the citizens of Europe for the multiple forms of cultural contact awaiting them on foreign shores. One such encounter is represented by the figure that we projected onto the map that is illegible to the viewer. Porter's drawing shows Mouina, the chief warrior of the tribe of the Tayehs, who acted as Porter's allies in his violent attack against the Typees. The naval officer had been stationed in the Caribbean with orders to fight British warships in the War of 1812, but he had left his position, sailed round Cape Horn, and subsequently went exploring in the Pacific. Mouina, together with the other indigenous allies, witnessed Porter's official ceremony of taking possession of Nukuhiva, the main island of the Marquesas, in the name of the United States of America. He may have been puzzled by this strange rite but he was also eager to join the strangers with their impressive weaponry in their march against his enemies, the Typees. The latter were less impressed than Mouina by American guns; according to Porter, whose knowledge relied on the faithfulness of his British translator, they responded to American threats by saying:

> that as to myself and my people, we were white lizards, mere dirt; and as the most contemptible epithet which they could apply, said we were the posteriors of the privates of the Taeehs. We were, said they, incapable of standing fatigue, overcome by the slightest heat and want of water, and could not climb the mountains without Indians to assist us and carry our arms; and yet we talked of chastising the Typees, a tribe which had never been driven by an enemy [...]. (Porter 364)

Mouina assisted Porter in 'pacifying' the Typees by burning and pilfering their villages.

We may read the geographer's 'empty' window, map, and gaze as a sign of the artist's secret recognition of the silences of the Western logic of representation. The native warrior, by inhabiting that 'empty' space, may be said, following Homi Bhabha's famous dictum, to turn the ambivalence of the colonial site of enunciation into the grounds of intervention (Bhabha 97). Yet, Mouina should not be seen as a mere victim or antagonist of European aggression. Rather, this little story is a typical example of the mutual attempt to use a new situation to one's own advantage. Successive events, however, proved the futility of Mouina's hopes of turning the strangers into useful instruments of his own strategy: during the genocidal conflicts that followed, no distinction was made between former ally and former foe.[2]

The virtual encounter between Mouina and Vermeer's geographer symbolizes our understanding of cultural encounter as a mutual affair, as a by-product of an expanding world that has set into motion a series of complex processes of interaction. The image also suggests the centrality of acts of writing, performance, and representation in the history of cultural encounters. The *tabula rasa* of the geographer's map-in-progress is effectively contrasted by the native warrior's body, which is totally covered with tattoos. As Porter informs us, every line had its meaning, and no two people had the same tattoos. In other words, Mouina's body is a medium for a very individual set of inscriptions, and in this forms a counterpart to the geographer's map, whose inscriptions, though illegible to us, imply the claim to absolute objectivity. However, because the indigenous tradition of tattooing and reading tattoos has been interrupted by many decades of colonial domination, Mouina's body-writing is today as unintelligible as the geographer's map.

We owe our knowledge of Mouina less to Porter's imperialist ambitions than to his concurrent desire to present himself as a competent scholar of other cultures. His narrative is both a war report and a protoethnographic description of

---

2   The best account of the history of the Marquesas is the late Greg Dening's *Islands and Beaches.*

the customs of the Marquesans. These two discourses collide at times in Porter's text by producing strange paradoxes and ruptures – for example when he admires the high civilizational standard and regularity of the Typees' settlements and buildings but declares the historical inevitability of setting fire to their villages in the same paragraph (an idea later dubbed "manifest destiny") (Porter 400). Acting out the imperial project on South Pacific beaches rather than drawing precise lines in domestic discretion (as Vermeer's geographer), Porter is faced with the practical contradictions that the geographer may or may not divine in his moment of reflection – that the situation of contact never follows a preconceived script but is always unpredictable and messy.

The essays in this volume endeavor to locate themselves, in different ways, in the epistemological void or ambiguity symbolized by Vermeer's painting. Conceived within the theoretical and conceptual frameworks of a variety of disciplines, they are united by their attempts to explore the intersections between cultural encounters or cultural diversity and the emergence and circulation of scientific discourses. These intersections take various forms. First, Western scientific progress is unthinkable without the process of European expansion and the contact between European explorers, missionaries, traders, and soldiers with representatives of non-European cultures. No matter where we look – at the development of the Linnean botanical classification system, at zoology, at new discoveries in medicine, at theories of society and natural history – European scientific development has been crucially influenced by different forms of local knowledge from diverse places around the world.

Secondly, the perception and representation of other cultures are themselves informed by specific 'knowledges' about them. These knowledges rarely stand the test of reality; from antiquity up until today, images and assumptions about one culture were frequently transferred to another in European discourses about its 'others.' The 'scientific' discourses since the late eighteenth century, conversely, emphasized the differences between the 'races' of man and invented various hierarchical systems of classification in order for the West to reassure itself about its own cultural superiority. The study of cultural encounters has to take these facts into account.

Thirdly, as a consequence of these mutual impacts, and especially in light of the 'multiculturization' that has occurred in the sciences in recent decades, we can observe an increasing complexity of cultural interaction and in the discourses of scholarship: no longer is knowledge the exclusive domain of the former colonial metropolises, and the field of cultural discourse is now a highly contested realm. Former scientific classifications have become virtually defunct, and even those disciplines less concerned than anthropology or ethnology with exploring the idiosyncrasies of cultures have come to develop more heterogeneous forms of knowledge due to the global exchange of local practices, skills, and traditions (as can be observed, for example, in medical and environmental studies). The mathematical precision with which Vermeer's geographer was still able to represent the world is now frequently challenged by other concepts of truth, rationality, and order. To conceive of cultural contact as a two-way process – to leave behind an earlier dualistic paradigm of 'victors' and 'victims,' or of 'strong' and 'weak,' 'hot' and 'cold,' 'mobile' and 'static' cultures – is one of the most important achievements of recent theoretical discourse. In her analyses of European imperial travelogues, Mary Pratt spells out this notion of mutuality and reciprocity in the interaction between cultures. In adapting Fernando Ortiz's concept of transculturation, she expresses this idea in the now widely used term "contact zone/s," which she describes as "social spaces where disparate cultures meet, clash, and grapple with each other, often in highly asymmetrical relations of domination and subordination – like colonialism, slavery, or their aftermaths as they are lived out across the globe today" (Pratt 4). The essays collected here strongly confirm the necessity of a dialogic, and sometimes polyphonic, concept of cultural interaction.

The Professor and his Theory

It may still take a hard-core postmodernist to acknowledge the fact that science itself has become 'fuzzy,' not least as a result of its internationalization. Yet as early as 1964, Professor Lotfi Asker Zadeh, of the Department of Electrical Engineering at the University of California in Berkeley, formulated a new variation of mathematical set theory, which he decided to call "Fuzzy Sets" (Zadeh, "Fuzzy Sets").[3] The subsequently developed "Fuzzy Logic" made a significant impact on mathematics, computer technology, linguistics and, most notably, electrical engineering. Today, it is widespread in the construction of domestic appliances (such as washing mashines, air conditioners, heaters, and stoves), in transportation (trains, cars, and elevators), in entertainment electronics (cameras, mobile phones, video games, and radios), and in some advanced medical systems (Seising chapter 7).

It may at first seem surprising to encounter a mathematical term in the title of a volume on cross-cultural theory and its applicability to empirical research. Less surprisingly, the technical applicability of Zadeh's theory did not immediately appeal to engineers and consumers in the anglophone world: the designation comes across awkwardly. The term "fuzzy sets" initially coined by Zadeh even appeared to be a paradox: "fuzziness" is generally associated with confusion, irregularity, or incertitude, while mathematical sets only exist by virtue of the clearly defined attributes of their elements. Indeed, the term "fuzzy" is often used pejoratively, and Fuzzy Logic has been criticized as "unscientific" (Seising 227-8). Its relation to probability theory and its potential for handling larger problems are in fact still a controversial topic among mathematicians. Japanese engineers, however, had no such qualms and picked up the concept, so that by the end of the 1980s, "faaji"

---

3   Zadeh was not the first to devote himself to the phenomenon of imprecision. See below, as well as Seising 225-6.

had become a fashionable term and a symbol of intelligent technology in Japan. From there, it spread to other countries in Asia, and finally in the 1990s, to Europe and the USA (Zadeh in Ladan 70; Drösser 151-4).

Some have argued that the more immediate success of Zadeh's theory in the East was only possible because Asian thinking (and the mysticism of Buddha and Laotse in particular) is more ready to accept vagueness and imprecision, and that Fuzzy Logic may even constitute a clash between Eastern and Western belief systems on a technical level (Bart Kosko qtd. in Drösser 149-50). It seems doubtful that the astonishing career of Fuzzy Logic can be reduced to such essentialist categories. Rather, it obviously incorporates important elements of Western thinking: its basis, conventional set theory, was invented by the German mathematician Georg Cantor in 1874-97 (Drösser 150).[4] Others have speculated that Japanese engineers simply behaved according to the Western stereotype by appropriating Western technological innovation and subsequently developing marketable products based on it (Drösser 151). The 'missed opportunity' is openly regretted by some Americans: "[Fuzzy Logic] was one more technology the United States created and neglected, only to watch the Japanese pick up, nurture into profitability, and sell back to us" (McNeill and Freiberger 10). Irrespective of whether "the United States" really "created" technology based on Fuzzy Logic (or indeed, Fuzzy Logic itself), and leaving aside the implicit jibe against the (supposedly economically clever but intellectually dependent) Japanese engineers, the one thing that can safely be said is that the current widespread use and popularity of the concept, as well as its name, are both products of repeated cultural transfer between East and West.

Indeed, Lotfi Asker Zadeh himself is a product of cultural contact: born to a Russian mother and an Iranian father in Baku in Azerbaijan in 1921, he had to emigrate to Persia in 1931 with his family when Stalin's regime began to enforce a rigid migration policy. Zadeh grew up in Tehran during the reign of Reza Shah Pahlavi, studying at Tehran University, which at the time was deeply influenced by French culture. In 1944 – the year after the Tehran Conference (28 November and 1 December 1943) at which Stalin, Roosevelt, and Churchill planned their war strategy against Germany and also negotiated Iran's independence – Zadeh realized that he "could not do scientific work" in Iran, where only "becoming rich was possible," which he "did not want" (Zadeh in Ladan 71). He decided to emigrate again, this time to the USA, where he graduated in engineering from MIT and received his PhD from Columbia University. Zadeh married an American woman and until his formal retirement in 1991 taught and conducted his research at two American universities (first at Columbia, then at the University of California at Berkeley). Fuzzy Logic firmly established his academic renown, which brought with it numerous honors: honorary doctorates from universities as well as a host of medals and awards from research organizations and companies

---

4   This assessment is based on Drösser's discussion of the question.

in Asia, Europe, and eventually the USA. Quite clearly, Zadeh's celebrity status is a result of the globalization of the academic community and of global intellectual mobility.

During his lifetime, Zadeh has experienced a bewildering number of cultures (along with four languages and three different scripts) as well as ideological and religious creeds (Soviet atheism, Presbyterianism, Protestantism, Islam). When once asked in what way the exposure to so many different influences affected his life and work, Zadeh answered that "the question really isn't whether I'm American, Russian, Iranian, Azerbaijani, or anything else [...], I've been shaped by all these people and cultures and I feel quite comfortable among all of them" (Zadeh in Blair 49).

Zadeh's mathematical theory is based on a seeming paradox: it allows for calculations with variables that cannot be expressed in exact numbers – and it nonetheless produces exact results. The starting point for most explanations of Fuzzy Logic is that the classical tradition of logic (as founded by Aristotle during the fourth century BC and developed further by Descartes during the seventeenth century) relies on absolute terms ("exact reasoning"), which in some respects jars with human perception, thinking, and interaction – in other words, with real life:

> Clearly, the 'class of all real numbers which are much greater than 1,' or 'the class of beautiful women,' or 'the class of tall men,' do not constitute classes or sets in the usual mathematical sense of these terms. Yet, the fact remains that such imprecisely defined 'classes' play an important role in human thinking, particularly in the domains of pattern recognition, communication of information, and abstraction. (Zadeh, "Fuzzy Sets" 338)

To solve this problem of "imprecisely defined" groups, Fuzzy Logicians like Zadeh propose taking into account gradual variations ("approximate reasoning"), both with regard to the data on which calculations are based and to the truths established, thus avoiding binary oppositions and deliberately relying on vague values or ranges of values. So in Fuzzy Logical terms, a person could be "moderately" or "extremely beautiful," "rather tall" or "positively huge." As a result, any statement concerning groups of people does not necessarily have to be either "true" or "false." Instead, there can be "intermediate truth degrees": "a proposition may be more true than another proposition" (Hajek), and a statement may also be "a little bit true" or "mostly false." Fuzzy Logic is "an exact way of thinking about very ambiguous and obscure things" (Zadeh in Blair, "Interview").

By grouping people in imprecise categories like "beautiful" or "tall," Zadeh's seminal 1965 article acknowledged the double fuzziness of these categories: firstly, they are judgmental; beauty and tallness are always in the eye of the beholder and depend on individual perception, experiences, and preferences. Secondly, they are also relative categories in themselves, and cannot be defined in absolute numerical terms. Thus, the way modern washing machine technology relies on non-numerical variables, such as the degree of soiling of the textiles in the washing load, has become a favored practical example of Fuzzy Logic: no matter whether the clothes are "a little bit stained" or "very dirty," the machine will have to be set to exact values (or the calculation "defuzzified") for the necessary amount of detergent, the water level, and the temperature used. These values will have to be based on 'soft' criteria, such as experience and empirical observation, and they will have to be expressed verbally rather than numerically. Finally, it should be added that Fuzzy Logic not only addresses our imprecise use of language and dependency on individual perception. Our knowledge with regard to any given situation may also be incomplete or dated, so that conclusions or decisions may have to be drawn from or based on uncertain preconditions.

In the humanities, fuzziness as defined by Zadeh and others applies especially to language, where it is often used to identify semantic sets that cannot be defined exactly and that tolerate continuing degrees of inclusion or exclusion.[5] It has been crucial to linguistic prototype theory developed by the cognitive psychologist Eleanor Rosch in the 1970s (Rosch), and for a while attracted the interest of linguists (Lakoff).[6] Although linguists in general did not adopt the concept (Seising 250), ambiguity, vagueness, or contradictiveness can in fact constitute the appeal of language: pun, double entendre, or even the whole world of figurative language would not exist without such linguistic imprecision (Drösser 17-8).

The Fuzziness of Cultural Contact

Fuzzy Logic is certainly not the only concept that promotes notions of ambivalence and uncertainty in the so-called exact sciences. It was preceded, and probably influenced, by Werner Heisenberg's formulation of the uncertainty principle in physics (1927). Heisenberg had realized that the natural behavior of particles is disturbed and therefore altered by the very act of observation, and that it is only possible to determine either a particle's exact position or its speed of movement at any given moment, but never both simultaneously. This acknowledgement of a certain degree of inexactness by a representative of one of the most 'exact' sciences was subsequently adopted by many other disciplines. Unlike this revolutionary discovery in quantum physics, which greatly influenced philosophical thinking (e.g., Karl Popper) and postmodern literature (e.g., Thomas Pynchon), the concept of Fuzzy Logic was never widely received by scholars studying culture, remaining limited to the exact sciences mentioned above. This is all the more surprising since its invention and implementation were so deeply affected by cultural contact and transfer.

5   For initial positive reactions by one linguist and one cognitive psychologist to Zadeh's 1965 article, see Seising 225. Zadeh himself regards languages as an obvious field of application for Fuzzy Logic, see Seising 226 and 330-3.
6   Seising credits Lakoff with having first used the term "Fuzzy Logic."

For several reasons, the theoretical premises of Fuzzy Logic lend themselves particularly well to the analysis of cultural encounter situations. First of all, cultural contact can only occur between human individuals, not between abstract entities – cultures are always bound to agents, they do not float freely, as the anthropologist Johannes Fabian stresses in our first chapter. Cultural contact is therefore highly dependent on human perception, thinking, and interaction which, as Fabian demonstrates in his recent book *Out of Our Minds* (and as Joseph Conrad impressively showed in his late imperial novels) always include a component of unreliability, irrationality, and messiness caused by the strains of unfamiliar climatic and psychological situations. Hence, the analysis of cultural encounters requires tools especially suited to these extraordinary conditions.

Secondly, encounter situations are often complex; they rely on communication, both the verbal and nonverbal variations of which are fraught with misunderstandings and equivocality – yet they are real life situations and require concepts to understand them. Just like Fuzzy Logic, theories dealing with cultural contact should enable us to handle problems that involve vague or ambiguous constituents. But there are also limits to its applicability: the objective of cultural analysis is not (as in Fuzzy Logic) to facilitate the complexities of real life but to develop concepts for understanding them.

Thirdly, binary oppositions have recently been challenged in research addressing cultural contact situations, and a number of concepts have been introduced that allow for entanglement or mutual impact. Examples of such concepts would be hybridity, the middle ground, transnationality, transculturation, and *histoire croisée*. Phenomena of cultural 'impurity' or blending, which in the course of history have often been opposed in highly problematic ways (for example, in scientific racism), have generally been revalued and are today perceived as cultural givens that have shaped cultures in important ways.

Our use of the term "Fuzzy Logic" is motivated by a desire to offer an alternative to more frequently used metaphors in cultural and postcolonial studies. In spite of their usefulness in certain contexts (see the essays by Mühleisen and Schulze-Engler in this volume), terms such as "creolization" and "hybridity" tend to evoke problematic connotations and associations (for an extensive critique of their biologistic implications, see Young). It also seems important to us to avoid the language and logic of purity and homogeneity contained even in such terms as "blurred genres" (see Geertz). As mentioned above, even the term "fuzzy" conventionally has a pejorative ring, but it also is not explicitly related to any particular field of perception. In adopting the term "Fuzzy Logic" from the science of engineering, this volume seeks to stress that ambiguity, complexity, imprecision, and 'impurity' are the rule in the world of human relations, in spite of a dominant discourse – itself reaching back to antiquity – that insists on Manichean opposites, clearly defined divisions, and incontrovertible classification systems. The persistence of such discourses of purity, which associate cleanliness with stability and impurity with danger and social disorder (see Campbell 93 and Douglas), it seems to us, is the paradoxical – not to say paranoid – flip-side of the very 'impurities' produced by Western practices of forced migration, global traffic, territorial expansion (such as, for example, miscegenation, religious synchretism, and linguistic 'creolization'). The existence of such 'impurities' is continually being denied and abhorred by dominant Western cultural discourses. But even in the safe realm beyond the complexities of transcultural traffic, the example of music teaches us that 'purity,' far from being a natural fact, is a powerful ideology (and therefore 'real' in a certain way). As the ethnomusicologist Lars-Christian Koch pointed out in the discussion of his paper on Indian *srutis* during our conference, even the artificial sounds produced in the name of pure harmony during the classical period of European music are, mathematically speaking, impure.[7]

There can be no doubt that the applicability of Fuzzy Logic to cultural phenomena has its limits. The most obvious objection is that unlike the exact sciences, the humanities seldom operate with exact numerical values anyway. While we do not advocate the concept as a cure-all for cultural short-sightedness, we are convinced that the phenomena of intercultural mixture, blending, and indeterminacy, which this volume seeks to elucidate, amount to more than the widespread assertion that things are more complicated than commonly assumed.

The chapters in this volume have been arranged in geographical order, with the focus moving around the globe via four continents. The first, more general contributions reflect our ongoing concern with disciplinary traditions and the premises of research in the field of cultural contact. Johannes Fabian, one of the first scholars to have begun conducting the auto-critique of anthropology (see Fabian, *Time*), gives a rather personal account of the transformations and potential hazards of the concepts at the center of the volume: "culture," "encounter," "discourse," and "scholarship." He reminds us of the dangers residing in too much abstraction when talking about intercultural processes. Departing from Mary Pratt's definition quoted above, Fabian insists that encounters can only take place between people, never between cultures. He thereby challenges us to study those moments of human contact 'on the ground' and not to reduce their sociological and psychological effects to lofty theoretical formulas.

Fabian's *tour de force* through the history of anthropology since the 1960s is followed by an essay by Susanne Mühleisen discussing the emergence and critical potential of the concepts of "creolization" and "hybridity" from the late eighteenth century to modern linguistics. She documents, for example, the persistent antipathy and denigration of these "bastard tongues," themselves the result of European expansion. In modern linguistics, the struggle over how to categorize these languages continues, and apart from changes in terminology and figurative language, the basic epistemological categories have remained remarkably stable.

---

7 Recognizing 'purity' as the key metaphor of the popular ideology of cultural identity and alterity (see Douglas), it is interesting to note that the concept of "Fuzzy Logic" is often explained using the example of washing machines.

In the following chapter, Dominik Collet shows how strongly the European perception of foreign cultures, in the course of history, has relied on dichotomies and clear divisions that can be revealed as constructs: divisions between Europe and its 'others,' which are often combined with a denial of variation, amalgamation, or historic change. Collet reveals how the representation of extra-European cultures aimed at European audiences or addressees was (and still is) highly determined by European prejudices. These caused the extra-European situation to be rendered homogenous and simplistic, both on the synchronic and the diachronic level, for instance by blanking out multilateral relationships or historical development. This held true even for practitioners of cultural exchange who supplied early modern museums, the so-called curiosity cabinets (*Kunstkammern*), with extra-European objects for their collections. Moreover, the environment created in European museums can be argued to abet such biased views even today.

The fuzzification of cultural contact situations should heighten our awareness of the potential for minority groups to determine the representation of such situations, as Susanne Lachenicht's chapter on Huguenot historiography shows. From a comparative perspective, Lachenicht presents a few important qualifications of the prevailing opinion that the Huguenot diaspora was exceptionally quick to assimilate to its host societies in Europe and North America. Conversely, Lachenicht reveals how despite their moderate input in technology and financial capital, and also despite a persistently mixed perception by these societies, Huguenots were able to portray themselves as culturally superior. They managed to uphold their distinct identity across the centuries, and to preserve their peculiar historiography, parts of which they even succeeded in incorporating into their host societies' national historiographies.

The necessity to bring to the fore views diverging from the dominant representation of such situations also applies to the history of European expansion, and to the colonization of Africa in particular. In spite of the crucial role of colonialism in the process of globalization, as Benedikt Stuchtey demonstrates, the imperial philosophy of history was disputed during the age of Empire, even within the metropolis itself. Toward the close of the nineteenth century, French public moralists like the geographer Elisée Reclus believed that imperialism had landed the world in a crisis, and claimed that neither political control over extra-European territory nor the cultural 'Europeanization of the world' could resolve it. Proponents of empire viewed such criticism as a corroding force – although the criticism itself was far from unequivocal.

The recently edited *Acta Ethiopica*, which comprise a wide range of nineteenth-century diplomatic correspondence, reveal that the relationship with European colonial powers afforded the colonized opportunities for political agency, as Samuel Rubenson makes clear. Thus, like Johann Michael Wansleben, one of the early modern museum collectors traveling in Ethiopia and introduced by Collet, Ethiopian rulers chose to confirm a European myth. Instead of acknowledging the ongoing, friendly interreligious relationships between Christians and Muslims in

Ethiopia, they instrumentalized the myth of a Christian island surrounded by hostile Muslim nations to draw the colonial powers' intervention into local struggles.

While Europeans largely tended to ignore the history and development of African countries, they were acutely aware of the cultural heritage of ancient civilizations in Africa and Asia – which did not prevent them from entertaining serious misconceptions, and false expectations, engaging in cultural appropriations, and imposing Western ideas on Eastern cultural artifacts. An example from archaeology is provided by Stefan Altekamp, who discusses the restoration policy governing monuments from the Mesopotamian era in Iraq. Like other nations harboring ancient architectural structures within their territories, Iraq was confronted with the alternative of leaving the ruins of Babylon and other famous sites as they were – indulging in their special "aura of distance and respect" – or of restoring the sites completely or in part. As Altekamp shows, the scholarly debate over how to preserve a culture's ancient monuments, which was introduced into Iraq by the European colonial powers, is deeply entangled with questions of national identity and pride.

Three essays in this collection are dedicated to India. Andreas Nehring demonstrates Europe's long-standing fascination with the spirituality of India, whose civilizational status was considered by some colonial travelers and scholars as almost equivalent to that of Europe, while others (Humboldt and Hegel among them) insisted on Indian culture's lack of regularity and order. Regardless of their position in this debate, European scholars have produced a series of "mistaken readings" of Indian culture, as Gayatri Spivak and others have argued. In a rather intricate reading, Nehring traces Spivak's critical method in her deconstruction of Hegel.

The inability to accept manifest fuzziness as a cultural constituent becomes clear from Lars-Christian Koch's analysis of the use and scientific treatment of Indian music: for centuries, European musicologists in their obsessive quest for the exact size of the *sruti* (microtone) remained blissfully ignorant of the fact that Indian musicians – while regarding it as a vital ingredient in classical Indian music – cared little for such mathematical definitions and instead followed a pragmatic approach based on the teacher-pupil relationship.

Frank Schulze-Engler departs from the thesis that, contrary to a once dominant cultural discourse, the claim to "modernity" is not – and never has been – the exclusive privilege of the West. In a reading of two novels by Amitav Ghosh, he shows how intellectuals in the former periphery defamiliarize and parody the scientific and philosophical certainties of Europe. He reads Ghosh's fictions as aesthetic articulations of Bruno Latour's dictum that our world is increasingly faced with a "proliferation of hybrids" between different fields of science and social practice once considered to be mutually exclusive. Thus the novels, Schulze-Engler argues, are "excellent examples of the complexity involved in 'cultural encounters' in a world of decentered modernity."

North American indigenous cultures especially have often been regarded by Europeans as determined by a close relationship with nature (which seemed to exlude civilization) and as timeless, without a history of their own. Claudia Schnurmann introduces a frequently misunderstood but extremely significant aspect of the material culture of some North American Indians of the East Coast and eastern woodlands: wampum, or shell beads. She shows the uncertainty within European discourses in correctly classifying these objects, as well as their changing usage between different indigenous tribes (as payment, as spiritual object). Wampum, Schnurmann argues, is a perfect cultural broker which, for a time at least, facilitated trade between various parties (different Indian Nations as well as Europeans). Because it aided intercultural exchange and its significance depended on the respective context, wampum can be seen as a "fuzzy" object *par excellence* within the cultural contact zone.

In the final essay, Bruce Harvey explores the discovery of a very particular zone from the age of geographical discovery: the subterranean world comprising caves, coal mines, and geological deep-formations, which was readily appropriated into the cultural discourses of anthropology, archaeology, and the theory of the sublime. As Harvey explains, metaphors of depth – whether geological or historical – have abounded in theories of cultural difference ever since the early modern period and became fashionable in popular discourses of the nineteenth century. The imagery of depth, Harvey argues, offered the "necessary penumbra of shadow" against which "the Enlightenment directive to systematic visual clarity" could be defined in the first place. Though not predominantly concerned with the theme of cultural encounter, Harvey's essay, which again and again returns to the writings of Melville as symptomatic of the attitude toward "deep spaces" and "deep times," impressively illustrates the dependency of European scientific and philosophical-aesthetic discourses on the cultures and natural worlds encountered beyond the seas.

Historically speaking, cultural encounters and a keen recognition of the complexities of cultural interaction have become more relevant than ever before in today's globalized world while remaining woefully undertheorized in most (though not all) academic disciplines. It is the purpose of the present volume to establish an interdisciplinary forum within which to probe the potentials and the limits of concepts of cultural contact developed in various disciplines, as well as to address the complex ways in which scholarly disciplines and discourses have contributed to enabling, but more frequently to disabling, intercultural communication. No single vocabulary should be expected as the result of such an attempt – this would rather seem a relapse into the logic of pure classifications. Instead, this volume, as well as those that will follow in this series, is motivated by the desire to create a space for congenial intellectual exchange across cultures and disciplines. Such exchange becomes ever more necessary in a world that rapidly – as one result of European expansion – grows closer together. While this process remains fundamentally unfair in its distribution of wealth and human rights, we are now faced with the obligation to analyze, as Edward Said asserts, "the historical experience of empire as a common one" in spite of "the horrors, the bloodshed, and the vengeful bitterness" it has caused (xxiv).

References

Bhabha, Homi K. "Signs Taken for Wonders. Questions of Ambivalence and Authority Under a Tree Outside Delhi, May 1817." *Europe and Its Others*. Ed. Francis Barker, Peter Hulme, Margaret Iversen, and Diana Loxley. 2 vols. Colchester: University of Essex, 1985. 1: 89-106.

Blair, Betty. "Lotfi Zadeh. Short Biographical Sketch." *Azerbaijan International* 2.4 (1994): 49. Online-edition: http://www.azer.com/aiweb/categories/magazine/24_folder/24_articles/24_zadeh.html [02.09.08]

---. "Interview with Lotfi Zadeh, Creator of Fuzzy Logic." *Azerbaijan International* 2.4 (1994), 46-7, 50.
Online-edition: http://www.azer.com/aiweb/categories/magazine24_folder/24_articles/24/fuzzylogic.html [02.09.08]

Campbell, David. *Writing Security. United States Foreign Policy and the Politics of Identity*. Manchester: Manchester University Press, 1992.

Clifford, James, and George E. Marcus (eds.). *Writing Culture. The Poetics and Politics of Ethnography*. Berkeley: University of California Press, 1986.

Dening, Greg. *Islands and Beaches. Discourse on a Silent Land. Marquesas 1774-1880*. Chicago: Dorsey Press, 1980.

Douglas, Mary. *Purity and Danger. An Analysis of the Concepts of Pollution and Taboo*. 1966. Rpt. London: Routledge, 2002.

Drösser, Christoph. *Fuzzy Logic. Methodische Einführung in krauses Denken*. Reinbek: Rowohlt, 1994.

Dülmen, Richard van, and Sina Rauschenbach (eds.). *Macht des Wissens. Die Entstehung der modernen Wissensgesellschaft*. Köln, Weimar, Wien: Böhlau, 2004.

Fabian, Johannes. *Time and the Other. How Anthropology Makes Its Object*. 1983. Rpt. New York: Columbia University Press, 2002.

---. *Out of Our Minds. Reason and Madness in the Exploration of Central Africa*. Berkeley: University of California Press, 2000.

Foucault, Michel. *The Order of Things. An Archaeology of the Human Sciences*. New York: Vintage, 1970.

Geertz, Clifford. "Blurred Genres." *American Scholar* 49 (1980): 165-79. Rpt. in *Local Knowledges. Further Essays in Interpretive Anthropology*. New York: Basic Books, 1983.

Hajek, Petr. "Fuzzy Logic." *Stanford Encyclopedia of Philosophy*. Online-edition: http://plato.stanford.edu/entries/logic-fuzzy/ [02.09.08].

Klein, Bernhard. *Maps and the Writing of Space in Early Modern England and Ireland*. Houndmills, Basingstoke: Palgrave, 2001.

Ladan, Anna. "We All Have a Duty of Leaving our Ideas Behind. A Conversation with Creator of Fuzzy Logic Lotfi Zadeh." *Journal of Automation, Mobile Robotics and Intelligent Systems* 1.4 (2007): 70-2.
Online-edition: http://jamris.org/issue_04_2007.php [02.09.08]

Lakoff, George. "Hedges. A Study in Meaning Critieria and the Logic of Fuzzy Concepts." *Journal of Philosophical Logic* 2 (1973): 458-508.

McNeill, Daniel, and Paul Freiberger. *Fuzzy Logic. The Revolutionary Computer Technology that is Changing Our World*. New York: Simon & Schuster, 1993.

Porter, David. *Journal of a Cruise Made to the Pacific Ocean* (1815). Ed. R.D. Madison and Karen Hamon. Annapolis, MD: Naval Institute Press, 1986.

Pratt, Mary Louise. *Imperial Eyes. Travel Writing and Transculturation*. London: Routledge, 1992.

Rosch, Eleanor. "Natural Categories." *Cognitive Psychology* 4 (1973): 328-50.

Said, Edward W. *Culture and Imperialism*. London: Chatto & Windus, 1993.

Seising, Rudolf. *Die Fuzzifizierung der Systeme. Die Entstehung der Fuzzy Set Theorie und ihre ersten Anwendungen – Ihre Entwicklung bis in die 70er Jahre des 20. Jahrhunderts* (= Boethius. Texte und Abhandlungen zur Geschichte der Mathematik und der Naturwissenschaften 54). Stuttgart: Franz Steiner Verlag 2005.

Young, Robert. *Colonial Desire. Hybridity in Theory, Culture and Race*. London: Routledge, 1995.

Zadeh, Lotfi Asker. "Fuzzy Sets." *Information and Control* 8 (1965): 338-53.

CHAPTER ONE

You Meet and You Talk. Anthropological Reflections on Encounters and Discourses

JOHANNES FABIAN

Anthropology and Interdisciplinarity

The plain language of the title of this essay may sound a bit irreverent; it reflects an attitude I have begun to develop toward inter-, multi-, trans- and ultimately nondisciplinary programs. More than ever before, our work – academic research, publishing, and teaching – is carried out under institutional pressure on established disciplines to create interdisciplinary spaces as ways to prove themselves in the competition to acquire resources. The game can be interesting and intellectually invigorating but it should not make us forget a lesson we ought to have learned from a long history of colonial exploration and expansion: inevitably, it seems, spaces become territories, exploration turns into occupation. However, as I ponder this connection between inquest and conquest I find a significant difference between disciplinary and interdisciplinary projects, one that encourages me to remain open for, and ready to contribute to, undertakings such as our symposium. Disciplines and interdisciplinary programs both mark and occupy spaces, but they differ in their temporal orientation. Disciplines emerge, change, and proliferate – they seldom disappear. Interdisciplinary programs are inherently ephemeral. They are projects that can end. In fact, they should end if they are to be carried out as innovative endeavors. If it succeeds in subverting expectations or pretensions that equate marking spaces with claiming territories to be ruled by scholarly discourses, then interdisciplinarity can open spaces of freedom. This is the perspective from which I respond to the invitation to contribute a few thoughts on "cultural encounters and discourses of scholarship."

As an anthropologist, a representative of a discipline that has long claimed to ground its discourse on cultural encounters, I should be able to talk about such encounters from experience – and eventually I will – but I am mindful of the possibility that I may be expected to play another part often assigned to anthropology, namely that of providing theory and methods that can be transported and used across disciplinary boundaries. Long ago, G. Gusdorf observed that linguistics (or philology) took on such a vehicular function and became a *sabir épis-*

témologique, facilitating intellectual trade between disciplines. His phrasing expressed a certain disdain, and I must confess to similar feelings with regard to anthropology. Anthropology is not, or should not be, in the catering business. Culture theory and ethnography, to mention only two of our bestselling "exports," are anything but easily exportable commodities. Formulating anthropological theories and devising research methods are *practices*. Both are deeply situated, one could say implicated, in historical and political processes. Their transfer to other fields can be effected only by two operations (or a combination of both): in a quasi-economic mode, by stripping them of their use value and making them into commodities, or by that literary mode of transportation we usually call *metaphoresis* (a term whose literal meaning came back to me when I noticed it on delivery vans and trucks in Greece). Either way, as intellectual merchandise or as figures of speech, when anthropological concepts of culture and ethnographic forms of inquiry are adopted outside of anthropology they deserve the same rigorous critique to which they have been submitted inside the discipline.

Cultural Encounter

My first encounter with encounter occurred in the course of dissertation research on a religious movement in Africa. This was at a time (in the mid-1960s) when anthropology in the US was at the height of its modernity. Culture *contact* and *clash*, notions that had been prominent since the 1930s were beginning to look old-fashioned. The theoretical challenge was to explain culture *change*, a concept that took its urgency from the then reigning Parsonian paradigm of structuralism-functionalism: culture and society (but also religion, ideology, and art, to name the topics of a series of classic essays by Clifford Geertz) were approached as *systems* whose fundamental characteristics were external boundaries, internal structures, and the maintenance of equilibrium within the system. True, it was also said that these systems had to be dynamic in order to maintain boundaries and equilibrium and that they were subject to processes of evolution imposed by changes in their environment. However, in anthropology, attempts to integrate Weberian notions such as the concepts of rationalization and the *Eigengesetzlichkeit*, or logic of meaningful symbols irreducible to functional demands, left us at a loss when it came to understanding cultural creativity of the kind that we began to see everywhere in the (former) colonial world. Phenomena such as cargo cults and prophetic-charismatic, often millennial, movements were no longer curiosities but became a testing ground for our theories of culture and society.

The movement I studied, called Jamaa (Swahili for family), emerged around 1950 among Catholic married couples in the mining towns of Katanga, in the southeastern part of what was then still the Belgian Congo. Its founder was Placide Tempels, a Franciscan missionary who had become famous as the author of *La Philosophie Bantoue* (1945).[1] What distinguished Tempels from other late colonial writers was his passion when he argued that the colonial *oeuvre civilisatrice* was bound to fail unless colonizers and colonized encountered each other "metaphysically" (his term), that is, on the level of their deepest philosophical ideas. Knowledge of these deep ideas was for Tempels a means to a utopian end. Intellectuals who read his book focused on the *means*; sixty years after it was first published, *La Philosophie Bantoue* is still discussed by African philosophers and writers on African philosophy. The powers that were – the dominant factions in the colonial administration, the industrial establishment, and some ecclesiastic authorities – saw the *end* Tempels had in mind. They understood the subversive, indeed revolutionary potential of his vision of deep encounter with Africans and reacted in concert by removing him, at least for a while, from the colony. They were unable, however, to prevent a transformation that occurred in the years of his exile in Belgium. The missionary ethnographer and expert on African thought turned into a charismatic prophet. He returned to the Congo with a universal message, still religious in idiom but humanist in essence, that eventually made him the leader of the Jamaa which, at its height in the 1950s and 1960s, attracted some 200,000 followers. *Rencontre*, encounter, was a key concept of the movement's teachings and ritual initiation. Not contact between cultures but deep mutual understanding between husband and wife, between initiating and initiated couples, as the way to "become human" was to be assured by encounter. Tempels probably was not aware (nor was I when I did my research) that his discovery of encounter as an event and a praxis was part of a wider and eventually global trend in social psychology and psychiatry promoting group encounter as a form of therapy whose popularity shows no signs of abating in the present.

What are the theoretical and conceptual lessons to be learned from this story? In what way is it relevant to the idea of "cultural encounter?" At the very least it should make us wary of any casual use of the phrase. "Encounter" is a concept that carries a heavy historical and ideological load, and the same goes for "cultural." A generation ago, "cultural encounter" had a predecessor, "colonial encounter," a phrase that achieved wide notoriety when it appeared in the title of an influential critique of anthropology's implication in colonialism (edited by Talal Asad, 1973).[2] Before that, the concept of the "colonial situation" signaled the dawning of historical and political consciousness, especially in the sociological study of cults and movements (Balandier, Wallerstein). If the connections I am making here are correct, it would follow that "cultural encounter" cannot count as a neutral, purely analytical concept. It is always in danger of serving as a euphemism for violent events or states that have perpetrators and victims.

---

1 For the full text (in French, Dutch, and English) as well as exhaustive information on Tempels and the reception of his work, see http://www.aequatoria.be/tempels/HomeEng.html [29.08.08]

2 When I checked with Talal Asad he confirmed that the phrase was used more for convenience than as a target of critique.

In sum, as an anthropologist I cannot but take a critical view of "encounter between cultures." One may prefer its irenic connotations to talk about clash of cultures or, to evoke a phrase of recent notoriety, war between cultures. The real problem with bringing encounter and culture together may be that in "encounter between cultures" culture is deployed as if the term had a commonly accepted meaning. The contrary is the case. Nowhere is the notion of culture more debated, contested, and sometimes outright condemned than in fields that label themselves "cultural," such as cultural anthropology and cultural studies. Which brings me back to my earlier assertion that talk that has cultures encounter each other is essentially metaphorical. What is wrong with that, one may ask. Nothing, as long as a metaphor is a vehicle for, not an obstacle to, understanding. To put it bluntly, cultures are neither entities nor agents. They cannot clash or be at war, nor can they encounter each other; only people can, singly and collectively. What we may imagine as cultural encounter (poetically at best, demagogically at worst) cannot be found and studied "on the ground" (or "in the field") except in actions or events that can be ethnographically or historically documented. Of any other understanding one could say that it has no empirical referent. Which would seem reason enough to banish "encounter between cultures" (as well as "cultural encounter") from empirical scholarly discourse.

But, as may be suspected from the story I told about my first encounter with encounter, the verdict I just pronounced does not mean that I am about to close the books on the issue. In an essay titled "Inquiry as event: About encounters and the making of knowledge in Africa" (Fabian, *Memory Against Culture*, chapter 12), I recently reflected on the role of encounters in three projects: a history of the exploration of Central Africa based on a critical rereading of a corpus of travelogues (Fabian, *Out of Our Minds*); a study of the History of Zaire, narrated and represented in one hundred paintings by a popular artist from the Congo, Tshibumba Kanda Matulu (Fabian, *Remembering the Present*); and in my work on the Jamaa movement. In interpreting the wealth of material I found in the first and second projects I concentrated on reports and representations of *encounters as actual events*, as happenings but also as purposeful practices and staged performances. Above all, I examined *the epistemological significance of encounters*, that is, the role meetings between travelers and Africans in the first case, and between the protagonists of Tshibumba's *History of Zaire*, played in the production of (proto)anthropological and popular historical knowledge. When I tried to bring my findings together with what I knew about *rencontre* in Jamaa doctrine and ritual I saw an interesting analogy: not unlike the prophet of *rencontre*, the scholar whose work starts with, and builds on, encounters ("scholar" taken in a wider sense that includes protoethnographers and popular historians) must find ways to render unique happenings repeatable and make fleeting moments last. The charismatic leader's solution was to ritualize encounter, the protoethnographers turned meetings into an instrument of inquiry, while the popular historian used the topos of fateful confrontations to structure his narrative. All of this (ritual, method, topology), I think, is food for thought when it comes to understanding contemporary theories and practices of ethnography. One could say that anthropology has ritualized field research; meeting people and conversing with them became a method. Still, the idea of encounter as something that can but does not have to happen when two parties meet ought to remind us of the inherently precarious and contingent nature of our work.

Let me stop here and take stock of what I hopefully achieved by taking you through the steps that made me discover and reflect on encounter in the course of my work. I wanted to show that encounter should not be used casually; it is a term loaded with connotations, some of which – the "colonial encounter" was my example – are manifestly ideological; others are dubiously metaphorical (when they suggest that cultures encounter each other), falsely neutral (when they posit the facticity of encounters), and outright obfuscating (when they conceal domination and violence). Critique of ideological uses, I suggested, can begin when we move from encounter as an idea to encounters as events that can become objects of scholarly inquiry. Even that, at least in my own experience, makes the concept hardly less tricky, especially when we consider its epistemological significance. We sense that there is a difference that appears as obvious as it is difficult to put into words. Epistemologically, we could say, meetings can become encounters when they produce knowledge. However, since it is not knowledge in general we have in mind but specific, disciplined knowledge (the kind that disciplines produce), this lands us in quandary: encounters happen, they cannot be planned and what happens in encounters cannot be controlled. Are we ready to admit that ethnographic knowledge is happenstance?

Scholarly Discourse

There are concepts that are good to think of but not so good to think with. I fear that "cultural encounters" may be one of them. What about "scholarly discourses," pronounced on cultural encounters? A facile answer could be that discoursing about doubtful objects is pointless. It has its partisans among observers of a postmodern anthropology that seems to have lost faith in culture, the guiding concept of our discipline since its modern beginnings. Anthropology, they say, is headed for self-destruction. I do not accept such a conclusion because I do not accept its premise that cultures must be empirical entities if they are to be objects of scholarly inquiry. The history of our discipline shows that anthropology has always made, construed, rather than found its object. Construction (or constructedness) is not an antonym of reality; it is, short of naive realism and equally naive empiricism, a realistic view of the processes by which we come to produce what we present as scholarly and, let us not be squeamish about it, scientific knowledge. This reflects my understanding of the epistemological foundations of anthropology; it is the position from which I now want to offer some thoughts on discourse. Again, keep in mind that I speak as an anthropologist and ethnographer.

When the concept of discourse entered theory and informed practices of research in our field this happened in more than one way.[3] In my own work I can retrace two major lines, which I will now sketch as briefly as possible. The first one goes back to developments in the US that took place in the 1940s and 1950s and were represented by projects in cultural anthropology (in "culture and personality" studies to be exact) and in linguistics. As stated in the title of a book edited by Margaret Mead and Rhoda Metreaux, *The Study of Culture at a Distance* (1953),[4] the aim was to produce knowledge about other cultures in situations where the usual methods of ethnographic inquiry could not be applied because the researcher's society was at war with the targets of research. The key concept at the time was "national character," a kind of deep cultural personality structure that made the Japanese, Germans, and not much later the Russians behave the way they did. These anthropological attempts (such as the "Harvard Project") to get at the jugular of the enemy's culture – most famous among them Ruth Benedict's *The Chrysanthemum and the Sword* (1946) – were made at about the same time as, and had actual connections with, the services linguistics was called upon to lend to the US "war effort" by developing methods for cracking the codes that were employed by the enemy in espionage and military communication.

When the hot war turned cold, discourse – the idea and the term – took center stage in the work of the linguist (and anthropologist) Zellig Harris, a teacher of Noam Chomsky at the University of Pennsylvania. The challenge now was no longer so much to crack codes but to provide theoretical foundations for putting computer technology to the tasks of information gathering, especially from sources in Russian. The field of machine translation emerged and continued to draw on the latest theoretical developments in thought about language (notably transformational or generative linguistics).[5] These two kinds of war efforts (as they were thought of and called) by anthropologists and linguists, both supported by generous funding from political and military agencies and foundations, were not only eminently practical, they also had a profound and long-lasting influence on theories guiding scholarly discourses about other cultures. They certainly favored positions that were eventually criticized as "culturalism." In spite of such criticism they continue to have proponents in anthropology and other fields.[6]

---

3   For a recent comprehensive assessment of "discourse" see Blommaert.
4   See also the review of that book by A. F. C. Wallace. For an exemplary critical assessment of this period in the development of a theory of culture see the article by Federico Neiburg.
5   John Hutchins is of one of the foremost experts in that field, see http://www.hutchinsweb.me.uk/ [29.08.08]. In a brief summary he tells the history of machine translation up to the present, including its more recent turn to statistical methods.
6   Not to mention "customers" – see the debates in US anthropology about historical and current relations with intelligence agencies (with numerous publications, David Price has become the expert in this field).

As far as I know, anthropologists did not use discourse to designate either their object or their mode of inquiry until later, for instance when Clifford Geertz stated: "[T]he aim of anthropology is the enlargement of the universe of human discourse" (Geertz 140). Linguists, though they may have started out calling for discourse analysis, pursued a nondiscursive kind of scholarship seeking to create highly formalized models of language that all but eliminated speaking and communication as objects and modes of inquiry. While it could be said that both sought encounter with other cultures (encounter as an idea), the historical-political context of the time made it imperative to turn a vice – the fact that war made communicative interaction (encounter as event and practice) impossible – into a virtue. This was done by keeping language separate from speaking and by conceptualizing culture in such a way that another society could be studied "at a distance." That did not bode well for anthropology and linguistics as scholarly discourses of cultural encounters. Leaving linguistics aside for the moment, in anthropology culturalist theorizing exacerbated a glaring contradiction between scholarly discourse and research practice. As I stated in *Time and the Other,*

> [on] the one hand we dogmatically insist that anthropology rests on ethnographic research, involving personal, prolonged interaction with the Other. But we then pronounce upon the knowledge gained from such research a discourse which construes the Other in terms of distance, spatial and temporal. (Fabian, *Time and the Other* xli)

Some took this as a condemnation, a sort of final verdict on the modernist discourse of anthropology; most, I like to believe, heard it as a call for resolving the contradiction I had identified.[7]

When, after this necessary detour through a chapter in the history of culture theory, I now look once more at my own work I find that the concepts of "discourse" and "encounter" guided me in exploring three distinct but interconnected theoretical directions. The first goes back to the critique of anthropological and linguistic formalism that made us rediscover what its most influential proponent, the linguist and anthropologist Dell Hymes (1964), called the "ethnography of speaking."[8] In my research on the Jamaa I first concentrated on the movement's teachings as a "language" (later I would call it discourse) and a formal semantic analysis of its terminology was an important part of my dissertation (Fabian, *Jamaa*). But this "ethnoscientific" method left me dissatisfied and made me turn, following Dell Hymes's lead, from a quasi-linguistic to a sociolinguistic approach that allowed me to understand and represent both Jamaa doctrine and my ethno-

---

7 On this see Matti Bunzl's foreword to the second edition of *Time and the Other* (ix-xxxiv) and my essay "The Other Revisited."
8 At about the same time I became aware of Wilhelm von Humboldt's theory of language and of Jürgen Habermas' critique of positivism in the social sciences. I invoked Humboldt, Hymes, and Habermas in an essay in which I tried to lay the epistemological foundations for a language-centered and historical anthropology (Fabian, "History, Language, and Anthropology").

graphic research as communicative practices. "Ethnography of speaking" helped me to understand what had happened when I let my search for information on the movement be directed by the rules that governed Jamaa speech. Following these rules had practical consequences. For instance, although I met groups and individuals daily I never conducted an interview in the technical sense of the term. Eliciting information following a preset agenda, if not an actual list of questions, was not a form of communication practiced in the movement. Accordingly, the ethnographic documentation I brought back from field research consisted above all of recordings of communicative events that produced texts belonging to distinct genres (such as instruction, testimony, and the interpretation of dreams) whose emergence and differentiation allowed me to understand Jamaa discourse as communicative practice.

If there was "cultural encounter" in my project it was not with Jamaa doctrine as a "semiotic" object of interpretation (to invoke Geertz again).[9] It was a meeting or a confrontation of discourses – the discourse of a prophetic movement's teachings and the discourse of an anthropologist's research project. That confrontation had consequences. It took a while but eventually I realized that the encounter with the Jamaa had changed my theoretical orientation. When I noticed that I was not the only student of prophetic movements to whom this had happened, I invited others to report on their experiences. Eventually, five of them contributed essays to a collective volume called *Beyond Charisma. Religious Movements as Discourse* (Fabian, *Beyond Charisma*).[10] In my introduction I found in discourse a concept that made it possible to grasp the theoretical implications of our experiences, which were by no means identical but clearly had a common theme: the pursuit of ethnographic knowledge as an encounter between discourses rather than the imposition of one on the other. This move to discourse was in part inspired by Michel Foucault, whose *Archaeology of Knowledge* (1969) I had just read. "In part" because I was at that time less interested in his discovery of "epistemes" and regimes of knowledge than in what he had to say about the difference between "discursive fact" as the object of language analysis and the "description of the events of discourse" (Foucault 27). Whether or not I interpreted that distinction accurately, it made me state:

> In other words, "discourse" points to a social practice located, so to speak, between the levels of dumb (i.e., speechless) "behavior" and abstract, disembodied language (or "grammar") ... "discourse" carries connotations of activity in space and time, of unfolding in processes of in-

---

9   I should say "not only;" after all I had shown that it was possible to analyze the terminology of teaching as a "doctrinal system" (Fabian, *Jamaa* ch.3).

10   The contributors were James Fernandez, Paul S. Breidenbach, William J. Samarin, John M. Janzen, and Roy Wagner. It is gratifying to note that our efforts of almost a generation ago continue to inspire students of religion. See *Being Changed by Cross-Cultural Encounters*, edited by Young and Goulet (1994) and *Extraordinary Anthropology*, edited by Goulet and Miller (2007).

ternal differentiation, and of openness to response and argument from an audience. (Fabian, *Beyond Charisma* 28)[11]

Discourse served me in conceptualizing the object of my critique in *Time and the Other. How Anthropology Makes its Object*. The target was not one or the other school of anthropology but an all-pervading characteristic of my discipline, which has been to place societies we study in a time other than our own. I call such a discourse "allochronic." In addition to its analytical and epistemological meanings, discourse now signaled awareness of relations of power that are involved when we pronounce what we know about other societies. Discourse not only helped me to bring the target of critique into focus, it also made me attentive to what I called discursive (or rhetorical) devices, that is, specific ways in which anthropology had succeeded in keeping its object at a safe distance. If Foucault's writings influenced the arguments of *Time and the Other*, it was more through their spirit than their letter.

In later work I spoke of colonial discourse rather than just colonialism, for instance, when I wrote on colonial linguistics and the social history of Swahili in the Congo. But it seems the longer I tried and the further I went in translating programmatic criticism of anthropological discourse into ethnographic and historical writing the less use I had for the term in its abstract and ahistorical meaning. A series of studies on contemporary African culture (popular historiography, painting, and theater) directed my attention to two theoretical issues that I should like to address, however briefly, because I think that both need to be considered in these reflections on cultural encounters and scholarly discourses.

The first came to me when, in the course of work with popular actors, I had to face more directly than in other projects the performative, that is, nondiscursive aspects of cultural practices and productions. Much of ethnographic research, I realized, puts the anthropologist in a role that Victor Turner (albeit in a more narrow sense) had defined as that of an "ethno-dramaturg." Not unlike directors of film and theater, ethnographers are *metteurs en scène* of performances of culture and this, I suggest, ties in with some of our earlier observations on encounters as events or happenings.

The second issue came up when I wrote on two remarkable works of Congolese popular history, a history of colonization with a focus on the town of Elisabethville/Lubumbashi, commanded by an organization of former domestic servants (1990), and a history of the country (then called Zaire), painted in one hundred pictures and narrated by a local popular artist (1996). In both cases the "ethnographic material" consisted of fully developed discourses rather than the usual information or documentation a researcher assembles during field work. Even more than in the situation we had reflected on in our collective volume on

---

11 Recently, two commentators on my work noted that "discourse" no longer appears in the index of a later book even though I continue to address issues I discussed in earlier writings (Goulet and Miller 13, n4).

the encounter between prophetic-charismatic and scholarly discourses, these studies of popular historiography made me realize that a hierarchical theoretical position, no matter whether it aims at scientific explanation or at hermeneutic interpretation, could and should not be maintained. To deny or neutralize "for analytical purposes" the challenge posed by encounter of discourses at eye-level would amount to negating the event-character and historicity of such "cultural encounters."

Conclusion

Where did these different trains of thought about encounter and discourse leave me? How do the views I hold inform my current work? And why should my rather personal account speak to problems that presumably occupy the participants of this conference?

Let me begin with two assertions: First, neither scholarship nor culture should be the premises of our work; they are our problems. Whenever we feel safe in our disciplines and are at ease with the concepts such as culture (and encounter) we may assume that something has gone wrong. That was the valid point in critiques of anthropology as a colonial enterprise.[12] Second, when we talk and write about cultural encounters we should keep in mind that we are part of them. In matters human there is no safe distance between a discourse and its object. That is probably still more obvious to the anthropologist than to the historian or literary scholar, but anthropology cannot claim and should not be granted, as it were, special, much less exclusive, rights to the study of other cultures. This also harks back to remarks I made about the interdisciplinary popularity of anthropology. In my view, interdisciplinarity is not (or not only) about trading, importing and exporting *answers* but about sharing *questions*.

When all is said and done about the conceptual, historical, and political complexities of cultural encounters and scholarly discourses, the crucial issue is how to get from one to the other and back. What can scholarship build on when it pronounces its discourse about a culture? It was part of my story to tell you that anthropology's answer to that question has been field work (also called ethnography), practices that at one time were those of natural history but which are by now fairly generally recognized as interactive and communicative. Though we may still observe and collect data, we now think that it is events, actual meetings with our interlocutors that mediate rather than simply represent relations between knower and known. Once mediation became a central tenet of epistemology it was almost inevitable that our discipline rediscovered the significance of materiality in culture as well as in encounters with culture. Material culture studies, often ridiculed in modern anthropology as a kind of nineteenth-century survival

---

12 And in Edward Said's *Orientalism* (1978), later critiques notwithstanding. See also his later *Culture and Imperialism* (1993).

(it was Malinowski who spoke of "museum moles"), became an exciting field of inquiry, as did the rediscovery of the body (and gender) and of the senses (meaning senses other than vision) in the production of knowledge.

The literary turn in anthropology (and beyond) can remain a challenge if we are prepared to take another turn, this time from a literary and largely metaphorical to a literal conception of texts as material objectivations of culture that make it possible to ground our scholarly discourses in time and place, in events and actual encounters documented by texts. The virtual presence of texts, the possibility of writing in the presence of documents that are available in their entirety to writers *and* readers, may make us return to the ancient genre of *commentary* as a literary form of ethnography.[13] Informed, nonauthoritative commentary could help us avoid the closures and delusions of scholarly discourses about cultural encounters.

References

Asad, Talal. *Anthropology and the Colonial Encounter.* New York: Humanities Press, 1973.

Balandier, Georges. *Afrique Ambiguë.* Paris: Plon, 1957.

Benedict, Ruth. *The Chrysanthemum and the Sword. Patterns of Japanese Culture.* Boston: Houghton Mifflin Company, 1946.

Blommaert, Jan. *Discourse. A Critical Introduction.* Cambridge: Cambridge University Press, 2005.

Bunzl, Matti. "Introduction." Johannes Fabian, *Time and the Other. How Anthropology Makes its Object.* Reprint. New York: Columbia University Press, 2002. ix-xlv.

Fabian, Johannes. *Jamaa. A Charismatic Movement in Katanga.* Evanston: Northwestern University Press, 1971.

---. "History, Language and Anthropology." Philosophy of the Social Sciences 1(1971):19-47.

--- (ed.). *Beyond Charisma. Religious Movements as Discourse. Special Issue of Social Research* 46, 1 (1979).

---. *Time and the Other. How Anthropology Makes its Object.* New York: Columbia University Press, 1992 [1983]. Reprinted 2002.

---. *Remembering the Present. Painting and Popular History in Zaire.* Berkeley: University of California Press, 1996.

---. *History from Below. The 'Vocabulary of Elisabethville' by André Yav. Texts, Translation and Interpretive Essay.* Amsterdam and Philadelphia: John Benjamins Publishers, 2000.

---. *Out of Our Minds. Reason and Madness in the Exploration of Central Africa.* Berkeley: University of California Press, 2000.

---. "The Other Revisited. Critical Afterthoughts." *Anthropological Theory* 6 (2006): 129-52.

---. *Memory Against Culture. Arguments and Reminders.* Durham, NC: Duke University Press, 2007.

13 I have since tried to fulfil my prophecy, most recently in a book titled *Ethnography as Commentary: Writing from the Virtual Archive* (2008).

---. *Ethnography as Commentary. Writing from the Virtual Archive*. Durham, NC: Duke University Press, 2008.

Foucault, Michel. *The Archaeology of Knowledge*. New York: Harper & Row, 1976.

Geertz, Clifford. *The Interpretation of Cultures. Selected Essays*. New York: Basic Books, 1973.

Goulet, Jean-Guy A., and Bruce Granville Miller (eds.). *Extraordinary Anthropology. Transformations in the Field*. Lincoln, NE: University of Nebraska Press, 2007.

Hutchins, John. http://www.hutchinsweb.me.uk

Hymes, Dell. "Introduction: Towards Ethnographies of Communication." *The Ethnography of Communication*. Ed. John J. Gumperz and Dell Hymes. Menasha, WI: American Anthropological Association, 1964. 1-34.

Mead, Margaret, and Rhoda Metreaux (eds.). *The Study of Culture at a Distance*. Chicago: University of Chicago Press, 1953.

Neiburg, Federico. "Anthropology and Politics in Studies of National Character." *Cultural Anthropology* 13 (1998): 56-81.

Said, Edward W. *Orientalism*. New York: Vintage Books, 1979.

---. *Culture and Imperialism*. New York: Vintage Books, 1994.

Tempels, Placide. *La Philosophie Bantoue*. Elisabethville: Imbelco, 1945. Online-edition: http://www.aequatoria.be/tempels/HomeEng.html

Wallace, Anthony F. C. "Review of Mead and Metreaux." *American Anthropologist* 56 (1954): 1142-5.

Wallerstein, Immanuel. *Social Change. The Colonial Situation*. New York: Wiley, 1966.

Young, David E., and Jean-Guy A. Goulet (eds.). *Being Changed by Cross-Cultural Encounters. The Anthropology of Extraordinary Experiences*. Peterborough, ON: Broadview, 1994.

CHAPTER TWO

From Humboldt to Bickerton.
Discourses on Language Contact and
Hybridity

SUSANNE MÜHLEISEN

On Contact between Languages and Cultures

Without language contact and, by implication, cultural contact, no language would look the way it does in its present form. The history of a language is always a history of its linguistic contacts, too; at the same time, language contact is also one of the main catalysts of language change. The English language is a particularly good case in point: with its Germanic base and manifold influences from Romance languages, its scattered Scandinavian and Celtic lexical embeddings, and more recent loanwords from a multitude of Asiatic, African, and Pacific languages, it provides evidence of how cultural encounters – not only in the form of friendly exchange but also as violent colonial domination – are mirrored in the contemporary lineaments of the language.

One may ask, however, where 'normal' results of language contact – borrowings or linguistic convergences, for instance – end and where we should speak of the emergence of a new language. To put it differently: to what degree can a language incorporate elements from one or several others without counting as a 'hybrid construct'? Opinions on this issue differ considerably. As we can see in the following statements of two significant nineteenth-century linguists, such disagreement has a long tradition. While Max Müller, important scholar of Indian studies, notes that "there are no mixed languages"[1] (quoted in Thomason and Kaufman 1), his colleague Hugo Schuchhardt, linguist and tireless collector of language samples from around the world, came to the conclusion that "there are no completely unmixed languages"[2] (quoted in Thomason and Kaufman 1).

This paper provides an overview of the development of discourses on language contact, of the emergence of the concept of Creole languages, and of the contested criteria used to define such languages. These criteria will be scrutinized as to their ideological implications regarding language and they will be placed in the epistemological environment in which they occurred, from early nineteenth-

---

1 "Es gibt keine Mischsprachen."
2 "Es gibt keine völlig ungemischten Sprachen."

century discourses on language and hybridity to twentieth-century notions on universalist versus substrate influences on the formation of these languages. Finally, more recent debates on Creole exceptionalism will be considered.

Early Concepts of Creole Languages

The two nineteenth-century statements on language amalgamation quoted above were made at a time when the field of linguistics was developing an interest in a particular type of language that was the result of language contact, especially in the wake of European colonial expansion: so-called Creole languages. In contrast to other languages such as Latin or Greek, for example, these comparatively 'young languages' have the advantage that their origins can be traced and reconstructed, at least to some extent, which makes them an exciting field of research for linguists. What exactly, however, is a Creole language? The textbook answer, which can be found in copious numbers of works with titles like *Introduction to Linguistics* (e.g., Meyer 166), is rather straightforward: Creole designates a particular group of languages that developed out of special language contact situations, for instance, plantation slavery in the eighteenth-century Caribbean. Creoles can be traced back to Pidgin languages, rudimentary contact languages in their linguistic ancestry. If Pidgin is the sole language of the social group, it will become the mother tongue of the second generation of speakers. In the course of such nativization, the language undergoes restructuring and expansion. Creole languages are full languages and are able to fulfill all language functions.

For those linguists who actually work on these languages, so-called creolists, the issue is much more complex. After a period of affirmative use of the term Creole to confirm the legitimacy of those varieties conventionally named Pidgins and Creoles, it has come under attack within linguistic debates because of its lack of precision: should the criteria of definition be typological, genetic, or sociolinguistic? As David DeCamp summarizes:

> Some definitions are based on function, the role these languages play in the community: e.g., a pidgin is an auxiliary trade language. Some are based on historical origins and development: e.g., a pidgin may be spontaneously generated; a creole is a language that has evolved from a pidgin. Some definitions include formal characteristics: restricted vocabulary; absence of gender, true tenses, inflectional morphology, or relative clauses, etc. Some linguists combine these different kinds of criteria and include additional restrictions in their definitions. (3-4)

A good example that illustrates this predicament is the classic "Model for a Sociolinguistic Typology of Languages," which was created by William A. Stewart in the early 1960s and has since been revised twice:

Model	Attributes
I (1962)	1. *standardization* The existence of codified norms which are accepted by the language community 2. *vitality* The existence of a living community of native speakers 3. *historicity* Whether or not the language has developed through use of some ethnic or social group 4. *homogeneity* Whether or not the basic grammar and lexicon are derived from the same pre-stages of the language
II (1968)	**1-3 as in 1962, plus** 4. *autonomy* Whether or not it is accepted by the users as being distinct from other varieties
III (1971)	**1-4 as in 1968, plus** 5. *reduction* Whether or not it makes use of a smaller set of structural items and relations than some related variety of the same language 6. *mixture* Whether or not it consists essentially of items and structures derived from no source outside itself 7. *de facto norms* Whether or not it possesses norms of usage which, though uncodified, are accepted by the community

Table 1: Models for a Sociolinguistic Typology of Languages (Stewart)

The original model of 1962 attempted to classify the sociolinguistic status of language varieties by means of a set of attributes such as whether or not they: a) are standardized, b) are the native language of a living speech community, c) have developed 'naturally,' and d) have developed from one or multiple sources. The last characteristic in particular seems to have at first been invented especially to classify Creoles. It was also the first one to be dropped in the second model, most likely because homogeneity did not comply with any one 'type' exclusively – after all, English is also a language with more than one variety in its ancestry. As a result, the model was changed in 1968 and in 1971 (in Fishman). Other attributes were also redefined, for example, *historicity*, which at first meant having "developed through use of some ethnic or social group"; later on, the attribute was reclassified as meaning whether or not the community was concerned about finding a "'respectable' ancestry in times long past" for the language (Fishman 230) – which again made historicity a criterion of distinction between Creole and standard languages. The point here is that the model seems to match the negative perceptions of those varieties called Creoles rather than any 'objective' principles of classification.

The elusive character of Creole definitions led David DeCamp to the conclusion that "to a creolist, almost everyone else's definition of a creole sounds absurd and arbitrary" – yet "linguists all agree that there is such a group, that it includes many languages and large numbers of speakers," as he points out (3-4).

How can we explain this discrepancy between the firm conviction that there are such languages and the evident problem of defining a basis for classification? The discursive formation of the concept of Creole, I want to argue, is the key to this problem. In this article, I will look at three points concerning what I call the conception of Creole (cf. also Mühleisen), both in its physical origin and its mental representation: a) the etymological origin of the term Creole, b) the sociohistorical background, and c) the epistemological environment in which this idea was conceived.

Creole Etymology

Much of the confusion about the attempt to define Creoles as a group of languages arises from the unfortunate choice of a term which, long before its introduction to linguistics, was employed as a lay term for various references.[3] In the history of its use, the term Creole has undergone various semantic shifts that reveal not only a lot about the social history of the term but also about the attitudes with which it is associated.

As most established etymological sources (e.g., the *OED*) agree, the term 'creole' derives from Spanish *criollo* ('native') – adapted from Portuguese *crioulo* – and was first used to designate Spaniards born in the Americas in order to distinguish them from more recent settlers from Europe. D'Acosta's *Historia natural y moral de las Indias* (1590) is cited as the earliest source of its written use. At first, the term seems to have carried high prestige in the New World. For North American usage, *Webster's Dictionary* (2nd ed., 1934) gives a citation from George W. Cable's *Creoles of Louisiana* (1885) which states that the term was first used by French settlers, and "implied a certain excellence of origin" (1: 41). The particular French connection was soon modified to include persons of high social rank with French or Spanish ancestry, i.e., mostly plantation owners. Later, however, Cable elaborates, "the term was adopted by, not conceded to, the natives of mixed blood and is still so used among themselves" (Cable, 41). We can therefore observe a semantic shift here, from its early implication of an ancestral 'purity' to the later, explicit notion of mixed heritage.

While the term was at first only employed to refer to people, later uses also included attributional or adjectival meanings, as "belonging to or characteristic of a Creole" (*OED*, 1972, 1163 referring to vol II of *The Annals of Jamaica* by

---

3   Cf. also Mufwene (*Ecology* 9-11) on the intricacies of the use of the terms Pidgin and Creole.

Rev. G.W. Bridges). According to *Collier's Encyclopedia* of 1965, this has led to a confusion between person reference, i.e. "a Creole (person)" and adjective usage and may be responsible for the shift from European to mixed African/European person reference, "for it has been customary to apply the adjective to anything produced in the ex-colonies [...]. Thus, there are 'creole' eggs, 'creole' carrots, 'creole' mules, and, in the same adjectival sense, 'creole' Negroes, to differentiate the latter from the *bossals* imported from Africa." (429)

When the term was increasingly employed to refer to the speech of both black and white Creoles in the course of the eighteenth century, one may assume that it was first used in an adjective-like function, as the speech characteristic of a Creole person. As early as 1777, the Moravian missionary Christian Oldendorp distinguishes between metropolitan European languages and European languages in the West Indies. He notes that "only those people who learned to speak them in Europe can talk the pure European form of the language. On the other hand, the people who were born here – the crioles – do not speak the same kind of language." (ms. quoted in Holm 18-9). The contrast between the metropolitan languages and the speech of the Creoles is therefore much more marked than the speech used by black versus white inhabitants of the Caribbean territories. On the use of Creole by whites, Oldendorp remarks that children of European origin are usually brought up by black nannies and among black children, and that they therefore learn Creole first, if not exclusively.[4] (Oldendorp 358) The semantic shift the term has undergone is twofold. It has moved away from a designation of "purity" to a designation of "mixture," and the meaning has broadened, from person reference to include language.

The names of many Caribbean language varieties contain the term Creole as one element of a compound (e.g., Belizean Creole, Guyanese Creole), especially those that have been in continued contact with their lexifier. Because of the negative image associated with the term, there have been quite a number of suggestions for renaming the varieties, e.g., Jamaican Creole as "nation language"[5] – so far without noticeable success. This is not surprising, given that such a change in naming can only be successful if it is supported "from below," and if the change occurs gradually through broader usage rather than authoritative demand. The dilemma here becomes particularly evident if we reflect on the process of how the term came into being – not through legislation or on the basis of linguistic criteria, but via its manifestation in historical-colonial discourse. Categories, after all, take form not because they objectively exist, but because they have been created by humans. As George Lakoff remarks in *Women, Fire and Dangerous Things*, his seminal work on language and conceptualization, with regard to the relationship between metaphysics and epistemology,

---

4 "Die blanken [= weißen, S. M.] Kinder werden teils von Negerinnen gewartet, teils wachsen sie unter Negerkindern auf und lernen also zuerst die criolische oder Negersprache. Man trifft welche an, die keine andere recht können." (Oldendorp 358)
5 Cf. Brathwaite who introduced this term to refer to Jamaican Creole.

> it would be very strange to say that [...] a category [like a particular
> kinship category, S. M.] existed independent of human minds and human
> conceptual systems. In such cases, human minds have produced such re-
> alities. This is the case for institutional facts of all kinds. Institutions are
> created by people. They are culture-specific. They are products of the
> human mind. And they are real. (207)

And, one might add, they are here to stay. Once a category is established, it is extremely difficult to free one's mind from this classification or to avoid reference
to the established and named object.

Creoles and their Social History

The history of the term Creole shows that its origin is tied to the colonial situation. But not only that: it seems to be almost exclusively associated with plantation slavery. Salikoko Mufwene stresses the importance of the social and ethnic
distribution in the settler colonies and considers this as decisive for the terminological distinction between Creoles and other contact-based varieties:

> There are good socio-historical reasons why these varieties [e.g., in set-
> tler colonies like Australia, the U.S., S. M.] have not been called cre-
> oles: they developed in settings in which descendants of non-Europeans
> have been the minority; and they have not been disowned by Europe-
> ans and descendants thereof. Typically, creoles have been island and/or
> coastal phenomena, especially associated with the plantation industry of
> the eighteenth and nineteenth centuries. The other contact varieties do
> not have this typical genetic history. (*Jargons* 57)

In the final analysis, this argument implies, it is not only the language situation,
but rather the prestige of the social group of speakers that determines whether or
not a language is categorized as a Creole. The notion of Creole as the "language
of slavery" can best be observed in the heated arguments over Creole/Patois,
which are frequently conducted in the columns or "Letters to the Editor" sections
of Caribbean newspapers. The following examples are taken from the Jamaican
newspaper *Daily Gleaner/Sunday Gleaner.* In the first text, the author's aversion
is directed against those who

> would like to see Patois retained as part of our cultural heritage and be-
> lieve that it can occupy that honorable place alongside the teaching of
> standard English. I, on the other hand, take the view that if it is what is
> called our 'cultural heritage' it is a lousy heritage, reverent of slavery
> and that we keep on saying that it is a great thing, merely encourages its
> continued use until it will finally swamp what remains of standard Eng-
> lish in Jamaica. Of necessity, most people have inherited Patois but I see
> no reason to make a virtue of a necessity. (Cargill A8)

A concerned *Daily Gleaner* reader expresses a similar attitude, and views Patois/ Creole as a language of illiteracy and inadequacy:

> They [intellectuals, S. M.] speak of Patois as being a part of our heritage. This is true; its genesis is from our dark backward era when our ancestors were illiterate and unread. As a result, they were unable to properly pronounce all but the most basic of English words. The revisionists among us, in an attempt to advance their agenda, have put a new spin on this, and are attempting to romanticise this inadequacy of our ancestors by saying that it was their unique blend of English, Spanish, African dialect, etc. Their hypothesis is that Patois was consciously conceived out of an attempt to confuse 'backra' [= the white plantation owners, S. M.]. This is nonsense! It stands to reason that whereas there may have been minor elements of this along the way, the more plausible explanation surely must be due to an uneducated people's inability to properly pronounce English words. (Russell, "Letter to the Editor")

Such linguistic evaluations have a long tradition and can be traced back to eighteenth-century sources in West Indian plantation societies and their population. It may be significant that these attitudes toward language were most prominent at a time when the importing of slaves had already passed its peak and the plantation industry was thriving. The majority of documents, which brought 'home' evaluative reports of the manners and habits of the inhabitants of the West Indies, are either travel diaries (e.g., Nugent) or planters' reports (e.g., Leslie, Long). An outstanding example of the latter is Edward Long's three-volumed *The History of Jamaica* (1774), which offers a vast number of examples of contemporary attitudes toward language and also some interesting insights into the late eighteenth-century linguistic situation. Long distinguishes between "the Africans [who] speak their respective dialects, with some mixture of broken English" and the language of the Creoles which "is bad English, larded with the Guiney dialect, owing to their adopting the African words, in order to make themselves understood by the imported slaves, which they find much easier than teaching these strangers to learn English" (Long 426).

As already mentioned in Oldendorp's observations, the speech forms of slaves and those of the white Creole population were rather similar – a fact that was met with scorn and contempt by metropolitan travelers and West Indian planters alike. This is reflected in the following historical excerpts:

> The Creole language is not confined to the negroes. Many of the ladies, who have not been educated in England, speak a sort of broken English, with an indolent drawling out of their words, that is very tiresome if not disgusting. I stood next to a lady one night, near a window, and, by way of saying something, remarked that the air was much cooler than usual; to which she answered, 'Yes, ma-am, *him rail-ly too fra-ish*'. (Nugent 132)

The travel diary by Lady Nugent quoted above is certainly addressed to an (imaginary) metropolitan audience. The same can be said for the historical account of Jamaica, written by Charles Leslie in thirteen letters and published under various titles:

> To talk of a *Homer*, or a *Virgil*, or a *Tully*, or a *Demosthenes*, is quite unpolite; and it cannot be otherwise; for a Boy, till the Age of Seven or Eight, diverts himself with the Negroes, acquires their broken way of talking, their Manner of Behavior, and all the Vices which these unthinking Creatures can teach; then perhaps he goes to School; but young Master must not be corrected; if he learns 'tis well; if not, it can't be helped. After a little Knowledge of reading, he goes to the Dancing-school, and commences Beau, learns the common Topicks of Discourse, and visits and rakes with his Equals. (Leslie 36-7)

One of the recurring themes in these eighteenth-century documents is the fear of "contamination" of the white population by their black servants, be it the language, manners, or habits of the whites. The fact that Creole speech was not restricted to blacks, but was spoken by a substantial part of the plantation society, seemed to threaten the hierarchy of the colonial plantation society: if master and slave speak alike, how can the former uphold the social difference? Furthermore, a lot of underlying eighteenth-century philosophical assumptions are reflected by the fear that, alongside the speech of those held in contempt, one would also adopt "their Manner of Behavior, and all the Vices which these unthinking Creatures can teach." Such negative attitudes toward Creole by both the colonists and the metropolitan traveler were not merely matters of individual taste, but instrumental in eighteenth-century plantation society for a number of purposes. Apart from the already mentioned necessity of marking a (linguistic) distinction between the white and black population – despite the real situation – chauvinist ideas about "superior" versus "inferior" forms of language were used to reinforce stereotypes about Africans as childlike people barely capable of speech. These notions were important arguments in justifying the slave plantation economy and were in turn nourished by those defending slavery as an institution (such as, for instance, the planter Long). And finally, they also served to uphold a highly paternalistic and condescendingly protective stance toward colonial subjects.

The Notion of Creole and its Epistemological Environment

The negative evaluations of Creole documented above were not formed and formulated independently of the thinking of the particular historical period in which they emerged. The eighteenth century, i.e., the time when Caribbean creolization reached its peak, can be seen as a fruitful environment for expressing metropolitan contempt about the "colonial corruptions" of the English language. Pure economic envy – white Creoles in the West Indies were seen as rich and lazy – as well as the fear of a loss of control over the English language may be two reasons for this stance. But a look at the dominant Western concepts of language and culture during the eighteenth century may reveal further grounds for such disdain. As the work of Michel Foucault on the production of knowledge has shown, knowledge and belief systems always operate within their own epistemological environment – there are therefore no timeless truths.

First of all, we can note that in Britain the eighteenth century was the age of language standardization and language prescription. The printing press (and with it the growing need to create a more uniform written standard) had already existed for 250 years when this practical aspect of language usage was put into the prescriptive form of influential dictionaries (Samuel Johnson's *Dictionary*) and grammars (e.g., Bishop Lowth's *A Short Introduction to English Grammar*). This development had an enormous impact on the creation of language norms and, simultaneously, negative attitudes toward language (speech as well as writing) that deviated from the standard form. We can how linguistic ideology emerged from a practical standpoint and later began to serve as a justification of a particular language structure and use.

The Caribbean plantation society is a good example of the practical implementation of such a linguistic ideology: linguistic evaluations are made instruments for the legitimization and affirmation of social structure. Contemporary scholarly literature supported the application of distinctions of superiority and inferiority to metropolitan versus colonial/Creole populations. In his classic book on the origin and spread of European nationalism, Benedict Anderson suggests that the writings of Herder and Rousseau exerted a wide influence in creating such a distinction between Europeans and those born in the colonies. They claimed that climate and ecology had a profound and constitutive impact on character: "It was only too easy from there to make the convenient, vulgar deduction that creoles, born in a savage hemisphere, were by nature different from, and inferior to, the metropolitans – thus unfitted for higher office" (Anderson 61).

Linguistics as a scholarly field became highly popular and influential toward the beginning of the nineteenth century. The historical-comparative research of the time was dominated by the search for the origin of language in general and the relationship between individual languages. The ideal of a "highly developed" language was represented by the classical languages Latin and Greek, i.e., inflectional languages. This model influenced evaluative connections between the forms of a language and its stage of development. August Wilhelm von Schlegel, for instance, divides the languages of the world into three different classes: languages without any grammatical structure, those that employ affixes, and the inflectional languages:

> Today's languages and earlier ones spoken by the various people on this earth fall into three classes: languages without any grammatical structure,

languages that use affixes, and inflecting languages. Languages of the first class merely consist of words of a kind that are not capable of any development or modification. One might say that all words of such a language are roots, albeit infertile roots, which develop neither plants nor trees. (von Schlegel 187, my translation)[6]

The period of Romanticism saw language as an organic, developing body, closely connected to nation and culture as homogeneous entities. In such an organic view, "mixed languages" like Creoles would be seen as unnatural, disrupting the organic body of the language. This quote by Wilhelm von Humboldt illustrates this view on language contact and the mixing of languages in a general sense:

> One may take it as a firm principle that everything in language is based on analogy and that its structure is organic up to its smallest parts. Exceptions to this rule are found only in those cases where the linguistic development of a nation is disrupted, where one people borrow linguistic elements from another, or are forced to use another language wholly or partly. This occurs in all languages known to us today [...]. But whenever a language takes up a foreign element or mixes with another language, the assimilating activity starts at once. An effort is made to gradually change the matter that comes off second best in the mixing and to convert it into the analogous development of the other matter This mixing may thus result in shorter and longer analogous lines, but it does not easily result in completely inorganic matter. (von Humboldt 295, my translation)[7]

Von Humboldt does not make explicit reference to any particular languages here. He also concedes that borrowing elements from other languages is a common phenomenon. However, his idea of language as an organic whole nevertheless gives rise to the image of corruption, an idea often expressed in language attitudes

---

6   "Die Sprachen, die heute noch gesprochen werden und die früher bei den verschiedenen Völkern der Erde gesprochen worden sind, gliedern sich in 3 Klassen: die Sprachen ohne irgendwelche grammatische Struktur, die Sprachen, die Affixe verwenden, und die flektierenden Sprachen. Die Sprachen der ersten Klasse haben nur eine Art von Wörtern, die zu keiner Entwicklung oder Modifikation fähig sind. Man könnte sagen, dass alle Wörter einer solchen Sprache Wurzeln sind, aber unfruchtbare Wurzeln, die weder Pflanzen noch Bäume hervorbringen."

7   "Man kann es als einen festen Grundsatz annehmen, dass Alles in einer Sprache auf Analogie beruht und ihr Bau bis in seine feinsten Theile hinein ein organischer Bau ist. Nur wo die Sprachbildung bei einer Nation Störungen erleidet, wo ein Volk Sprachelemente von einem anderen entlehnt oder gezwungen wird, sich einer fremden Sprache ganz oder zum Theil zu bedienen, finden Ausnahmen von dieser Regel Statt. Dieser Fall tritt nun zwar wohl bei allen uns jetzt bekannten Sprachen ein [...]. Allein wo eine Sprache ein fremdes Element in sich aufnimmt oder sich mit einer anderen vermischt, da beginnen sogleich ihre assimilirende Thätigkeit und ihr Bemühen, nach und nach denjenigen Stoff, welcher in der Vermischung den kürzern zieht, so viel als möglich in die, dem andern eigentümliche analogische Bildung zu verwandeln, so dass durch diese Mischungen zwar kürzere und längere analogische Reihen entstehen nicht leicht aber ganz unorganische Masse zurückbleibt."

toward Creoles. Interpreted negatively, von Humboldt's "foreign element," which has come into the language via language contact, might appear not so much as an addition or a new creation, but rather as a harmful virus that affects the rest of the linguistic body as well.

Scholarly Discourse in the Twentieth Century: *Ab Ovo* Languages and the Search for a Linguistic Holy Grail

Looking back to the models for a sociolinguistic typology discussed at the beginning of this paper (Stewart, "Outline of Linguistic Typology," "Sociolinguistic Typology"), we see that they attempted to encode this idea of a "lack of purity" in Creoles in the attributes "homogeneity" (Model 1, 1962) and "mixture" (Model 3, 1971). Behind this implied absence of a pure origin we see another nineteenth-century concept. During that period of time, the notion of Creole languages became increasingly prominent in linguistics: it was part of the idea of a genetic relationship between languages that is expressed, for instance, in the family tree model or in concepts such as language families. Applied to the situation of Creole languages, one might state that these are languages with dubious parenthood, i.e., "bastard languages" – a term which has actually been used for Creole languages in various contexts (cf., for a recent example, Bickerton, *Bastard Tongues*). It is rather obvious that the metaphors used in the scholarly discourse on these languages are taken almost entirely from the field of biology. It does not come as a surprise that the concept of a "hybrid" language, a friendlier and more politically correct term compared to "bastard," is also a borrowing from botany. This choice of metaphor is by no means a coincidence. It illustrates how the emergence of a linguistic interest in these languages must be placed in a particular epistemological environment, one in which Darwin's evolutionary theory surfaces as well.

Darwinist Images and Creole Linguistics

Did this Darwinist view on language, and on Creoles in particular, survive into the twentieth century? Is there a tradition beginning in the eighteenth and nineteenth centuries that has shaped today's modes of Creole conceptualization? The interest of modern twentieth-century linguistics in Creole languages arose from various motivations: firstly, the waves of independence movements in the 1950s and 1960s were accompanied by a growing attention to colonial and then postcolonial language situations. Historical-comparative approaches to the analysis of Creole genesis, i.e., the origin and the exact composition of the languages, paid close attention to the contribution of the substrate languages – in the Caribbean Creole case, West African languages – thus attempting to correct notions of Creoles as merely incomplete and incorrect versions of the lexifier languages. One theory that arose out of this interest, the so-called substrate theory (e.g., Alleyne) claims, for instance, that grammatical and phonological structures of Caribbean Creole languages can be traced almost completely to grammatical and phonological structures of West African languages.

On the other hand, linguists noted similarities between Creoles in the Atlantic and the Pacific region that could not be explained by virtue of the involved 'parent languages' alone. This detail gave rise to the second major motivation for studying Creole languages: the idea that the parallel structures that could be found in Creoles all over the world[8] might, in fact, be universal language structures. The attraction of this idea is obvious: if Creole languages revert to universal structures in their formation, they can serve as material for clues to language origin in general. In other words, Creoles can be useful in the search for the Holy Grail in linguistics. This is also expressed in Bickerton's idea of the vicinity of Creoles and "*ab ovo*" creations of language: "Creoles are the nearest thing one can find to ab ovo creations of language, but they are not and cannot be purely ab ovo creations" (Bickerton, *Roots* 45). More than one century before, shortly after the publication of Darwin's *On the Origin of Species* (1859), Creoles had already been associated with *ab ovo* creations in this somewhat condescending statement by Alfred de Saint Quentin (1872):

> [Creole grammar] is, therefore, a spontaneous product of the human mind, freed from any kind of intellectual culture [...] But when one studies its structure, one is so very surprised, so very charmed by its rigor and simplicity that one wonders if the creative genius of the most knowledgeable linguist would have been able to give birth to anything that so completely reaches its goal, that imposes so little strain on memory and that calls for so little effort from those with limited intelligence. An in-depth analysis has convinced me of something that seems paradoxical. Namely: if one wanted to create ab ovo an all-purpose language that would allow, after only a few days of study, a clear and consistent exchange of simple ideas, one would not be able to adopt more logical and more productive structures than those found in Creole grammar. (quoted in DeGraff, *Origin of Creoles* 215, trans. DeGraff)

Influenced by Chomsky's idea of a human mental language program by means of which language acquisition is based on the generation of rules rather than imitation, Derek Bickerton formulated his Bioprogram Hypothesis. This theory basically claims that, on the road from Pidgin to Creole, children of Pidgin and multiple language speakers are exposed to such chaotic language input that, in the process of language acquisition, these children have to revert to fundamental universal structures in order to create a full language.

---

8 Derek Bickerton, the main promulgator of this idea, famously compiled a list consisting of twelve features in such "common structures" in creole languages.

> The idea that there is an innate bioprogram that determines the form of human language is still vigorously if often illogically resisted, threatening, as it seems, to free will, mental improvements, and the whole galaxy of human dreams and desires. [...] If it is the case that the creole child's capacity to create language is due to such a bioprogram, then [...] it would be absurd to suppose that this bioprogram functions only in the rare and unnatural circumstances in which the normal cultural transmission of language breaks down. (Bickerton, *Roots* 134)

It is only a small step from the search for universal structures in Creoles to the search for a primitive *Ursprache* ('original language') freed of all the ballast with which civilization has burdened languages. Again, it seems, the thinking is related to a rather biologistic, evolutionary idea of language. In the case of Creole languages, the reason for relating them to such *Ursprachen* is the fact that they are not inflectional languages, i.e., they have little inflectional morphology. In von Schlegel's words, they are languages that "merely consist of words of a kind, which are not capable of any development or modification" (cited above). The scholar's stance with regard to the question of Creole genesis thus becomes a highly ideological issue in which each party stakes their claims – usually supported by seemingly objective empirical data – on the proportional contribution of African and European languages as well as universal processes in the creation of Creoles.

Debates on Creole Exceptionalism

It is no surprise that recent debates on the issue of whether or not Creoles form a different type of language or are exceptional languages focus once again on the question of morphological complexity (cf. DeGraff, "Origin of Creoles," "Against Creole Exceptionalism," "Linguists' Most Dangerous Myth"; McWorther, "Identifying the Creole Prototype," "The World's Simplest Grammars," *Defining Creole*). Are Creole grammars really "the world's simplest grammars," as McWorther claims in one of his articles? His Creole prototype is characterized by three features that, he supposes, are shared by all Creoles all over the world. He also maintains that no language that has native speakers but does not have a pidgin ancestor can possess all three features: exclusive semantic compositional derivation, the absence of tone, and the absence of bound inflectional morphology. This claim has become the subject of fierce disputes, which are dominated, for example, by attempts to provide further evidence that Creoles do have some inflectional morphology. (cf., for instance, DeGraff "Origin of Creoles," Farquharson "Typology and Grammar"). In his critique of McWorther's "Identifying the Creoles," DeGraff argues for an ideological turn in the discussion of Creole languages, which have so far been treated as exceptional and special types (*Origins of Creoles* 227). Part of this turn is a "Cartesian critique," as a rational methodological doubt of linguistic views that are rooted in Darwinian evolutionary thought, and DeGraff cites contemporaries of Darwin, Hermann Osthoff, and Carl Brugmann to support his assessment:

> Language is not a thing which leads a life of its own outside of and above human beings, but [...] it has its true existence only in the individual, and hence [...] all changes in the life of a language can only proceed from the individual speaker; and second, [...] the mental and physical activity of man must have been at all times essentially the same when he acquired a language inherited from his ancestors and reproduced and modified the speech forms which had been absorbed into his consciousness. (quoted in DeGraff, *Origin of Creoles* 216)

But the idea of "language [as a] thing which leads a life of its own" is difficult to get rid of, as a brief glance at conceptualizations of language in any linguistic text book with its notions of the "life cycle of languages" or "language death" will verify. In a recent publication, Mufwene argues against the conceptualization of language as an organism. Instead, he encourages the reader to "think of language as a species" (*Ecology* 15-21). While Mufwene tackles many important issues in his book, the location of its main arguments in the biologistic and evolutionary tradition remains somewhat problematic.

Conclusion

The question of whether or not Creole languages are characterized by their lack of morphological complexity is, in my view, beside the point. The more interesting question to ask is why the concept of Creole languages as a particular type came into being. In other words, the issue is one of foregrounding epistemology over metaphysics (cf. Lakoff cited above). After all, no matter how much data one collects to prove or disprove that Creoles are capable of inflectional affixation, the fact remains that the category of a Creole does not simply exist as a reality outside of the human mind, but was created in a particular environment. One could thus conclude with Foucault that

> [the] question posed by language analysis of some discursive fact or another is always: according to what rules has a particular statement been made, and consequently, according to what rules could other similar statements be made? The description of the events of discourse poses a quite different question: how is it that one particular statement appeared rather than another? (Foucault 27)

My brief exploration of the past should have made clear that the concept of Creole has been constructed in a network of statements, and that the formation of Creole as an object has come into being under certain conditions and was instrumental in justifying of the colonial plantation economy. I have also demonstrated that the formation of the object "Creole" is rooted in a particular epistemological environment, at the turn from the Classical to the Modern episteme. The relationship with contemporary ideas in other sciences such as biology and, in particular, evolutionary theory is more than obvious and continues in the imagery of linguistic descriptions (e.g., "hybridity," "life-cycle of languages"). Because the concept of Creole was formed discursively, it cannot be simply abandoned. However, as I have tried to show elsewhere (Mühleisen), Creole discourse is an ongoing development. Processes such as new restructurings, new uses and users in the urban diaspora, new functions in fields like writing and translation are currently contributing to prestige changes that will gradually alter the concept of what really makes a Creole a Creole.

References

Anderson, Benedict. *Imagined Communities. Reflections on the Origin and Spread of Nationalism.* London: Verso, 1983.

Alleyne, Mervyn. *Comparative Afro-American.* Ann Arbor: Karoma Press, 1980.

Bickerton, Derek. *Roots of Language.* Ann Arbor: Karoma Press, 1981.

---. *Bastard Tongues. A Trailblazing Linguist Finds Clues to Our Common Humanity in the World's Lowliest Languages.* New York: Simon and Schuster, 2008.

Brathwaite, Edward Kamau. *History of the Voice.* London: New Beacon Books, 1981.

Bridges, George Wilson. The Annals of Jamaica. 2 vols. London, John Murray, 1928.

Cable, George Washington. The Creoles of Louisiana. London: Nimmo, 1885.

Cargill, Morris. "Corruption of Language Is no Cultural Heritage." *Sunday Gleaner* [Jamaica] 29 Oct. 1989, A8.

Collier's Encyclopedia, 24 vols. London: Crowell-Collier, 1965.

Darwin, Charles. *On the Origin of Species by Means of Natural Selection, or the Preservation of Favoured Races in the Struggle for Life.* London: John Murray, 1859.

DeCamp, David. "The Development of Pidgin and Creole Studies." *Pidgin and Creole Linguistics.* Ed. Albert Valdman. Bloomington/London: Indiana University Press, 1977. 3-20.

DeGraff, Michel. "On the Origin of Creoles: A Cartesian Critique of 'Neo'-Darwinian Linguistics." *Linguistic Typology* 5.2 (2001): 213-310.

---. "Against Creole Exceptionalism." *Language* 79.2 (2003): 391-410.

---. "Linguists' Most Dangerous Myth: The Fallacy of Creole Exceptionalism." *Language in Society* 34 (2005): 533-91.

Farquharson, Joseph. "Typology and Grammar: Creole Morphology Revisited." *Deconstructing Creole.* Ed. Umberto Ansaldo, Stephen Matthews and Lisa Lim. Amsterdam: John Benjamins, 2007. 21-37.

Fishman, Joshua A. "The Sociology of Language: an Interdisciplinary Social Science Approach to Language in Society." *Advances in the Sociology of Language I.* Ed. Joshua Fishman. The Hague: Mouton, 1971. 217-404.

Foucault, Michel. *The Archaeology of Knowledge.* Trans. A.M. Sheridan Smith. London: Routledge, 1972.

Holm, John. *Pidgins and Creoles.* Vol. I: *Theorie and Structure.* Cambridge: Cambridge University Press, 1988.

Humboldt, Wilhelm von. "Ankündigung einer Schrift über die baskische Sprache und Nation, nebst Angabe des Gesichtspunktes und Inhaltes derselben." 1812. Reprint. *Gesammelte Schriften,* vol. 3 Berlin: Akademie der Wissenschaften, 1903: 288-99.

Johnson, Samuel. *A Dictionary of the English Language: in which the Words Are Deduced from Their Originals, and Illustrated in Their Different Significations by Examples from the Best Writers. To which Are Prefixed, A History of the Language, and an English Grammar.* London: Printed for J. and P. Knapton; T. and T. Longman; C. Hitch and L. Hawes; A. Millar; and R. and J. Dodsley, 1755.

Lakoff, George. *Women, Fire and Dangerous Things. What Categories Reveal about the Mind.* Chicago & London: University of Chicago Press, 1987.

Leslie, Charles. *A New History of Jamaica.* 2nd ed. London: T. Hodges, 1740.

Long, Edward. *History of Jamaica, or General Survey of the Ancient and Modern State of that Island. With Reflections on its Situations, Settlements, Inhabitants, Climate, Products, Commerce, Laws and Government.* 1774. Introd. George Metcalf. 3 vols. London: Frank Cass, 1970.

Lowth, Robert. *A Short Introduction to English Grammar.* London: A. Millar; and R. and J. Dodsley, 1762.

McWorther, John. "Identifying the Creole Prototype: Vindicating a Typological Class." *Language* 74 (1998): 788-818.

---. "The World's Simplest Grammars are Creole Grammars." *Linguistic Typology* 5.2-3 (2001): 125-66.

---. *Defining Creole.* Oxford: Oxford University Press, 2005.

Meyer, Paul Georg et al. *Synchronic English Linguistics. An Introduction.* Tübingen: Narr, 2002.

Mühleisen, Susanne. *Creole Discourse. Exploring Prestige Formation and Change Across Caribbean English-lexicon Creoles* (CLL 24). Amsterdam: Benjamins, 2002.

Mufwene, Salikoko. "Jargons, Pidgins, Creoles and Koines: What Are They?" *The Structure and Status of Pidgins and Creoles.* Ed. Arthur K. Spears and Donald Winford. (Creole Language Library 19). Amsterdam: Benjamins, 1997. 35-69.

---. *The Ecology of Language Evolution.* Cambridge: Cambridge University Press, 2001.

Nugent, Maria Skinner. *Lady Nugent's Journal. Jamaica One Hundred Years Ago.* 1802. Reprint. Ed. Frank Cundall. London: Adam and Charles Black, 1907.

Oldendorp, Christian Georg Andreas. *Historie der caribischen Inseln Sanct Thomas, Sanct Crux und Sanct Jan.* 1777. Ed. Gudrun Meier, Stephan Palmié, Peter Stein and Horst Ulbricht. Kommentierte Edition des Originalmanuskripts. Erster Teil. Berlin: Verlag für Wissenschaft und Bildung, 2000.

Osthoff, Hermann and Carl Brugmann. *Morphologische Untersuchungen auf dem Gebiet der Indogermanischen Sprachen.* Leipzig: Hirzel, 1878-1910.

Oxford English Dictionary (Compact Edition), Oxford: Clarendon Press, 1972.

Russell, John. "Letter to the Editor: Patois Versus the English Language." *Daily Gleaner* [Jamaica], 8 February 2002.

Schlegel, August Wilhelm von. 1818. "Observations Sur la Langue et la Littérature Provençales." 1818. Reprint. *Sprachwissenschaft. Der Gang ihrer Entwicklung von der Antike bis zur Gegenwart.* Ed. Hans Arens. vol. 1. Frankfurt am Main: Fischer Athenäum, 1969. 187-91.

Stewart, William A. "An Outline of Linguistic Typology for Describing Multilingualism." *Study of the Role of Second Languages in Asia, Africa and Latin America.* Ed. F. A. Rice. Washington: Center for Applied Linguistics, 1962. 15-25.

---. "A Sociolinguistic Typology for Describing National Multilingualism." *Readings in the Sociology of Language.* Ed. Joshua A. Fishman. The Hague: Mouton, 1968. 531-45.

Thomason, Sarah G., and Terrence Kaufman. *Language Contact, Creolization and Genetic Linguistics.* Berkeley: University of California Press, 1988.

Webster's New International Dictionary of the English Language. 2 vols. 2nd ed. London: Bell et al., 1934.

CHAPTER THREE

The Museum Predicament.
Representing Cultural Encounter in
Historical and Contemporary Collections

DOMINIK COLLET

Ethnographical museums have recently become the target of severe and fundamental criticism. Their exhibitions have been blamed for stereotyping non-European people as primitive. The selection of exhibits has been held responsible for
the 'othering' of foreigners and constructing seemingly homogenous ethnicities
out of hybrid societies. They have been criticized for perpetuating the colonial
gaze of their founders and failing to address their own history, including the often
violent formation of their collections and their involvement in colonial exploitation. The very idea that exhibits could serve as 'cultural brokers' and museums as
places of cultural encounter has been questioned. Indeed the critique has been so
fundamental that museologists talk of "an epochal shift in museum history" (Kirshenblatt-Gimblett 369).

Remarkably, while the modern ethnographical museum's ability to serve as
a place of understanding has come under pressure, the interpretation of its early modern predecessors has shifted in the opposite direction. The museums or
'Kunstkammern' of the sixteenth and seventeenth centuries are no longer regarded as haphazard collections of quaint curiosities but as places of scientific discovery. Their exotic 'trifles' are now cast as crucial catalysts for the emancipation
from established authorities. The foreign objects unknown to ancient authors re-
putedly fomented an understanding of the world based on material evidence instead of established books. Accordingly, the stereotypical descriptions of contemporary travel literature are often contrasted with the factual, respectful, or apparently unprejudiced way early modern collectors looked at their exotic specimens
(Bujok 187ff.).

In this essay I will question the interpretation of early modern museums as
laboratories of evidence.[1] I will try to show that the 'research museum' remained
an ideal proposed in contemporary theoretical tracts, while a closer look at the actual practice of collectors suggests a view of the non-European world that was far
from unbiased. In fact, I hope to reveal some basic challenges to the representa-

---

1 For examples of the popular association of early modern museums with the laboratory
– the classic locale of the Scientific Revolution – see: Findlen, "Laboratorium" 194 and
Bredekamp, *Antikensehnsucht* 52ff.

tion of distant cultures in the museum. While some of these challenges can be attributed to the peculiarities of the early modern era, many originated in the museum environment itself and remain valid today.

Initially I will focus on three practicioners of early modern collecting and their work as cultural mediators between the Old world and the New: Caspar Schmalkalden (1616-73), Johann Michael Wansleben (1635-79), and John Winthrop Jr. (1606-76). I will analyze their opposition as arbiters between colonial fringe and the European collector and examine the displays that resulted from their work. In a second step, I will compare their activities with those of modern curators and draw some conclusions about the predicament of museums as they try to reinvent themselves as sites of cultural encounter.

Early Museums

The first European museums were founded in the second half of the sixteenth century. In contrast to earlier collections, these 'Kunstkammern,' 'repositories,' or 'cabinets' ordered their exhibits according to elaborate taxonomic systems. They were also far more accessible than their medieval predecessors. Instead of simply gathering the collector's favorite items, the objects had to be chosen and presented with the potential visitors in mind. Finally, their collectors pursued not just entertainment but hoped to facilitate learning and erudition. Public access, educative purpose, and a structured collection mark them as 'museums' in the modern sense. However, they differed substantially from our modern establishments. Very few were publicly owned or institutionalized. Most belonged to private 'virtuosi' and were frequently sold or disposed of after the death of the founder. Collectors and visitors also came from social backgrounds that were surprisingly broad for their time but far more limited than today's museum public. They included the nobility, wealthy tradesmen, and the odd scholar or artisan. Furthermore, early museums were substantially less specialized, with collections ranging from objects of 'art' such as painting and antiques to monstrous births, miraculous animals, exotic plants, and ethnographic material. In fact, the increase in non-European material reaching the Old World in the sixteenth century constituted one of the main reasons for their establishment (Collet 30-4).

Most museum owners displayed objects that popular travel reports praised as strange, rare, or beautiful. They aimed to illustrate established knowledge and provide a safe space for social intercourse. Travelers on their 'grand tour' of Europe quickly seized the opportunities these museums offered. The collections along their route allowed them to meet local notables and establish contacts quickly and efficiently. Together with the popular printed museum catalogues these visits created a network of collectors and virtuosi that stretched throughout Europe and across established social and religious divides. Many of the museums' visitors kept in contact long after their visits and went on communicating by letters. By relating what they had seen in other collections they helped to fashion a uniform type of museum.

Encyclopedic collections remained the dominant type of museum for more than two hundred years. However, at the beginning of the eighteenth century it became obvious that the collections had lost touch with the rapid development of science as well as new forms of social representation. The new focus on utility and separate scientific disciplines paved the way for more specialized collections. At the same time, demands for broader public access threatened the exclusive milieu of the virtuosi and the privately owned museum. The 'polyhistor' and the collector of rarities were soon regarded as curiosities themselves.

Correspondingly, the older research on early museums focused on the display of useless monstrosities and their failure to contribute to scientific progress (regularly attributed to the undue involvement of noblemen). In recent years the early museums have made a remarkable comeback in the history of science. Paula Findlen and Ken Arnold have argued that the study of the hitherto unknown products of America and Asia might have constituted a source of 'new' knowledge that encouraged the establishment of an equally 'new science' (Findlen, "Laboratorium" and Arnold, *Cabinets*). Other researchers looked at the exhibits of early museums in search of an alternative to the incongruent accounts of contemporary travel literature. The idea that material evidence from overseas might provide an unfiltered source of information, replacing the "superficial [...], imperfect [...], ambiguous" travel reports, has occasionally been voiced by early modern collectors themselves (Waller 338). As I will show, however, substantial obstacles frustrated these endeavors – the museum environment being one of them.

Caspar Schmalkalden

Caspar Schmalkalden was born in the small town of Friedrichsroda near the Thuringian town of Gotha in 1616. His father was the town's mayor and funded his son's initial training as a surveyor. In 1642 Caspar traveled to Amsterdam where he joined the Dutch West India Company, signing a five-year contract as a soldier. He was initially stationed in the Brazilian colonies the Dutch had recently taken from the Portuguese. Later he joined an expedition force to Chile. After his return to Europe in 1645, Schmalkalden opted for another contract, this time with the Dutch East India Company. During his journey he stayed in the nascent colony on the Cape of Good Hope and met the famous "Hottentots" (Khoikhoi) of Africa. After some time in Batavia (today's Jakarta) he joined in diplomatic missions to Aceh (now part of Indonesia) and the Dutch outpost Deshima in Japan. In 1648 he took up the comfortable position of a surveyor in Taiwan. When he finally returned to Europe he had seen a vast part of the Dutch colonial empire and the world then known to Europeans (Schmalkalden 7-29).

In 1653 Schmalkalden reached Gotha again. While the town had suffered heavily during the Thirty Years' War, it was now hosting the court of the young Dukedom of Saxe-Gotha. When Schmalkalden realized that Ernest I of Saxe-Gotha planned to establish a museum in his new residence, he quickly grasped the opportunity and donated several of his exotic souvenirs. In return, the Duke granted him the position of a court clerk and entrusted the traveler with the acquisition of exotic material for his collection.

As the Duke's agent, Schmalkalden went to Amsterdam to obtain some of the foreign objects he knew through his travels. At the Gotha court he was also famous for his stories on the "many and numerous marvellous plants, fruits and other rarities of the Indies." His colorful tales of the 'Indians' were eagerly listened to and even inspired others to travel as far as he had (Vogel, Preface).[2]

The short and neutral entries in the inventories of the ducal museum reflect very little of this contextual information. However, while in Gotha Schmalkalden drew up several manuscripts that not only covered his travels, but also contained information on Indian "rarities," their uses, and the Indians themselves. A comparison of the museum's inventories with Schmalkalden's "West and East Indian journey" reveals extensive correspondences (Collet 97-101).[3] Stripped of the framework of his travels to and fro, Schmalkalden's texts read almost like a museum catalogue. Each plant or animal is treated in a separate chapter containing a careful illustration along with information on nomenclature, physical form, habitat, and uses. Additional chapters focus on the Indian "nations" and their material culture, each including drawings of a male and a female figure displaying their essential ethnographic objects. A large number of these objects were on display in the ducal museum. When Schmalkalden felt that important pieces were missing, he tried to acquire them from Amsterdam's curiosity shops.[4]

In his texts Schmalkalden provided much needed details on the exotica. By the time the exhibits arrived in Gotha they had lost almost all contextual information beyond their physical shape and their 'Indian' provenance. To fill these gaps Schmalkalden employed popular narratives to endow them with a meaningful 'story.' The collection's Indian baskets were used by female cannibals to carry human flesh. The "bow and arrow of the wild people of East- and West-India" illustrated the supposedly violent nature of Indian societies as well as their primitive technologies, already obsolete in Europe.

However, Schmalkalden did not limit his moralizing stories to ethnographic objects. On the cashew plant he remarked that its fermented juice provided a potent drink for the famous Indian dances and added that "those that are able

---

2   For a comprehensive analysis of the Gotha museum and Schmalkalden's role, see: Collet 35-132.
3   For a shortened and modernized version of Schmalkalden's journal, see: Schmalkalden, *Kompass*.
4   Cf. the 1656 "specification of several Indian rarities to be obtained in Amsterdam" by Caspar Schmalkalden in: Thüringisches Staatsarchiv Gotha, GA E IV (Sun) 2a. For a modern edition of this text see: Collet 360.

to drink, vomit and drink again are regarded as jolly fellows. They make merry, dance, sing and jump about, dressed in colourful feathers day and night until their supply runs dry." Similarly, the plant's rather inconspicuous nuts illustrated the Indian's intellectual deficiencies. Schmalkalden asserted that they were used as primitive calendars to remedy the Indian's inability to count beyond five. Each year a nut would be kept, "so that, if you ask them their age, one cannot ask for the number of the years, but rather for the number of cashews they have since collected."[5]

Schmalkalden's texts transferred fragments of European popular culture such as the 'danse sauvage,' the 'wild man,' and the 'amazon' across the ocean. He then played with the principle of inversion, or a 'world turned upside down': 'Indian' women appeared aggressive instead of docile, their daily bread consisted of poisonous plants and the miraculous cassowary-bird fed on hot coals. Apparently harmless objects, such as the collection's pieces of cassava bread, cassowary eggs or cashew nuts thus turned into representatives of a primitive, violent, and alien world that was not just foreign but the 'other' of Europe.

The presentation of exotic material in the museum mirrored Schmalkalden's textual interpretation. The selection of objects centered on material that appeared primitive to European eyes, just as Schmalkalden focused on Brazilians, 'Hottentots,' or Formosans instead of city-dwelling people. Schmalkalden's clear separation between Europe and the Indian 'other' was reflected in the absence of exhibits that could be associated with Indo-European contacts, hybridization, missionary activities, or trade. The museum also reflected Schmalkalden's opposition of a dynamic Europe with a static 'India' by excluding all material that reflected the dramatic changes of the colonial world.

This divide was emphasized further by the presentation of non-European material on a separate table in the exhibition room. Similarly, the museum's inventories listed "exotic, Indian and other foreign things" ("von Außwändischen Indianischen und sonst frembden sachen") apart from the European exhibits. As a result, overseas ethnographic material was associated with plants, animals, and nature, while European material was routinely divided into natural and man-made objects. The inventorie's short entries also followed Schmalkalden's homogenizing approach, by reducing the non-European world to a single 'other.' Most material in that category was simply listed as 'Indian' with no further indication of geographical provenance. In fact, the separation was less geographical than religious, integrating material from the non-Christian fringes of Europe into the

5   "[...] und welche das meiste sauffen, sich übergeben und wieder darauf sauffen können die werden für wackere Kerls geachtet. Sie machen sich lustig und frölich, sie tantzen, singen und springen mit ihren bunden federn gezieret nacht und tag, so lang als etwas [von dem Cashew-Wein, D.C.] vorhanden ist [...] Darumb, wenn man von ihnen zu wißen begehret, vor wie viel jahren was oder das andere geschah oder wie alt einer seÿ, muss man nicht nach der Zahl der jahre, sondern nach der Zahl der Castanien fragen, so sie seither der Zeit daswegen gesammlet haben." Caspar Schmalkalden, "West- und Ostindianische Reisebeschreibung" in: Forschungsbibliothek Gotha, Chart B 533 fol. 12ff.

'Indian' category. It closely mirrored Schmalkalden's characterization of all 'Indians' as heathens, negating their religious diversity.[6]

The museum thus presented the non-European world as a primitive, homogeneous, static land of heathens fundamentally different from the Old World. It captured little of the dynamic colonial life in the early seventeenth century that was characterized by emerging colonial societies, hybrid ethnicities, rapid Christianization, the creation of new artistic styles and forms of social organization, as well as the introduction of new crafts and European flora and fauna.

Accordingly, a closer look quickly reveals that Schmalkalden's text contains almost no original material. Instead of relying on his personal experiences, he in fact preferred to compile information from the authoritative travel accounts in the Duke's library. All accounts of animals, plants, Indians and their way of life are copied – often literally – out of popular books. Schmalkalden's contributions were limited to brief accounts of his travels, some anecdotes, and the mottos accompanying the drawings of 'Indian nations.' In a few cases he decided to correct or mitigate some reports. More often he eagerly supported the interpretation offered by his sources, particularly on the uncivilized and brutal nature of the Indian people. Accordingly, his caption for the illustration of a male Brazilian reads: "We go naked, knowing nothing of money. Only bow and arrow support us in the field. We crave for human flesh, be it arm or leg. Let it be cooked quickly so we can gorge ourselves on it." (Figs. 1 and 2)[7]

Copying from other, more respected authors was common practice in Schmalkalden's time. What is more surprising is that he chose to copy illustrations too. A large number of them came from the popular *Historia Naturalis Brasiliae* of Georg Marcgraf and Wilhelm Piso. Other illustrations were drawn from established museum catalogues or engravings in the ducal library. Although he often had the opportunity to study real specimens in the museum, Schmalkalden preferred to copy printed works. Even in those cases where he had brought the objects to Europe himself, he looked to reputable publications for inspiration instead. In fact, he later decided to replace the drawing of a rhinoceros he had acquired from a Chinese painter for the more conventional illustration by Albrecht Dürer (Collet 123-8).

As a traveler and eyewitness Caspar Schmalkalden provided stories for the exotic exhibits removed from their original contexts. Through careful selection, presentation, and his accompanying texts, he marked them as representatives of an alien world that he delineated as the 'other' of Europe. His stories were therefore prescriptive rather than descriptive: he drew on popular travel accounts and

---

6   Cf. the "Inventarium über Die KunstCammer ao. 1656" in: Thüringisches Staatsarchiv Gotha, GA YY VIIIa No. 2/9 p. 51f. and 70.

7   "Wir gehen nackendt her und wißen nichts vom gelde, Mit Pfeil und bogen nur, marschiren wir zu felde, Uns schmeckt das Menschen fleisch, es seÿ arm oder bein So mus es baldt gekocht undt aufgefreßen seÿn." Caspar Schmalkalden "West- und Ostindianische Reisebeschreibung" in: Forschungsbibliothek Gotha, Chart B 533 fol. 18r. For a detailed analysis of Schmalkalden's sources, and a reproduction of his drawing see: Collet 113-28.

Figs. 1 and 2: 'Tapuya' couple with their possessions. Drawings by Caspar Schmalkalden based on illustrations of Albert Eckhout's oil paintings in Piso and Marggraf 280. Forschungsbibliothek Gotha Chart B 533 fol. 18 and 20.

books instead of experience and observation. Neither his employer nor the Gotha court regarded such an approach as flawed or disreputable. On the contrary, Schmalkalden's active espousal of established stereotypes earned him a respectable position and the support of his superiors. The fate of his fellow courtier Johann Michael Wansleben illustrates how fragile his position might have been had he chosen to question the expectations of those who had stayed at home.

Johann Michael Wansleben

Johann Michael Wansleben was born in 1635 in a small village close to Gotha. He briefly studied theology and oriental languages at the University of Königsberg before he set his mind on traveling to distant lands instead. At first, however, these ambitions were frustrated by his failure to secure a position with the Dutch India companies in Amsterdam, and in 1663 he was forced to return to Gotha (Pougeois, *Vansleb*).

Some time before, the court had enjoyed the visit of a rare guest from Ethiopia. A certain Abba Gregorius had come to Gotha at the behest of Hiob Ludolf, a scholar of the Ethiopian language and councilor to Duke Ernest I. The dark-skinned African caused quite a sensation in the small town. As he knew no Latin or German he could only communicate through Ludolf using the gi'iz, an old Ethiopian language, which neither of them had used in oral communication before. Ludolf had taken advantage of this fact and embellished Gregorius' tales in order to "draw from him an answer comfortable to his own inclinations" (Johnson 154-7).[8] He quickly managed to convince the pious Duke that the remote African kingdom was home to a Christian faith closely resembling their own Lutheran beliefs. Ludolf was eager to portray the Ethiopians as "witty and good-natur'd, not given to quarrels [...] being naturally Lovers of Justice and Equity, and very desirous of Learning" (Ludolf 392). Consequently he remarked that sending an embassy to these 'African Lutherans,' could initiate a Protestant mission as well as an alliance against the Turks, whose recent incursions into Moravia had threatened all of Thuringia. He did not fail to mention the area's enormous gold deposits and hinted at the chance to acquire rare marvels for the sovereign's museum.[9]

The Duke finally settled on Wansleben as envoy to Africa's Christians. To prevent diplomatic tensions with the Catholic princes and the Turks, Wansleben was to travel incognito. In June of 1663 he set out for Egypt via Italy. Unlike Schmalkalden he did not travel in a controlled colonial environment, but in hostile territory. Accordingly, Wansleben quickly had to come to terms with the fact that Ludolf's ideas had been mere fables. He was surprised to find Ethiopian monks in Alexandria living harmoniously alongside their Muslim neighbors. These clerics were quick to point out that the Turks were in fact less of an archenemy to the Christian 'Emperor' of Ethiopia than a respected source of trade and income. To Wansleben's profound irritation, he later discovered that a major part of the trade by the supposedly benign and pious Ethiopian ruler consisted of his own Christian subjects, whom he sold as slaves to Muslim masters. The monks also unsettled Wansleben's belief in their allegedly 'Lutheran' understanding of Christianity: they proved to be just as unwilling to distinguish between Lutheran and Catholic 'Franks' as Europeans were between American and Asian 'Indians.' Undeterred, Wansleben continued his travels up the Nile. Only after he had ascertained that the Ethiopians would indeed bar him from entering their territory, and his Ethiopian guide had cheated him out of his remaining money, was Wansleben forced to return, bankrupt and in ill health, to Alexandria and then to Italy.[10]

When Wansleben sent a long account to Gotha, detailing the complex situation in the Orient and excusing his inability to deliver the expected rarities, he met with little sympathy. Instead, the court was quick to blame the messenger. They settled on Wansleben's supposedly unsteady character as the cause for the failure of the expedition rather than their own premises. His reports on the shifting

---

8 The quotation by Samuel Johnson paraphrases a scathing letter to Ludolf by the Paris orientalist Ludwig Piques. For an analysis of Ludolf's views on Ethiopia, determined by his theological convictions see: Uhlig, *Theologia*.

9 For Ludolf's instructions to Wansleben and reports on the expedition's potential see: Forschungsbibliothek Gotha, Chart A 101 and Chart A 102.

10 For Wansleben's initial handwritten travel report see: Forschungsbibliothek Gotha, Chart A 101 fol. 99-141. He later published a revised Italian version as: Wansleben, *Relazione*.

boundaries and 'third spaces' between Christians and Heathens, friends and foes, were ignored and quickly forgotten.[11]

Wansleben had, however, learned his lesson well. He briefly invented a noble title, converted to Catholicism, joined the Dominican order and started a new life. After some time as an expert eye witness at the courts of Florence and Rome, he managed to obtain another mission, this time for the French minister Colbert. In 1672 he went to Egypt once more. This time, however, he took care to limit himself to the rarities and information his employers were expecting. He carefully stuck to the ever popular mummies, stuffed crocodiles, and heathen idols, and quickly managed to establish himself as an agent for several European collectors.[12]

In Gotha, the museum continued to present the non-European world as the stereotypical other. None of its later acquisitions ever reflected the multifaceted reality described in Wansleben's initial report. Instead, the princes of Saxe-Gotha collected many more exotica that supported the interpretation Schmalkalden had distilled from popular travel accounts. The Duke's subjects donated similar material and praised the marvelous objects on display (Collet 77-83).

It might be tempting to attribute this stereotypical and increasingly anachronistic presentation in Gotha to the representational rather than scientific interests of its noble owner or its geographical isolation from Europe's major ports. However, an analysis of John Winthrop's involvement with the museum of the Royal Society of London, planned as a research collection by the leading 'new scientists' of a colonial power, reveals striking similarities.

John Winthrop Jr.

John Winthrop Jr. was born in Suffolk, England, in 1605 but went to America with his father in 1631. John Winthrop Sr. was soon elected governor of the Massachusetts colony and his son took the same office in Connecticut in 1657. Four years later he traveled back to England in an attempt to gain a favorable charter for the young colony from the restored monarch Charles II. During his stay he became acquainted with the fellows of the incipient Royal Society for the Improving of Natural Knowledge. As the members had set their minds on establishing a research 'repository' and hoped to gather material from all corners of the world, Winthrop was seen as a promising contact and possible source of exotic material. In 1663 he was elected the society's first overseas fellow and later contributed American rarities over the course of many years (Winthrop, *Correspondence*).

The London fellows were nursing ambitious plans for their museum. The curator, Robert Hooke, insisted that "the use of such a collection is not for Di-

---

11 For an account of Wansleben's fall from grace in Gotha, see: Stein, "Wansleben."
12 For lists of Wansleben's rarities see: Omont 2: 887, 893, 901-4, 910, 916 as well as
    Pougeois 436, 439-42, 460, and his own travel account: Wansleben, *Relation*.

vertisment, and Wonder, and Gazing, as 'tis for the most part thought and esteemed, and like Pictures for Children to admire and be pleased with, but for the most serious and diligent study of the most able Proficient in Natural Philosophy." Instead of entertainment and illustration he hoped for research and experiments. These plans fitted well into the fellows' general call for a scientific renewal (Waller 338).[13]

One project in particular was to be based on the new museum: the initiation of a new 'natural history' that would include all the recently discovered parts of the world. The fellows hoped that this enterprise would demonstrate the virtues of a 'new science' based on facts rather than scholarly dispute. By working with physical objects instead of dubious reports or outdated texts, they planned to eliminate the divisive discussions that plagued the scientific debates of their day and the English post-Civil-War society in general. Accordingly, the fellows discouraged debate and favored a scientific practice geared toward fact-finding rather than interpretation. The museum's material objects seemed to be perfectly suited to put this method to the test.[14]

By the time John Winthrop returned to America he had received a preliminary questionnaire detailing information and objects to be sent from Connecticut. The society's secretary, Henry Oldenburg, later provided further examples of the "chief raritys" the fellows wanted "for ye inriching of ye History of Nature (whose composure is one of the maine things, they have in their eye)" (Hall 2: 149f.). They asked for popular curiosities as well as maps, samples of soil, mineral ores, and examples of the natural resources found in New England (Winthrop, *Correspondence* 8 and Hall 2: 149f.; 5: 422-6; 6: 594f.). However, transatlantic communication proved to be difficult and erratic. Several parcels miscarried, were lost or spoiled by seawater. It took almost five years for Winthrop's first rarities to arrive in London. When they were shown during the meetings, the parcels were found to contain many established collectables: a bird's nest curiously formed in the manner of male genitalia, rattlesnake skins, the strangely shaped "head of a deare, which seemeth not an ordinary head," the ubiquitous Indian bark baskets, as well as a bow and arrows. In his complementary letters, Winthrop could only provide limited information beyond names and the occasional anecdote detailing the items' miraculous qualities. When the Londoners asked him for details on locations, the indigenous names, or proof of these reported qualities Winthrop readily admitted his own ignorance. He claimed that "some Indian," who could not be

---

13 For a general analysis of the Royal Society's museum and its scientific uses see: Hunter, *Science* 135-50.
14 On the project of a natural history based on the museum's specimens see the letter of Henry Oldenburg to Robert Boyle in: Hall 3: 31-4. On the development of experimental science in order to soothe divisions caused by the Civil War, see: Shapin and Schaffer, *Leviathan* 337-43.

found again, had given the specimens to him, or that they had come from "remote Inland parts little discovered."[15]

Furthermore, while Winthrop was happy to contribute curiosities, he remained conspicuously elusive on all questions concerning cartography or mineral resources. A closer look at the situation in New England suggests that this was not accidental. Winthrop was well aware that the 'Royal' Society was very close to the monarch and his colonial administration. While in London, he himself had proposed projects on mining and surveying in New England under the joint stewardship of the colonial councils and the Royal Society. By the time Oldenburg's questions reached him, however, New England's position had changed dramatically. The King's administration was now set on regaining control in the colonies, some of which had been founded without royal consent during the Commonwealth era. Accordingly, the English fleet that in 1664 had taken the Dutch colony of New Amsterdam, which bordered on Connecticut, carried Royal commissioners. Their duties included the settling of Connecticut's borders with the colony now renamed New York, resolving similar disputes with its other neighbors, and establishing the colony's taxable resources, such as the mines and smelting works Winthrop had encouraged. The drawing of maps or a 'natural' history of resources had suddenly become a delicate and politically sensitive project (Woodward, *Utility*).

It is therefore hardly surprising that Winthrop preferred to send harmless curiosities that he knew would appeal to the sizeable group of fellows who were ambiguous about the official 'experimentalist' agenda. The fellows' reaction illustrates his success. His wondrous rarities were shown to a delighted audience in London. Some were even presented to the king and his court – unintentionally confirming Winthrop's reservations. The initial questions on more factual matters were quickly forgotten. When the fellows printed a list of Winthrop's curiosities in their *Philosophical Transactions* without detailed descriptions or illustrations, they obviously hoped to encourage similar shipments, not to initiate experiments. None of the specimens were ever tested for their reputed medical or occult 'qualities.' Instead, many of Winthrop's miraculous stories about the distant worlds featured unchecked in the society's publications (Winthrop, *Extract*).

Winthrop was not the only correspondent who employed rarities as decoys to divert attention from more delicate topics. Philippo Vernatti, an official of the Dutch East India Company, used similar tactics and curtly reminded the fellows that his employers prohibited the sending of any information or objects "necessarie to the Conservation of health or acquisition of wealth." Many others followed

---

15 See Winthrop's correspondence with Henry Oldenburg in: Hall 3: 525f.; 5: 422-34; 6: 253-7; 7: 142-5, 201-3, 221-4, 568f.; 8: 265ff., 305; 13: 402-5.

the same path and confirmed established narratives of India's otherness based on hearsay instead of autopsy.[16]

The objects that reached the Londoners adhered to a narrow canon of collectable exotica. Instead of broadening the collection into a comprehensive survey of the material world, the correspondents doubled and trebled objects already present. Additionally, most of the objects carried little documentation. The odd pieces of information that the fellows did receive proved to be stereotypical and impossible to verify. In the very few cases in which the fellows decided to check on the reputed qualities of exotic objects, they met with little success.[17] Their specimens proved incapable of refuting the stories that figured so strongly in the mutually corroborative reports of travelers, explorers, and donors.

Those fellows set on experimental research quickly realized that their initial hopes of using the museum as a research collection could not succeed. It proved impossible to just 'read' the objects as a 'book of nature' instead of established literature. Consequently, most exotic objects were shown at a meeting only to disappear forever into the museum holdings. After some years the plans for a new natural history of the world were tacitly abandoned. While the members used the exotic objects as a source of entertainment, their scientific work increasingly focused on better-documented European material. The museum gradually developed into a popular meeting place, whereas experiments continued to be performed in the controlled environment of private laboratories. Neither Robert Boyle's corpuscular theory of poisons, Robert Hooke's microscopical observations, John Ray's history of plants nor Francis Willughby's history of birds and fishes drew on the repository's specimens. Instead, the authors preferred to work with their own material in the calm seclusion of their private studies.[18] When visitors began to flow into the museum in the late seventeenth century, none of them observed any remarkable differences between this collection, once planned as the birthplace of a 'new science,' and other conventional cabinets of rarities.[19]

16 A copy of the questions addressed to Philippo Vernatti and a list of the established but harmless rarities he sent in return can be found in the Royal Society Archives London, Classified Papers XIX No. 9. Several other replies along these lines have been preserved in other parts of the same volume.

17 The cautious tests of the reputed 'Makassar poison' on cats and dogs are a case in question. Even though all of the animals escaped unharmed, the fellows could never exclude the possibility that they had simply received the 'wrong' specimen. Birch 2: 21, 314, 318. Although no results had been ascertained, the garish stories about the poison were later included as facts in: Ray vol. 3, appendix 87.

18 Collet 305-12, and Hunter 153ff. For an analysis of the early modern 'laboratory' as a carefully controlled space, separate from more public places such as museums, see: Shapin, "House."

19 For contemporary reports on the collection see: Hatton 2: 666-86 or Colsoni 12f.

Staging Separation

Caspar Schmalkalden, Johann Michael Wansleben, and John Winthrop Jr. were all practitioners of cultural encounter. Schmalkalden accompanied diplomatic missions to Aceh and Japan and lived in the hybrid colonial societies of coastal Brazil and East India. Wansleben spent months outside the safety of colonial rule, learning to make a place for himself among Turks, Copts, and Arabs. Winthrop regularly dealt with native American representatives and successfully exploited rivalries between hostile Indian tribes during King Philip's War. None of them drew on these experiences during their involvement with early museums. Rather, their displays followed and illustrated the established alterity narratives of travel literature.

To this end they carefully selected, classified, and recontextualized the overseas material record. They portrayed the non-European world as a primitive, homogeneous, and heathen 'other' of Europe – without cities or complex societies, without Christians or European involvement, without rapid socioeconomic changes or emerging multiethnic identities. This way they corroborated the Europeans' belief in their own superiority. They also provided material 'evidence' to legitimize colonial conquests and the ensuing exploitation and enslavement of indigenous peoples.

In their presentations, Europe's 'internal other' – witches, beggars, and amazons – moved overseas along with acts of violence, superstition, promiscuity, and gluttony. In their portrayal of the 'Indian' we can glimpse a reflection of the Europeans' own immorality as well as their attitudes toward their own minorities, religious dissenters, and their deviant popular culture. Projecting internal conflicts abroad provided museum visitors with a framework that made the distant world intelligible. It also allowed them to imagine the war-ridden, religiously, politically, and socially divided Old World as a civilized and unified 'Europe.'[20]

While many cultural brokers in the environment of Europe's museums employed literary narratives because they trusted reputable books more than individual objects or their own limited experiences, some knew the world to be more complex than the monolithic discourse on alterity and otherness suggested. However, Wansleben's case illustrates that it was seldom sensible to question the established prejudices of collectors. In order to forge a career out of curiosities or to deflect unwanted attention it was far more profitable to back up conventional imaginaries.

Most collectors welcomed this illustrative approach. It allowed them to visualize distant worlds in the manner of other famous collections or reputable books. While the princes of Gotha compiled reports on collections they had visited, so that missing exhibits could be acquired accordingly, the fellows of the Royal Society browsed popular travel books in search of marvels to add to their museum.

---

20 Cf. Collet 332-55. For the concept of the 'internal other' see: Hillerbrand, "Other."

Visitors also supported the stereotypical presentation of distant territories by do-
nating similar objects as a token of gratitude. They expected a collection to display devilish idols, feather 'crowns,' or colorful and exotic garments and shells –
the absence of which was noted and criticized.

Collectors who tried to broaden the established canon met with substantial difficulties. The trading network only provided a limited range of well-known collectables as dealers concentrated on objects known to turn a profit. Even if they
could acquire other exotica, the fragmented nature of colonial trade prevented
them from obtaining meaningful information about the objects. The use of personal instead of trade networks did little to alleviate these impediments as overseas correspondents often protected new colonial loyalties through carefully fil-
tered communication.

Under these circumstances it proved impossible to use exotic objects for a scientific survey of the material world and its inhabitants. The deficiencies of colonial trade systems and overseas communication meant that objects arrived in Europe in a decontextualized and empty state. Such objects could not simply be
'read' like a 'book of nature.' The notoriously variable natural history needed
careful contextual documentation. Such information had to be provided by agents
and mediators, and few of them shared the basic conceptions of a 'new science'
that preferred objects and experiment over the printed word. Those who did often
realized that this knowledge could easily be used against them and chose a strategy of loyal noncooperation. Most information these mediators provided was geographically vague, culturally insensitive, and based on literature instead of autopsy. They conclusively disrupted attempts to recombine information and objects in
the museum environment.

Instead of providing a fresh and unbiased look, early museums portrayed distant lands as Europe's primitive other. They presented non-Europeans as static,
timeless, and heathen people close to nature. They ignored the actual diversity
and complexity of indigenous societies as well as the rapidly changing colonial
world, the emerging hybrid societies, and the dramatic environmental transformations. Instead of cultural encounter early museums presented cultural separation.

Museum Traditions

Some characteristics of this presentation were decidedly early modern. The division of the world into Christians and heathens reflected the split of Europe along
Christian religious denominations and the dominant role of religion in identity
politics. The fragile and often erratic transnational communication was a result of
limited technological resources. The resulting poor documentation of objects in
turn fostered the prominent position of self-fashioned 'experts.' Many collectors
also shared the early modern preference of books over individual experience and
the opinion that objects served as illustration rather than evidence.

Other mechanisms are, however, part of any museum environment: all collecting is inherently conservative (Sommer 46). Its aim is to preserve, not to create knowledge. Museums are also intrinsically inert. As a collection grows, its subsequent rearrangement becomes increasingly difficult. To reorganize an established taxonomic system or change the bias of a collection requires substantial effort. Consequently, many modern museums continue to present exhibitions that were conceived a century ago and uphold acquisition policies established by their founders.[21]

Furthermore, all museums have to reduce complexity in order to create exhibitions at all. In order to simplify, many curators of ethnographic material still choose to construct homogeneous 'ethnicities' along the 'one tribe, one style' paradigm. To this end they use typifying displays that transform individual objects into representatives and marginalize all supposedly 'hybrid,' individualistic, or 'unauthentic' material tainted by European influences. As a result, they ignore most contemporary non-European cultures and thus continue to exclude the very people they claim to represent (Ivanov 356-62; Brutti 243ff.).

What museums frequently prefer is older, supposedly traditional material. Such objects are often considered to be free from 'foreign' influences. At the same time, they appeal to collectors because of their rarity – a feature that is always appreciated in a museum. Because older ethnographical material is often difficult to acquire, the objects of earlier collections remain in high demand. Reservations about their dubious documentation and primitive bias are often put aside because of their high visual appeal, their association with famous collectors, and their popularity with visitors. Indeed, such objects have become so prominent in modern museums that many descendants of those portrayed now identify with this primitivist and partial selection of their ancestors' material culture.[22]

Finally, the expectations of visitors always affect a museum's composition and arrangement – even more so now that most museums are publicly owned and financed. Visitors to an ethnographic museum still count on being entertained, not confused. Instead of being confronted with the discomforting reality of exploitation and continued deprivation, they look forward to leaving the museum with an upbeat message. Many visitors also expect an ethnographical museum to visualize supposed differences between 'us' and 'them' – a concept that is now so firmly

---

21 For the 'longue durée' of exoticist acquisition policies see: Schade, "Merkwürdigkeiten," and Ivanov, "Aneignung."

22 A prominent example is 'Montezuma's feather crown' of Central American origin, now in the Kunsthistorisches Museum in Vienna. It was first documented in a sixteenth-century Austrian collection and constitutes a typical example of the 'othering' views of early collectors. They regarded such 'crowns' as the equivalents of European royal insignia, familiar in their function yet pleasingly different and emblematic of the supposed inferiority of the Indian people. Mexican lobby groups have now appropriated the spurious association of this poorly documented object with the Aztec leader and consider it a vital part of their cultural patrimony, demanding its repatriation. The issue has been debated repeatedly in the parliaments of both Mexico and Austria, sparking international tensions. An abstract of the debate can be found in: Dellemann, "Federn."

established that it has resulted in the physical separation of museums presenting European and non-European material.[23]

So, even though the publicly owned, institutionalized museum in a Western democracy differs substantially from its seventeenth-century ancestors, many parameters have remained unchanged. Ethnographical museums still reduce the complex encounter with foreigners to stereotypes of the other. Exhibitions continue to present non-European people as homogenous units of timeless, primitive villagers in unity with the animal world, while the people they claim to portray remain excluded from the exhibition process.

New Approaches

In recent years, however, museums have come under intense pressure. Critical museologists, as well as the influence of postcolonial and subaltern studies have challenged the way museums work. Some of the debated issues are questions of participation, power, and agency, the repatriation of patrimony, and the selection, labelling, taxonomy, and nomenclature of exhibits. Several museums have tried to address these criticisms and reinvent themselves. Some have transformed into virtual museums, shedding their inflexible permanent collections. Others have become museums of themselves, exhibiting their own history rather than their objects (Kirshenblatt-Gimblett 361).

By far the most popular approach for ethnographical museums has been to reclassify their exhibits as 'art.' The recently established Musée du Quay Branly in Paris is one of the most prominent institutions to embrace this approach. Its collections reassemble material taken from two older colonial museums. The exhibits are now displayed as aesthetically charged, individual specimens spotlighted in a manner usually reserved for European art. This move has undoubtedly managed to question the dichotomy between 'Natur'- and 'Kulturvölker.' It has also challenged the notion that hold that 'primitive' societies are incapable of producing artworks.

The aestheticizing approach has, however, failed to placate the critics. Many have voiced their disapproval because institutions such as the Musée du Quay Branly fail to provide adequate contextual information. The colonial history of the exhibits, their original use, cultural background, and religious meaning, as well as the people behind them, remain opaque. Instead the objects are again classified according to a fundamentally European concept: aesthetic 'quality.' As in older ethnographic museums this has privileged supposedly 'pure' styles and familiar

---

23 On the frustrations of challenging the modern museum visitor's dichotomous views, see Ivanow 368, and Brutti 245, who also report on the unwillingness of many collectors to travel lest it spoil their image of the distant world. On the emphasis of recent projects on providing an upbeat message for commercial or political reasons, see: Grewe 13 and Riechelmann 44.

figurative exhibits at the expense of performative art, objects that blend cultural influences, and the people living in today's entangled societies (Riechelmann, "Kunst" and Brutti, "Kritik").[24]

Other museums, such as the National Museum of the American Indian in Washington, D.C., have tried to focus on participation and heritage rather than aestheticization. These institutions promote the participation of the people they portray through the concept of 'community curators.' They aim to present diversity instead of artificial homogeneity and encourage the careful documentation of their selection process. Occasionally they experiment with new museological methods, such as the multiple labelling of objects (Kirshenblatt-Gimblett 374). At the same time they have become foci for identity politics, sometimes to the point that they confirm rather than criticize established narratives. In Washington a point in question is the museum's naturalistic architecture and display design, which purports to represent the supposed affinity of American Indians with 'nature' – a claim many descendants (including the architects) have appropriated irrespective of its demeaning origins.[25]

While these new approaches address at least some of the problems modern institutions have inherited from older collections and the museum environment, many museums continue to employ more traditional forms of presentation. They yield to loopholes in the documentation, the rigid expectations of paying visitors, and museum traditions such as the privileged role of curators or the established separation of European art museums and non-European ethnographical museums. As recently as 2005 an exhibition entitled 'African wildlife' toured several German museums. Its diorama-style displays included several life-size figures of primitive Africans, dressed only in leather loincloths and equipped with bow and arrow as well as calabashes (Fig. 3).

The accompanying texts identified the figures as "bushmen" of Africa, a "continent of magic and fascination."[26] The blatant association of non-European people with animal life and nature, their presentation in a timeless, geographically vague setting, as representatives of supposedly homogenous ethnicities, with

24 Lorenzo Brutti pointedly observes that the re-branding of ethnographical objects as art was motivated less by postcolonial theory than by a flourishing market for 'primitive' or 'tribal' art, which thrives on its supposed 'otherness,' following the modernists of the early twentieth century. He also sees the redemption of ethnographic objects as 'art' as a symbolical counterweight to rigid anti-immigrant policies. Brutti wryly remarks that the clean, aseptic displays of the Musée Quay Branly provide safe spaces of alterity. They successfully purge the objects of their association with foreigners, who many visitors consider as troublesome and threatening outside of the museum. For a similar aestheticizing redesign of the Ethnologisches Museum in Berlin that masks the colonial genesis of the collection, see: Brückmann, "Material."

25 For a critical account of the National Museum of the American Indian's failure to extend its reflexive museology to the presentation of its collection's history, see: Zittlau, "Heye."

26 The fact that the creators of the exhibition and its exhibits failed to understand the fierce criticism of some visitors, who later hid the figures under blankets, denouncing their racist connotations, only serves to illustrate the resilience of established museum traditions. For a report on the protests see: http://de.indymedia.org/2005/07/123673.shtml [04.09.08]

Fig. 3: 'Bushmen' with calabash, bow and arrows. Display of the exhibition 'African Wildlife.' Erfurt 2005.

no indication of interaction or cultural contacts would not feel out of place in a seventeenth-century museum. In fact, the Africans displayed in 2005 were noticeably close to the seventeenth-century illustrations of 'Indian cannibals' by Caspar Schmalkalden.

Conclusions

Early museums of the sixteenth and seventeenth centuries have undergone a dramatic reinterpretation. Instead of haphazard collections of the odd and the monstrous, early museums are now seen as laboratories of evidence. This turn has been characterized by paying increased attention to the collections' non-European objects. The presence of this 'new' material has been cast as a catalyst for an equally new science. By drawing attention to the deficiencies of ancient authors, exotic exhibits might have supported a shift from bookish scholasticism to observation, experience, and experiment. Their physical presence supposedly offered an unfiltered, direct view of the foreign world, eliminating the need to consult the biased travel literature – a program sometimes proposed by early modern collectors themselves.

A closer look at the actions of agents and collectors reveals that this optimistic program was thwarted by substantial problems: long-distance communication proved fragile, trading-networks offered a limited scope of material and little possibility of asking questions; as objects arrived devoid of contextual information, collectors had to rely on intermediaries to make them speak. However, agents such as Caspar Schmalkalden, Johann Michael Wansleben, and John Winthrop Jr. chose to corroborate existing narratives of otherness by projecting Europe's 'inner Indians' onto the new worlds. They did so out of careerism, to protect their colonial interests, or because they trusted reputable books more than individual specimens. Their views were supported by rigid expectations of visitors, the example of other famous museums, and the mutually corroborative reports of colonial correspondents and travel narratives. Under these circumstances even the Royal Society of London, a prominent institution with support from a large colonial power, failed to harvest exotic objects for empirical research. Instead, the presentations of early museums reduced the cultural encounter to stereotypes of the other. Contact, entanglement, and the resulting 'play of differences' were replaced by strict separation.

While some of the problems can be attributed to early modern infrastructure and scientific methods, many others originate in the museum environment itself. A look at modern museums illustrates that they face many of the same issues as their early modern antecedents: objects fail to provide self-explanatory 'imprints' of culture, missing out on important parts of human interaction. Instead, museums still have to make their objects speak through selection, presentation, and contextualization. To deliver a simple story they construct homogeneous ethnicities out of hybrid identities and distill types out of individual objects. This imagined 'other' continues to be set against the European 'self' by highlighting perceived differences as well as physically separating domestic and foreign material. The exclusion of all material tainted by cultural encounter bars non-European people living in today's entangled societies from participating in their own representation and masks the negative results of contact: exploitation and colonial rule. Stressing separation instead of entanglement suits the expectations of visitors, allowing them to define their identiy in contrast to a perceived other. It also supports long established, resilient museum traditions, acquisition policies, and presentational techniques.

In fact, many of the issues debated in ethnographical museums point to more general problems museums have with contextualizing objects and representing diversity rather than constructing 'masterpieces' aloof from their environment, chosen by a narrow circle of museum professionals anticipating the wishes of a limited public. The challenges these institutions face are so fundamental that maybe, instead of asking ourselves whether early collections were almost as efficient as today's museums, we should question whether modern museums are in fact 'modern' at all.

References

Arnold, Ken. *Cabinets for the Curious. Looking Back at Early English Museums*. Aldershot: Ashgate, 2006.

Birch, Thomas. *The History of the Royal Society of London for Improving of Natural Knowledge, from Its First Rise* [...]. 4 vols. London: Millar 1756f.

Bredekamp, Horst. *Antikensehnsucht und Maschinenglauben. Die Geschichte der Kunstkammer und die Zukunft der Kunstgeschichte*. Berlin: Wagenbach 2000.

Brückmann, Thomas. "Exotisches Material. Über den Kolonialismus in der Ethnologie und ethnologischen Ausstellungen" *Jungle World* 25 Apr 2007 http://www.jungleworld.com/Seiten/2007/17/9828.php. [04.09.08]

Brutti, Lorenzo. "Die Kritik. Ethnographische Betrachtungsweisen des Musée du Quay Branly aus der Perspektive eines teilnehmenden Beobachters." *Die Schau des Fremden. Ausstellungskonzepte zwischen Kunst, Kommerz und Wissenschaft*. Ed. Cordula Grewe. Stuttgart: Franz Steiner Verlag, 2006. 231-52.

Bujok, Elke. *Neue Welten in europäischen Sammlungen. Africana und Americana in Kunstkammern bis 1670*. Berlin: Reimer, 2004.

Collet, Dominik. *Die Welt in der Stube. Begegnungen mit Außereuropa in Kunstkammern der Frühen Neuzeit*. Veröffentlichungen des Max-Planck-Instituts für Geschichte 232. Göttingen: Vandenhoeck & Ruprecht, 2007.

Colsoni, François Caspar. *Le Guide De Londres. Dedié aux Voyageur Etrangers. Il Apprend Tout ce qu'il y a de Plus Curieux, Notable & Utile dans la Ville* [...]. [Den Haag 1699].

Dellemann, Anne. "Fremde Federn." *IKA-Zeitschrift für Internationalen KulturAustausch* 67/68 (2007): 34-5.

Findlen, Paula. "Die Zeit vor dem Laboratorium. Die Museen und der Bereich der Wissenschaft 1550-1750." *Macrocosmos in Microcosmo. Die Welt in der Stube. Zur Geschichte des Sammelns 1450 bis 1800*. Ed. Andreas Grote. Opladen: Leske & Budrich, 1994. 191-208.

Grewe, Cordula. "Between Art. Artifact, and Attractions. The Ethnographic Object and Its Appropriation in Western Culture." *Die Schau des Fremden. Ausstellungskonzepte zwischen Kunst, Kommerz und Wissenschaft*. Ed. Cordula Grewe. Stuttgart: Franz Steiner Verlag, 2006. 9-44.

Hall, Alfred and Marie Boas Hall. *The Correspondence of Henry Oldenburg*. 13 vols. Madison, WI and London: University of Wisconsin Press and Taylor & Francis, 1965-86.

Hatton, Edward. *A New View of London, or an Ample Account of that City*. 2 vols. London: Chiswell, 1707.

Hillerbrand, Hans J. "The 'Other' in the Age of the Reformation. Reflections on Social Control and Deviance in the Sixteenth Century." *Infinite Boundaries. Order, Disorder, and Reorder in Early Modern German Culture*. Ed. Max Reinhart. Kirksville (MO): Sixteenth Century Journal Publishers, 1998. 245-70.

Hunter, Michael. *Science and the Shape of Orthodoxy. Intellectual Change in Late Seventeenth-Century Britain*. Woodbridge: Boydell, 1995.

Ivanow, Paola. "Aneignung. Der museale Blick als Spiegel der europäischen Begegnung mit Afrika." *Studien zu Rassismus in Deutschland*. Ed. Susan Arndt. Münster: Unrast, 2001. 351-71.

Johnson, Samuel. *A Voyage to Abyssinia. Translated from the French*. 1735. The Yale Edition of the Works of Samuel Johnson 15. New Haven, CN: Yale University Press, 1985.

Kirshenblatt-Gimblett, Barbara. "Reconfiguring Museums. An Afterword." *Die Schau des Fremden. Ausstellungskonzepte zwischen Kunst, Kommerz und Wissenschaft.* Ed. Cordula Grewe. Stuttgart: Franz Steiner Verlag, 2006. 361-76.

Omont, Henri. *Missions Archéologiques Françaises en Orient aux XVIIe et XVIII Siècles.* 2 vols. Paris: Imprimerie Nationale, 1902.

Pougeois, Alexandre. *Vansleb savant orientaliste et voyageur sa vie sa disgrace, ses oeuvres.* Paris: Didier, 1869.

Ray, John. *Historia Plantarum Species hactenus editas aliasque insuper multas noviter inventas & descriptas complectens* [...]. 3 vols. London: Faithorne, 1686-1704.

Riechelmann, Cord. "Geschichtslose Kunst. Zwei Pariser Museen beschäftigen sich mit Ethnologie und Migration." *iz3w* 306 (2008): 42-5.

Schade, Anette. "'Merkwürdigkeiten' aus Tonga und Viti. Ein Beitrag zur Ankaufspolitik von Ethnographica der königlichen Kunstkammer zu Berlin, 1800-1830." *Baessler-Archiv* N.F. 47 (1999): 189-221.

Schmalkalden, Caspar. *Mit Kompass und Kanonen. Abenteuerliche Reisen nach Brasilien und Fernost 1642-1652.* Ed. Wolfgang Joost. Stuttgart and Vienna: Erdmann, 2002.

Shapin, Steven and Simon Schaffer. *Leviathan and the Air-Pump. Hobbes, Boyle, and the Experimental Life.* Princeton: Princeton UP, 1985.

Shapin, Steven. "The House of Experiment in Seventeenth-Century England." Isis 79 (1988): 373-404.

Sommer, Manfred. *Sammeln. Ein philosophischer Versuch.* Frankfurt a. M.: Suhrkamp, 1999.

Stein, Hans. "Die Biographie des Orientreisenden Johann Michael Wansleben (1635-1679). Eine 'chronique scandaleuse'?" *Ernst der Fromme. Staatsmann und Reformer 1601-1675. Wissenschaftliche Beiträge und Katalog zur Ausstellung.* Ed. Roswitha Jacobsen. Jena: Quartus, 2002.

Uhlig, Siegbert. *Hiob Ludolfs "Theologia Aethiopica."* 2 vols. Wiesbaden: Steiner, 1983.

Vogel, Johann Wilhelm. *Gewesenen Fähndrichs und Bergmeisters, in Dienst der Edl. Niederl. Ost=Indischen Compagnie, anietzo F. G. Cammer=Meisters zu Altenburg, Zehen=Jährige, Jetzo auffs neue revidirt- und vermehrte Ost=Indianische Reise=Beschreibung* [...]. 1690. Altenburg: Richter, 1716.

Waller, Richard. *The Posthumous Works of Robert Hooke. Containing his Cutlerian Lectures and Other Discourses, Read at the Meetings of the Illustrious Royal Society* [...]. London: Smith & Walford, 1705.

Wansleben, Johann Michael. *Nouvelle Relation, en Forme de Journal, d'un Voyage Fait en Egypte en 1672 et 1673.* Paris: Michallet, 1677.

---. *Relazione Dello Stato Presente Dell'Egitto* [...]. Paris: Cramoisy, 1671.

Winthrop, John. "An Extract of a Letter by John Winthrop Esq. Governour of Connecticut in New England, to the Publisher Concerning Some Natural Curiosities of Those Parts, Especially a Very Strange and Very Curiously Contrived Fish. Sent for the Repository of the R. Society." *Philosophical Transactions of the Royal Society of London. Giving some Accounts of the Present Undertakings, Studies, and Labours, of the Ingenious, in many Considerable Parts of the World* 5 (1670): 1151-3.

Winthrop, Robert Charles. *Correspondence of Hartlib, Haak, Oldenburg and other Founders of the Royal Society, with John Winthrop, Governor of Connecticut,*

1661-1672. Reprinted from the Proceedings of the Massachusetts Historical Society. Boston: John Wilson and Son, 1878.

Woodward, Walter W. *"Matters of Present Utility." John Winthrop Jr., The Royal Society, and the Politics of Intelligence in Restoration New England*. Forthcoming.

Zittlau, Andrea. "George Gustav Heye and the National Museum of the American Indian – Collecting the Collector." *Copas* 8 (2007). http://www-copas.uni-regensburg.de/index.htm?articles/issue_8/Andrea_Zittlau.html [04.09.08]

CHAPTER FOUR

Culture Clash and Hubris. The History and Historiography of the Huguenots in Germany and the Atlantic World[1]

SUSANNE LACHENICHT

Identity, rather than easily defined, was and is contested ground and only certain identity constructs provide access to a society's resources and power. Identities emerge when subjectivity of individuals intersects with narratives of history and culture in relationships which are constantly modified by individual men's and women's agency, by their interests, life-course projects, and everyday dealings. The polyphonic and hybrid identities constructed by gatekeepers and lived by common people are reproduced/modified with each new generation raised in the memory-keeping institutions of families and schools. Reduction of multiple identities to one identity, whether personal and local or societal and national, involves a simplification of the complex, the multiple, the many-cultures, to a generic construct in accordance with socially accepted discourse and group-specific interests of the reductionists.

Dirk Hoerder, "Transcultural States"

Given the powerful sexual, psychological and affectative functions of "homeland", it is hardly surprising that "foreigners", "strangers" or "newcomers" are often identified negatively as "the other" and used to construct the collective identity of "the self". This is not to justify racism or xenophobia, merely to suggest that the social construction of "home" uses fears and passions that are deeply etched in human emotions and weaknesses.

Robin Cohen, *Global Diasporas*

An "Address from Protestants in France to [the English King] Charles II, praying for liberty to remove into Ireland," most likely written in the early 1680s, is one example, among others, that displays a very self-confident refugee people: Huguenots were proud of their French Reformed culture and of what they considered to be the specific traits of their nation:

1   This article presents results from my book entitled *Hugenotten in Europa und Nordamerika. Immigrationspolitik und Integrationsprozesse in der Frühen Neuzeit (1548-1787)*, forthcoming 2009. Some of these results have already been published in Susanne Lachenicht. "Huguenot Immigrants and the Formation of National Identities." *The Historical Journal* 50.2 (2007): 309-31.

Christian charity, Sire, the example of your ancestors and the well-being of your state invite you to meet their expectations and to support them in their designs, because apart from the blessings of Heaven and the love of all Protestants, of which His Majesty disposes, the number of your subjects and of the amount of your income could increase with the accession of a nation whose industriousness and labour would produce in little time affluence, riches and safety by cultivating the soil which Your Majesty will allow them, by their application to the trade and their vigilance, and their fidelity.[2]

Beginning with the *Grand Refuge*, as the exodus of 150,000 to 200,000 Protestants from France following the Revocation of the Edict of Nantes in 1685 was called, the Huguenots became a diaspora. In exile, their pastors attempted to forge a national identity for the French "elect," the martyrs of the Protestant faith, and the "best subjects" of their respective rulers (see below § 2). One hundred years after the beginning of the *Grand Refuge*, we still find this Huguenot self-confidence in all countries of refuge, as the Berlin example, dating from 1782, shows:

The refugees originating from a country where polished manners are much more developed than anywhere else, whose language is refined and since the century of Louis XIV has manifested its being refined in masterpiéces of eloquence and poetry, are not likely to take the citizens of their countries of refuge as a model, but hope to serve them as a model in many different ways. (Erman and Reclam 1: 302)[3]

This extract of the *Mémoires pour servir à l'histoire des réfugiés français dans les états du Roi de Prusse*, a nine-volume history of the French refugees in Brandenburg-Prussia, written by the two fourth-generation pastors Jean Pierre Erman and Pierre Chrétien Frédéric Reclam, displays an even stronger self-confidence in the Huguenots' specific qualities.

Protestants who left France in the aftermath of the Revocation of the Edict of Nantes in 1685 chose uprootedness, the loss of their local and regional identities, economic and social insecurity, and sometimes poverty, in order to safeguard their religious identity. Did they lose their cultural identity as well in their coun-

---

2 "La charité Chrétienne, Sire, l'exemple de vos ancestres, et le bien de vôtre état vous invitent a leur être propre et a les encourager [les Protestants français] dans leur dessein car outre les benedictions du ciel et l'amour de tous les protestants, que V. M. peut s'atirer, le nombre de vos sujets et de vos revenus peut s'acroître notablement par l'accession d'un peuple dont l'industrie, et le travail sera capable d'apporter dans peu de temps l'abondance, la richesse, et la s(o)ureté par la culture des terres que V. M. leur permettra de planter(,) par leur application au commerce et par leur vigilance, et leur fidelité." Quotations translated by the author.
3 "Les réfugiés, sortant d'un pays où la politesse des moeurs avoit fait plus de progrès que partout ailleurs, parlant une langue cultivée et dès lors fixée par les chefs-d'œuvre que l'éloquence et la poésie produisirent pendant le beau siècle de Louis XIV, bien loin d'être dans le cas de se modeler sur leurs nouveaux citoyens, pouvaient espérer au contraire de leur servir à plus d'un égard de modèles."

tries of refuge? The examples of Brandenburg-Prussia, Ireland, England, and the English colonies in North America suggest that the memory of the Huguenots and the making of their own history in the diaspora preserved their French and French Reformed identity to some extent, an identity that was celebrated as being superior to all other European and American identities.

The Huguenots were successful in preserving – *mutatis mutandis* – their diaspora identity through commemorating their persecution, their resettlement, and the roles they chose to play in the countries of refuge. But to what extent are the Huguenots' history and their memory of their own history identical? And to what extent is today's Huguenot historiography the result of successful French Protestant hagiography and myth making?

Encounters and Culture Clashes

The Huguenots' pastors and military leaders, "gatekeepers," such as Henri Massue de Ruvigny and Henri de Mirmand, would have preferred to settle French Protestants in the diaspora in entirely separate communities, as a separate "nation," following medieval models for the accommodation of religious minorities, the Spanish *aljamas* (BibSHPF, Papiers Court, Copies Cote 615, no. 15) serving as one example. However, the exiles in England, Ireland, and North America had to face other solutions. In Brandenburg-Prussia and several other German states, the French refugees were granted privileges that indeed enabled them to form a "state within the state." The so-called French *colonies* had their own administration, a separate jurisdiction under French law, their own churches and educational system. In England, Ireland, and North America, the governments allowed the Huguenots their own churches and consistories. However, in law, administration, the economy, and to some extent in religious matters, French refugees were expected to integrate into state and society.

Despite the Huguenots forming their own *colonies* in Brandenburg-Prussia, they were not in a position to avoid all contact with German subjects. French servants in German households, German servants in French households, journeymen and masters in the guilds, and workers in the manufactories had daily encounters with the "other." Germans and French were confronted with each other, just as the French faced encounters with the English and the Irish in the British Isles, and Indians, African slaves, and European settlers in North America.

Negative perceptions of the French in diaspora can be found in English, Irish, North American, and German contexts. In 1576, the *Lord Keeper* Francis Bacon accused the French refugees in England of holding dubious loyalties:

> If the ffrenche denizen's hart continue naturally ffrenche and lovinge to his owne Cuntrye Then can he not Love our Cuntrye nor be meet to be amongst us, yf he be unnaturall and can find in his hart to hate his

owne Cuntrye then will he not be trustie to *our* Cuntrye and so more un-meet to Lyve amongst us. (in Yungblut 36)

Again in England in the 1570s, some inhabitants of the City of London complained about "[...] the contynuall and daily resort of strangers of divers nacons unto this cytty [...] [being] the cause of great scarcety of victuals raiseinge rents and contynuall encreasing of begger idle vagabonds and theeves of our own countreymen and nacon" (Luu 160). A year later, more inhabitants of the City of London wrote a letter to Queen Elizabeth stating about the French refugees:

[They] ought not to be in companies or Societies [...] [yet] they are a common wealth within themselves, trade in partner shippe with strangers, and as factors for whole cittyes, comerce with us for nothing that they can have of their own nacon, though they be denizen'd or born heere amongst us, yett they keep themselves severed from us in church, in government, in trade, in language and marriage. (Luu 160)

By the 1620s, these prejudices had not changed: "[They] combyn'd themselves togeather, they marry not with our nation, they sett their owne people aworke in all sorts of trades [...] they alter not their affection, their apparrell [...] language [...] nor conforme themselves to our churches [and] gouvernment" (Luu 160).

As late as 1710, French refugees in London were perceived as a society *en vase clos* and as a threat to the host society, as the *Letter to the French Refugees Concerning Their Behaviour to the Government* indicates: members of the host society – in this case presumably represented by an Anglican pastor – suspected the French Protestants of being Republicans, who "think that they only are the Children of Grace, the particular Favourites of Heaven, and therefore that all the Right of Dominion and Power belongs peculiarly to themselves." According to the author, the French Protestants in England were "a separate Body in the Nation, not only by [their] manner of dwelling near one another, but by [their] assembling together in [their] French Churches, and also by [their] distinct Language." He continues in his *Letter to the French Refugees*:

[...] because you are universally naturaliz'd, and thereby intituled to the same priviledges enjoy'd by the Natives of this Land; there must be no distinction made between you and other Her Majesties Subjects: And if there be any difference amongst us in points of Church Government, or in Matters relating to the Constitution and Laws of these Realms; ther's no doubt but your Prudence and Duty, if not your Inclination, should oblige you to side with such as are Establish'd by Law rather than with those which are only tolerated. (*Letter to the French Refugees* 8)

In Brandenburg-Prussia, Lutheran pastors preached against French Calvinists whom they perceived as heretics. In Magdeburg, the German population feared that the French refugees would expel the town's German inhabitants (Hartweg, *Hugenotten(tum)* 30). Conflicts arose over different food habits, the French

Protestants' breweries and separate economy in Magdeburg, as well as different burial customs. The guilds vehemently opposed French Protestant techniques and the competition arising from the presence of French weavers, goldsmiths, hatmakers, and other craftsmen (Mittenzwei 128-9). French Protestants were accused of luxury habits, of hedonism, and of having introduced effeminacy to Brandenburg (Hartweg, *Hugenotten* 11-12). Up to the second and third generation of the *refuge* in Brandenburg, negative perceptions of the French prevailed (Tollin 1: 376, 391).

In England, pity and compassion toward the persecuted French Protestants co-existed with an "anti-Huguenot undercurrent" (Thorp) that, from the 1680s, defamed the refugees as "papists in disguise" (de Beer 302-7). As "the very sum of their nation" the refugees were "of dull Genius, mean capacities, and rude Deportments and Behaviors" (Thorp 371-4; Kidd chapt. 9). Their presence, it was claimed, threatened English society, as their arrival was thought to have further increased overpopulation and the scarcity of bread and housing in London. Furthermore, their craftsmanship meant unwelcome competition for English craftsmen. From time to time, negative perceptions of the French refugees led to revolts against Huguenot settlements and individual craftsmen. In 1682, the inhabitants of Norwich accused the French Protestants of working for less money than their English colleagues and employing too many apprentices. In Rye, Huguenots were physically attacked on their way to church (Thorp 571-2). Particularly during the reign of William III, Englishmen feared the growing influence of his *alien* entourage, largely consisting of Dutch, German, and French Calvinists. In 1693-94, Sir John Knight, MP for Bristol, attempted to prove that the French refugees' presence was damaging the English economy through overproduction and their ignorance of the English guilds' rules (Thorp 576-8).

From the perspective of the Anglican Church, the French refugees reinforced the presbyterian element among England's Dissenters, as Bishop Morley of Winchester put it in a letter to the Bishop of London, Henry Compton (Oxford, Bodleian Library, Rawlinson MSS 984 C, fol. 50). Many Anglicans disapproved of the French Calvinists being exempted from the penal laws against nonconformists, particularly as English Dissenters used French Churches in England for their services.[4] Anglicans published pamphlets reminding French refugees of the necessity of Anglican conformism, and of the "unity and peace" of the Protestant churches in England (Bingham 337). Furthermore, French Protestants in England were accused of not respecting the Day of the Lord. Generally, it was assumed that their persecution in France had been the result of the Huguenots' ungodly behavior prior to 1685 (*Lettre d'un ministre anglican* 1). It also becomes evident that English society did not necessarily appreciate the Huguenot and Jewish presence in the country from a theatre play published in 1748: *A Winter Evening's Conversation in a Club of Jews, Dutchmen, French Refugees, And English Stock-*

---

4   Letter dating from 12 November 1683. Oxford, Bodleian Library, Rawlinson MSS, 984 C, fol. 48.

Jobbers, At a noted Coffee-House in Change-Alley. Here, French refugees are accused of only pretending to be religious refugees. The reason behind their flight to England, as suggested by an Englishman in the play, was economic interest (*A Winter's Evening Conversation* 17). These negative stereotypes coexisted with more positive depictions of the French refugees. John Toland, familiar with a number of nonorthodox French refugees in England, described them as "industrious" and "peacable subjects" who would bring prosperity and wealth to England (Toland 56-7).

In the English colonies in North America, in this case in Boston, French refugees were perceived as "French Catholics in disguise who were sent by the Antichrist to multiply the colony's woes" (Butler 73-4). In the Hudson Valley, English settlers depicted their Huguenot fellow settlers as the "French ennemi and traitor" who would deliver the colonies to France in case of a French invasion (Wheeler Carlo 27).

Contrary to the implication of the second epigraph of this chapter, not only receiving societies but also diasporic groups use the "other," including the receiving societies, in order to construct the collective identity of the "self." The Huguenots' prejudices toward non-Protestants is evident, particularly in the Irish context: with the numerous attempts to settle French Protestants in Ireland in the 1680s, 1690s, and then again from the 1720s to the 1750s, the Huguenots' military leaders and pastors adopted the Protestant Anglo-Irish attitude toward Ireland's Catholic majority. The "Irish Popish" were described as "disloyal subjects to the crown," "non-industrious" people, "lazy," and only interested in "planning plots and rebellions to throw off the yoke of the just British domination." Of all the Catholics in the world, the Irish were elected as the most "ignorant and bigoted nation." And as it seemed "unlikely that the Papists would ever accept a Protestant government and therefore would rather try to extinguish their governors," some Huguenots suggested that the English crown should "establish new colonies of Protestants to counterbalance and if necessary to fight the growing power of popery in Ireland" (*Address from Protestants*). The Catholic population in Ireland had no rights to property and estates. The French Protestants thought that Ireland, a country "where milk and honey flow," should be 'handed over' to them as being more worthy. Because the Huguenot petitioners considered themselves to be superior to the Irish in character and manners, they defended their right to settle on Irishmen's estates. Therefore, in addressing the English government, Huguenots advised officials on how to get rid of the "originaires du pays" in favor of the new French Protestant settlers (Mémoire pour encourager les Protestants fol. 101).

While it is obvious that French Protestants perceived Catholics in Ireland and Catholic settlers in North America in negative, stereotypical terms, they held similar views with regard to other Protestants as well. In Brandenburg-Prussia, we find German Lutherans being depicted as "miserly" people: "A German who invites you for dinner will serve tasteless stews and soup which will taste like water, and he will tell you that the latter is very good for your health."(Mauvillon 247).[5]

Among the French stereotypes about the English, we find the "sincerité angloise" and the "liberté angloise." Those virtues naturally attracted the French refugees, as, from their own perspective, they shared this same sincerity.[6] Other French refugees were more critical of the English nation: Pierre Desmaizeaux accused them of being "extremement dégénerés" ("extremely degenerate") and of having no "veritable zele pour leur Patrie" ("lacking in true patriotic zeal"). According to Desmaizeaux, the English also had no "principes d'honneur et de vertu" ("principles of honor and virtue") (BL, Add. 61655, Political tracts by Pierre des Maizeaux, 1710, ff. 181-99 b).

In the North American context, Huguenot settlers most readily adopted other white settlers' attitudes toward African slaves and America's First Nations and established themselves as slave owners. Only a few Huguenot pastors, such as Elie Neau in New York and Daniel Bondet in New Rochelle, engaged in catechizing and baptizing Indians and African slaves. According to Elie Neau, Indians and African slaves were as capable of the "bien moral" as white settlers. However, Huguenot pastors did not engage in missionizing efforts in order to free slaves. Following the standards of the Anglican Church and the Society for the Propagation of the Gospel in Foreign Parts (SPG), Huguenot pastors, working as SPG missionaries, attempted to free souls, not bodies.[7]

In South Carolina, the Huguenot pastor Francis Le Jau depicted the Yammassee Indians as the white settlers' "neighbours." To the SPG, Le Jau complained about the little support he gained from white settlers in his efforts to missionize the First Nations. Prior to the warlike conflicts between white settlers and First Nation peoples, starting in 1715 in South Carolina, Le Jau described the Yammassee as "honest" and "polite" people with "noble and virtuous principles."[8] Only after 1715 did these perceptions change, as Le Jau now wrote about the "Indians' natural pride & malice."[9]

In spite of official conformism and the service of French pastors in the Anglican Church and the SPG, for some Huguenot ministers the Anglican Church was not only a persecutor of Presbyterians but also too close to Catholicism. They compared the English *Test Acts* to the French crown's efforts to financially relieve

---

5 "Un Allemand qui vous invite à manger, vous régalera avec des ragouts fades, et des soupes qui sentent l'eau tiède, A l'entendre, il n'est rien de meilleur pour la santé"

6 Letter of Antoine Augustin Bruzens de la Martiniere to Pierre Desmaizeaux, 6 May 1739, British Library (BL), Desmaizeaux Papers, Add. 4285, fol. 204.

7 SPG series A1, Copies of the letters received and sent, 1702-06, no. 106, 10 July 1703 (New York): Elias Neau (French Catechist) (to Mr. John Hodges).

8 London, Lambeth Palace Library, Fulham Papers, vol. IX: South Carolina, ff. 31-2: Francis Le Jau to Bishop Compton, St. James, Goose Creek, 27 May 1712, and SPG Papers series A 5, Copies of the letters received and sent, 1708-09, letter of Le Jau to SPG, 5 August 1709.

9 SPG Papers series A 10, Copies of the letters received and sent, 1714-15, letter of Le Jau to SPG, 10 May 1715.

French Protestants after they had converted to Catholicism (Memoirs of Reverend Jaques Fontaine 133). As late as 1718, according to the (officially) conformist French pastor Jean-Armand Dubourdieu in London, the Anglican Church, being not a truly Calvinist church, was "not yet ripe for, or worthy of so great a Blessing," which should have been the union of the French and Anglican Churches (Dubourdieu, *An Appeal* 90). While the Anglican Church did not accept passive obedience toward a tyrannical ruler by its members, such obedience was mandatory from the viewpoint of the truly Calvinist churches (Dubourdieu, *La faction de Grande Bretagne* 14, 18). In New York, the *Église du Saint Esprit's* consistory opposed the French pastor Louis Rou, perceiving him as an "Anglican sympathiser" (Wheeler Carlo 111). As late as the 1760s, some French Protestants, if only a minority, supported New York's French Church financially so "that the said Church shall continue to be moderated and governed in Peace, conformable to the Discipline of the Reformed Churches of France" (*Abstracts of Last Wills* 4: 418). In 1763, the New York *Église du Saint Esprit* rejected Anglican conformity, in spite of financial problems and decreasing numbers in membership:

> Not that we consider the Anglican Church not to be a true Church of Jesus Christ, Our Lord; but out of respect for our predecessors who established and founded our Church, we desire to conserve and maintain her the way she had been established, which was the unanimous desire of all members of the consistory. (*Registre des Résolutions du Consistoire de l'Église Françoise de la Nouvelle York, 1723-1766*, entry 8 January 1764)[10]

The French Reformed identity had to be preserved in honor of the persecuted ancestors, as also becomes evident from John Pintard's letters dating from the 1830s: "How can I abandon the Church erected by my pious ancestors!" As a fourth generation Huguenot descendant, Pintard felt obliged "to uphold the Church of my Forefathers & to pay my adoration where our pious ancestors poured forth their orisons [sic] to our Heavenly Father" (Pintard 1: 3-4).

Contrary to what historiography has stated about the French refugees' religious conformism in England, Ireland, and North America, many French pastors and/or the churches' consistories indeed attempted to establish a "France protestante à l'étranger" (François, *La Mémoire Huguenote* 235), even after the Anglican Church's attempts at conformism had increased with the 1660s and then again in the early eighteenth century (Lachenicht, *Differing Perceptions*).

In all countries of refuge, the French Protestants depicted themselves not only as the only true Protestants and as "God's elect," but also as "industrious people" who enriched the host countries with their crafts, trade, and special skills (Erman

---

10 "[...] non que Nous ne Regardions l'Église anglicane comme une véritable Église de Jesus Christ notre Seigneur, mais par le Respect pour nos predecesseurs qui ont Etably & fondé notre Église, que nous desirons de conserver & Maintenir sur le meme pied qu'elle est établie, ce qui a été le sentiment unanime de tous les Membres du Comité."

and Reclam 1: 152). Their virtues, furthermore, consisted of their "love for the truth," their "piety," and their "frugality." They were:

> [...] assiduous, active, free of vanity, distraction and a taste for luxury, their amusements being simple, their gaiety innocent and unaffected just like their leisure activities; in their business affairs they display honesty and a sense of duty so that in this regard their reputation like their name is the guarantor of these virtues. (Erman and Reclam 1: 183-5)[11]

According to their pastors, even fourth generation French Protestants had better manners and customs than the people in any other nations (Mauvillon 91-2). Regarding themselves as culturally superior, the Huguenots assumed that they would reward their host countries for their compassion and the asylum granted with their contributions and achievements.

Preserving Identities – Hubris and Early Historiography

As Kotkin argues, economically successful diasporas are likely to possess three characteristics, namely: a) a strong identity; b) an advantageous occupational profile; and c) a passion for knowledge. Whether a strong identity is derived from internal clannishness, external rejection, or a combination of the two, a definite ethnic identity engenders distance from the larger society that can be used for creative and productive purposes.

Preserving and reinforcing the French Protestant identity in the diaspora was mostly the work of the Huguenots' social, military, and intellectual elites. Most important in creating narratives about the French Protestants' exclusive identities were sermons (delivered in church and also available in printed versions), published memoirs, pamphlets, petitions, theological and philosophical writings, private memoirs, and correspondence intended for the guidance of family and acquaintances – such as the well-known memoir of Jaques Fontaine in Cork, dating from the early 1700s, or the autobiographical accounts of the escape of Marie de la Rochefoucauld, dame de Champagné (Chappell).

From the mid-sixteenth century, narratives about the distinct French Protestant identity were being composed, both in the diaspora and at "home." Shaped by their persecution in France and the political and religious conflicts during the French Wars of Religion (1562-98), the French Protestants added a French Protestant national identity to their local and regional identities. One common standardized language had fostered a sense of unity among French Protestants from as early as the 1530s: Pierre Robert Olivetan had translated the bible from Latin

---

11 "[...] laborieux, actifs, éloignés de l'esprit de vanité, de dissipation & du goût de luxe, leurs amusemens étoient simples, leur gaité fraiche & sans apprêt & leurs plaisirs des délassemens; dans les affaires ils portoient l'honnêteté & la droiture & telle étoit à cet égard leur réputation que leur nom étoit le garant de ces vertus."

into French and services were held in French Protestant churches all over France in one and the same French tongue. Thus, every French Protestant in France had knowledge of one unifying language that coexisted with the regional dialect or patois (Birnstiel, *Dieu* 110-22).

From a theological perspective, French Calvinists defined themselves as God's "elect," the only true Christians on Earth. Their persecution, their martyrdom for the true faith were "a sort of test that God imposed upon the elect" (Diefendorf 42; Birnstiel, "La Naissance" 23-4; Birnstiel, "La France" 39; and Racaut, "Religious Polemic" 29-43). In France, but particularly after 1685 in the countries of refuge, Huguenot military leaders also promoted French Protestant patriotism. On the one hand, French Calvinist writers advanced claims of being subjects of the French king, ready to shed "all their blood in the interest of His Highness and his State." On the other hand, French Protestants in France made it clear that there were limits to their loyalty to the king who, as they perceived it, did not rule over their religious beliefs (Basnage de Beauval 41). As long as the crown respected the French Reformed faith, the king was assured of French Protestant support within France. As a result, French Protestants could identify themselves as French patriots throughout the Wars of Religion in France without necessarily being fully loyal to the crown.

In 1680, Pierre Jurieu, a French Protestant refugee in the Netherlands (United Provinces), wrote: "We are as much French as we are French Reformed Christians" (Jurieu 125). And the pastor Elie Benoist (1640-1728), a Huguenot migrant in Delft (United Provinces), noted in his *Histoire de l'Édit de Nantes* (1693-95) that the Edict of Nantes (1598) had guaranteed Protestants equal rights with all other subjects of the monarchy. Therefore, the Edict of Fontainebleau (1685) could be considered an illegal act because by law the French Protestants could not be deprived of their entitlement to be French subjects (Benoist 321). Since the Calvinists' love for France did not involve any respect for the French king, they experienced no difficulty in opposing Louis XIV and his successors. From the French Protestants' perspective, they were not fighting against the French nation but against a king who, by revoking the Edict of Nantes, had forfeited his legitimacy as their ruler. Their mission was similarly represented when, from 1688 onward, Huguenot regiments helped William of Orange battle the Jacobite armies in both England and Ireland.

From the beginning, political and military support of the government and particularly the rulers of their host countries became one of the general patterns in French Protestant narratives in exile. Humble petitions to the king, panegyrics, and flattering sermons sustained this group's loyalty to their new monarch or prince and can be found in all countries of refuge (Drelincourt, de Gaultier).

However, panegyrics and loyalty to the new prince were not sufficient to gain and preserve privileges for the diasporic group. From the 1690s onward, Huguenot pastors engaged in writing their host countries' histories in which they integrated their own narratives about the French refugees' special contributions to the rise of the host nation. The Huguenot historiographers of the *Grand Refuge* followed traditions as established by Jean Crespin's *Histoire des Martyrs Persecutez et Mis à Mort Pour la Verité de l'Evangile, Depuis le Temps des Apostres Jusques à l'An 1574* (Geneva 1582) and Nicolas de Gallars' *Seconde Apologie ou Defense des Vrais Chrestiens, Contre les Calomnies Impudentes des Ennemis de l'Eglise Catholique* (Geneva 1559). In 1688, the French Reformed pastor François de Gaultier published his *Histoire Apologétique*, followed, in 1690, by Charles Ancillon's *Histoire de l'Ètablissement des François Refugiez Dans les Etats de Son Altesse Electorale de Brandebourg.* These two historians of the refuge developed two *topoi*: the French refugees' gratitude toward the Elector (or the ruling prince) and the special contribution made by Huguenot cultural and economic superiority, i.e., the French Protestants' "civilizing power" (Ancillon 8; Gaultier 41-5). Prussian memoirs and historiography, not the least that written by King Frederick II himself (Hartweg, *Hugenotten(tum)* 333), most readily accepted these Huguenot narratives, as the memoirs of the Gentleman of the Bedchamber von Pöllnitz, dating from 1750, show (Glatzer 52).

In London, during the first decade of the eighteenth century, the French refugee Pierre Desmaizeaux worked on his *Histoire & Sur les Interests de la Grande Bretagne*, while his compatriot Abel Boyer published his *History of King William the Third* and the *History of the Reign of Queen Anne Digested into Annals*. Paul Rapin's *History of England*, including the reign of William III and Mary II, was published posthumously in 1727. English Whig historiography adopted some of the narratives as established by Huguenot historiographers in Britain: the special role Huguenot regiments had played during the Glorious Revolution and the French churches' Anglican conformism (Macaulay 2: 675-81, 732-4, 868; 3: 1074-7, 1084; 4: 1678-80, 1690, 1875, 1880-1). However, England proved to be somewhat fickle, as it depended on the ruler's and his Parliaments' often changeable attitudes about whether the French Protestants were perceived an asset for the country or not. However, in the British Isles, Whig historiography, presenting Huguenots as promoters of French culture and artistry, and as strong allies in the defense against Jacobite invasions, proved to be stronger than the Tories' disbelief in the necessity of Protestant immigrants in England. While there is no question that Huguenot regiments helped William III in his efforts against Louis XIV and the Jacobites, there are obvious doubts about the Huguenots' Anglican conformity in the first half of the eighteenth century (Gwynn, *The Ecclesiastical Organization* 404-5, Lachenicht, *Hugenotten* chapt. 4). However, up to the present day, despite the French refugees' being perceived as Republicans and Presbyterians in England in the late seventeenth and the first half of the eighteenth century, they are rarely integrated into histories of Irish or English dissent (Barnard, McClendon, Keeble, Oliver MacDonagh).

In those Huguenot narratives that were made available to the public between the 1680s and about 1760, the trope of being loyal adopted subjects, and the rulers' better subjects, coexisted with claims that the French Protestant faith was superior to all others and that their French culture and prowess in crafts and commerce also made them superior to other subjects (Yardeni 47). These elements feature not only in narratives composed by authors of the first generation, but were reiterated by writers of the second, third, and even fourth generations in exile, as they proclaimed to be "French at heart." The Huguenot narratives modified through the experience of persecution and exile defined their brethren as being simultaneously loyal subjects to the sovereign of their host country as well as French nationals, or, as the Berlin pastor Jean Henry put it as late as 1814, they were "François de la monarchie prussienne" ("French of/within the Prussian monarchy") (Henry 31, 38, 47).

Integration and Assimilation

Significant social endogamy as reflected by the low number of intermarriages in the countries of refuge (within the French Protestant churches) indicates that at least up to the 1750s, narratives encouraging French refugees to preserve their exclusiveness might have been accepted by a majority of exiles. In Britain, Ireland, Brandenburg-Prussia, and some rural settlements in the Hudson Valley and South Carolina, up to the 1720s, the number of Huguenots who married non-Huguenots was small, amounting to only six percent of the refugees. Between the 1720s and the 1750s the rate of intermarriage increased (twelve to twenty percent). However, in Brandenburg-Prussia, the French Protestants' spiritual leaders refused to marry outside the Huguenot society (Lachenicht, *Migration* 52-3). Huguenot elites endeavored to promote intellectual networks all over Europe and also in the overseas colonies, and at the same time the majority of the Huguenots refused to link their families with non-Huguenots and in everyday life remained a separate society. Maintaining these boundaries through social endogamy was considered essential to sustaining the narratives of exclusivity and superiority.

However, the French Protestants' "national identity" came to be challenged from within. In 1700, while seventy percent of all Huguenot refugees in Berlin still accepted Holy Communion within a French Reformed church, these numbers had declined to a mere twenty-one percent by 1795 (Birnstiel, "Dieu" 121). With the second generation of the diaspora, mostly from the 1720s and the 1730s, Huguenot churches in London, Dublin, Berlin, and New York faced increasing disintegration. While some churches had already closed in the 1730s, most survived up to the late eighteenth century, and some far into the nineteenth century. However, with the third and fourth generations, Huguenot churches not only lost members. In England, Ireland, the Protestant German States, and North America, the 1760s and 1770s brought about the loss of French as the everyday language of the majority of the refugees' descendants. Even in relatively closed Huguenot societies, such as New Paltz and New Rochelle in the Hudson Valley, and some towns in Brandenburg's Uckermark, intermarriage with non-French settlers increased simultaneous to the language shift. While some communities were quicker than others in dissolving the cohesion of the French Protestant diaspora, the third and fourth generation made it clear that in all countries of refuge, the French Protestants were in danger of losing their identity. Even in Berlin, where according to many scholars the process of assimilation was slowest,[12] in 1772, fifty percent of all marriages celebrated in French Reformed Churches were marriages between Germans and descendants of Huguenot refugees. In the 1780s this increased to sixty percent, and in the 1790s to seventy percent. In 1785, the Berlin pastors A.R. Bocquet and Pajon berated the Huguenots for the loss not only of their language but also of French Protestant virtues such as modesty, probity, frugality, industry, and moderation (von Thadden 187-8).

The conformist French Church of the Savoy in London was one of the first to be hit by the lingering process of disintegration. Its consistory's analysis of the reasons, as exposed in a letter to the Bishop of London, reads as follows:

> We may impute the diminishing of the contributions of the Church of the Savoye particularly to its situation; as this side of the town has increased, the French Refugees have retired to the Extremities of it, where there are Churches new established, and where the houses are cheaper than in the Strand or there about. And as for the income of the other Churches, t'is easy to imagine, that it being now 45 years since the beginning of the Refuge, the number of those, that come out of France, are considerably diminished: their children brought young or born in England are very much dispersed in several places, and having professions, which oblige them to be incorporated to the Nation, are become as English as themselves; in so much that those, who are not in a condition to contribute towards our churches have left them, and the number that frequent them must of course decrease every day.[13]

Generally, French Protestants were torn between their economic survival and preserving their French Protestant identities. Onward migration, a result of, e.g., the crisis of the silkweavers' industry in Spitalfields (London), and return migration to France for economic reasons furthered the French diaspora churches' disintegration as much as the need to integrate into the existing English economy, culture, and society. Identities are primarily about survival, the survival of individuals and the survival of entire groups. However, if the preservation of group identity no longer serves the economic survival of its members, the cohesion of diasporic groups weakens, as Joyce D. Goodfriend has shown for the New York Huguenot community, the loosening of whose internal bonds was already apparent in the first generation (242-50). Neither negative perceptions of the other nor cultur-

---

12 For a revision of assimilation patterns in the countries of refuge see Lachenicht, *Hugenotten* chapt. 4.

13 London, Lambeth Palace Library, Fulham Papers, Papers of Edmund Gibson, Bishop of London, Ref. FP Gibson 2, 1713-48, fol. 153.

al conflicts and clashes could prevent the French Protestants from integrating and amalgamating with other immigrants and the host societies.

Making History

By the outbreak of the French Revolution in 1789 and the arrival of French Catholic *Émigrés* in England, Brandenburg-Prussia, and North America it became obvious that the Huguenots in the diaspora, now mostly the fourth and fifth generation, had become integrated into the host societies. How could the group's churches and privileges be conserved if there was proof that the Huguenots no longer formed an exclusive group and no longer shared one common French Protestant identity? Narratives about an exclusive and distinct French Protestant identity had to be adapted to changed historical circumstances.

To this purpose, the above mentioned Huguenot pastors, Erman and Reclam, emphasized in their *Mémoires* the benefit that the Prussian state of 1685 had derived from the arrival there of the French refugees. The two pastors argued that the French Protestants quickly became model subjects for less educated Germans, and that it was their standing apart as a privileged group that had made it possible for them to present an example in civil and economic living to the Prussian population at large (von Thadden 195). Negative perceptions of 'otherness,' conflicts with and within the host societies, the refugees' initial poverty, problems in integration, typical of the first decades after the arrival of the refugees, were erased from such narratives. As Viviane Rosen-Prest put it: Erman and Reclam's *Mémoires* were less concerned about the French refugees' history than about a history of their successful immigration and integration (Rosen-Prest 182). In 1792, Erman was nominated Historiographer of Prussia, a position that enabled him to integrate his contribution to the *Mémoires* into Prussia's official historiography. Late eighteenth-century Huguenots thus also offered Prussian historians a particular narrative – which included the myth of their active role in cultivating Prussian virtues – to be integrated into the emerging grand narrative of the nation as a whole.

This proposition emerged most clearly in 1814 in the course of the debate between David-Louis Théremin and Jean Henry over the extent to which Huguenots should preserve their distinctiveness. Théremin favored full integration, arguing, in German, that Prussia, threatened by Napoleon and the French, needed to consolidate itself as a unified nation with its own distinctive language and culture (Théremin 29-30). Even under these circumstances, his opponent, Jean Henry, encouraged Huguenots to retain their distinct identity, pointing to the fact that it was their difference as a community that had made their substantial contribution to the enrichment of the Prussian culture and economy possible. Such assertions enabled Henry to argue that the privileges that had always been enjoyed by the Huguenots in Brandenburg-Prussia should be continued, because it was from their position of privilege that they had made their particular contribution to the strengthening and enrichment of the Prussian state (Henry 48-9, 64-71). This line of argument would have been especially pertinent at this point because five years previously, in 1809, Prussian reforms had deprived the Huguenots of most of their privileges and placed them on a more equal footing with the remainder of the Prussian population.

As the Huguenots increasingly lost their privileges and their distinctive characteristics of language and culture within a host state, they had to rely on the fostering of memory and heritage as a means of salvaging something of a 'Huguenot identity' within the community into which they had assimilated. Such efforts were especially evident in the centennial year of 1785, but became more generally evident from the mid-nineteenth century to the 1880s in almost every country in which Huguenot communities had endured. New histories of the *refuge* appeared, such as Edouard Muret's *Geschichte der Französischen Kolonie in Brandenburg-Preußen, unter besonderer Berücksichtigung der Berliner Gemeinde*, reiterating *topoi* as developed by Ancillon and de Gaultier and adapted to the Prussian *Zeitgeist* in Erman and Reclam's *Mémoires*.

As the French Protestant churches, hotbeds for the preservation of a French Reformed identity, lost their members, new institutions had to be created in order to safeguard the memory of the persecution and the diaspora of the French Calvinists. From the second half of the nineteenth century onward, Huguenot descendants in every country in which their ancestors had found refuge began to publish church registers, consistory minutes, and memoirs as a means of memorializing the special contribution that the Huguenots had made to the greatness of the nation-states that had provided them with a new home. They began to establish Huguenot societies associated with particular states *and* with the general diaspora. Thus, in 1883, the Huguenot Society of America was established in New York, the Huguenot Society of London was founded in 1885, and the German Huguenot Society was instituted in 1890 (van Ruymbeke, *Minority Survival* 13). This trend persisted into the twentieth century with, for example, the launching in 1922 of the Huguenot Society of the Founders of Manakin in the Colony of Virginia, and in 1975 of the *Nederlandse Huguenoten Stichting*.

In Brandenburg-Prussia, between the end of the nineteenth century and 1945, the French Protestant identity in Brandenburg-Prussia began to contribute to a symbiotic relationship between Prussian patriotism and German nationalism. It became the view among Germans of Huguenot descent that Prussian and German virtues had been deeply influenced by the French Reformed spirit since the 1660s. Their arrival in Brandenburg-Prussia, mostly after 1685, was seen to coincide with Prussia's rise to power, which in teleological national histories of the nineteenth and early twentieth centuries was seen to have culminated in German unification in 1871 (François, *Vom preußischen Patrioten* 205). In this way they defined themselves, both under the Kaiserreich and during the Nazi Regime, as Germans of French Protestant descent who had become the 'best Germans' (Centurier 215-6).

In North America, both American and American Huguenot historians of the nineteenth century, as Bertrand van Ruymbeke has stated, incorporated the Huguenots "into the White-Anglo-Saxon Protestant model" (van Ruymbeke, *Minority Survival* 15). In the 1830s, George Bancroft, in his *History of the United States*, painted an extremely positive portrait of the Huguenots as a virtuous nation, sharing many attributes with the Puritans without displaying the latter's "bigotry" (181, 183). Negative stereotypes described earlier, about the French "ennemi" and "traitor" in North America, came to be deleted from these histories. In Charles W. Baird's *History of the Huguenot Emigration in America* (1885), the Huguenots were celebrated as the founders of tolerance, and of the love of freedom and beauty in North America (1: 482). At this point in time, the Huguenots' quick assimilation into American culture and society had become a narrative pattern. Furthermore, the French Protestants' history in North America contributed to the myth that America "was peopled largely by settlers fleeing religious persecution and yearning for the opportunity to worship openly and without fear" (Murrin 19). As Bertrand van Ruymbeke has argued, American historians – in some ways similar to their Prussian counterparts – of the nineteenth century were convinced that French Protestants had impregnated the American national character with specific desirable traits: religious freedom, economic success, perseverance, and the entrepreneurial spirit. Thus, it became possible to represent the Huguenots as "the essence of what America is all about" (van Ruymbeke, *Minority Survival* 16).

In the Irish case, the state church wished the Huguenot refugees to assimilate with and consolidate the Protestant ascendancy within a predominantly Catholic country. Evidence, particularly that concerning the assistance offered by several Huguenot regiments to William of Orange in overcoming the Catholic threat, was cited to show that they had contributed to the Protestant cause (Hylton 179).

However, more recent research suggests that the economic, military, and cultural contributions that the Huguenots offered their countries of refuge have, for a long time, been exaggerated. Comparative approaches to the history of minorities and immigrants in Europe have provided evidence that other migrant groups, often despised by the host societies, such as the Palatines, Ashkenazi Jews, Poles, Irishmen, and others, made contributions equally significant as those made by the Huguenots (Ashelford; Birnstiel and Reinke; Crouzet; Gwynn, *Huguenot Heritage* 98-100, Jersch-Wenzel; Mittenzwei). The "quick assimilation paradigm," reiterated by the Huguenots and national historiographies in England (Yardeni 20, Gwynn, *Huguenot Heritage* 213), Ireland, and North America (Butler) has also been strongly challenged. New research suggests that in all countries of refuge a slow process of 'creolization' led to the French Protestants' final assimilation during the nineteenth century, with the 1760s and 1770s representing a crucial phase of change and crisis for French Reformed group cohesion and identity. While some communities were quicker to "vanish" (Butler 148-9), such as the Huguenot community in the Narragansett, others, such as those in the Hudson Valley, were slower, and followed the same rhythm of assimilation as many Huguenot communities in Brandenburg's isolated Uckermark (van Ruymbeke, Wheeler Carlo, Lachenicht).

None of these observations are intended to belittle the fact that Huguenots in many ways enriched the countries to which they fled. However, they were not the only immigrants to do so. More work needs to be done to integrate immigrant groups and the roles they played in the making of Europe and the Americas into the history of the so-called Western World. Other diasporic groups, such as Black slaves in North America and the Caribbean, whose military and spiritual leaders, or "gatekeepers," were less influential than those of the Huguenots, have to be considered, too, as having contributed – through their distinct skills and qualities – to the change and/or enrichment of the European and the American culture and economy.

While the Revocation of the Edict of Nantes in 1685 has more often than not been interpreted as putting an end to the French Protestant faith in France, historians such as Philippe Joutard have suggested that the Revocation came to safeguard and to revive a French Protestant "nation" and identity that was – during the seventeenth century – in decline (Joutard 12-3). Primarily through their pastors, French Protestants in exile or in the diaspora formed a "nation abroad" that was to develop a very strong and lasting identity in a transnational and supranational context, reviving Protestantism in France and impregnating the national histories of their host countries with their distinct national character, while simultaneously safeguarding their own Huguenot identity in many places for at least four generations.

The memory and historiography of the Huguenots shows that historiography is one important tool that enables diasporas and nation-states to preserve their identities: "Memory is not necessarily authentic, but rather useful" (Said 179). However, questioning these myths and historiographies is one of the crucial responsibilities of historians. Cross-cultural studies, comparative studies, and the border crossing of historians will lead to a revised and multidimensional perspective on the histories and the role minorities and diasporas played in the making of Europe and the Americas.

References

Primary Sources

Manuscript Sources

New York Historical Society (NYHS). *Registre des Résolutions du Consistoire de l'Église Françoise de la Nouvelle York, 1723-1766.*

Oxford, Bodleian Library, Ms. Rawl A 478. *Address from Protestants in France to Charles II, praying for liberty to remove into Ireland, 17th c.*

Oxford, Bodleian Library, Rawlinson MSS, 984 C.

Paris, Bibliothèque nationale, *Mémoire pour encourager les Protestants à venir habiter en Irlande, 17th c.*, Fonds Français Ms. 21,622: no. 551. fol. 101.

Paris, Bibliothèque de la Société de l'Histoire du Protestantisme Français (BibSHPF), *Papiers Court*, Copies, Cote 615 No. 15.

Printed Sources

Abstracts of Last Wills. Vols. 1-15. New York: New York Historical Society, 1892-1907.

Ancillon, Charles. *Histore de l'Établissement des François Refugiez dans les États de son Altesse Electorale de Brandebourg.* 2 vols. Berlin, 1690.

Basnage de Beauval, Henri. *Tolérance des Religions.* Rotterdam, 1684.

Benoist, Elie. *Histoire de l'Edit de Nantes* 3 vols. Delft, 1693-1695.

Bingham, John. *The French Churches Apology for the Church of England: or, The Objections of Dissenters against the Articles, Homilies, Liturgy, and Canons of the English Church, Consider'd and Answer'd upon the Principles of the Reformed Church of France. A Work Chiefly Extracted out of the Authentick Act and Decrees of the French National Synods, and the most Approved Writers of that Church. By J. Bingham, M.A. and sometime Fellow of Univ. Coll.in Oxford.* London, 1706.

Boyer, Abel. *History of King William the Third.* 3 vols. London, 1702/1703.

---. *History of the Reign of Queen Anne Digested into Annals.* 11 vols. London, 1703-1713.

Drelincourt, Peter. *A Speech made to His Grace the Duke of Ormond, Lord Lieutenant of Ireland, and to the Lords of His Majesties most Honorable Privy Council. To return the Humble Thanks of the French Protestants lately arriv'd in this Kingdom; and Graciously Reliev'd by them. By P. Drelincourt Domestick Chaplain to His Grace the Duke of Ormond, and Chantor of Christ Church. Published by Special Command.* Dublin, 1682.

Dubourdieu, Jean-Armand. *La Faction de Grande Bretagne Caraceterisée & Confondue ou Sermon sur ces Paroles de la 2. Epitre de St. Paul aux Corinthiens Chap. 11 V. 26. En Perils entre faux Freres. Où l'on Réfute ce qu'il y a d'Essentiel dans le Discours du Docteur S.—L. sur ces Mêmes Paroles. Prononcé le 7. de Juin, Jour Marqué par Sa Majesté, pour Rendre Graces à Dieu du Succés de nos Armes contre les Rebelles.* London, 1716.

---. *An Appeal to the English Nation or The Body of the French Protestants, and the Honest Proselytes, Vindicated from the Calumnies cast on them by one Malard and his Associates, in a Libel Entitled, The French Plot Found against the English Church.* London, 1718.

---. *Histoire & Sur les Interests de la Grande* Bretagne. London, no year.

Erman, Jean Pierre, and Pierre Chrétien Frédéric Reclam. *Mémoires pour Servir à l'Histoire des Réfugiés Français dans les États du Roi de Prusse*. 9 vols. Berlin, 1782-99.

Gaultier, François de. *Histoire Apologétique, ou Défense des Libertez des Eglises Réformées de France [...] avec un Recueil de Plusieurs Édits, Déclarations et Arrêts [...]*. Amsterdam, 1688.

Henry, Jean. *Adresse aux Églises Françoises des États Prussiens en Réponse à l'Écrit Adressé en Allemand en cette Année sous Titre d'Appel aux Communs Françoises de la Monarchie Prussienne par un de leurs plus Anciens Pasteurs*. Berlin, 1814.

Janssens-Knorsch, Uta (ed.). *The Life and "Memoirs Secrets" of Jean Des Champs (1707-1767), Journalist, Minister, and Man of Feeling*. Amsterdam/London: Hollan University Press, 1990.

Jurieu, Pierre. *La Politique du Clergé de France*. Amsterdam, 1680.

A Letter to the French Refugees Concerning their Behaviour to the Government. London, 1710.

Lettre d'un Ministre de l'Église Anglicane, a un Ministre Francois Refugie, sur le Peu de Respect pour le Jour du Repos, qu'on a Remarqué en quelques uns de ses Compatriotes, qui font Gloire d'Avoir Abandonné leur Patrie pour la Cause de la Religion Reformée. London, 1703.

Mauvillon, Edouard. *Lettres Françoises et Germaniques ou Réflexions Militaires, Littéraires et Critiques sur les François et les Allemands*. London, 1740.

[Pintard, John]. *Letters from John Pintard to his Daughter Eliza Noel Pintard Davidson, 1816-1833*. 4 vols. New York, 1940.

Rapin, Paul. *History of England: As well Ecclesiastical as Civil*. London, 1727.

Théremin, Daniel Louis. *Zuruf an die französischen Gemeinden in der preußischen Monarchie von einem ihrer ältesten Lehrer*. Berlin, 1814.

Toland, John. *The State-Anatomy of Great Britain, Containing a Particular Account of its Several Interests*. London, 1716-1717.

A Winter Evening's Conversation in a Club of Jews, Dutchmen, French Refugees, and English Stock-Jobbers, at a noted Coffee-House in Change-Alley. By which the whole Secret of the Late Subscription is Laid Open, the Character of a Worthy Magistrate Vindicated, and the True Cause of our Agreeing so Precipitately to the Preliminaries, Detected. London, 1748.

Secondary Sources

Ashelford, Joan. *The Art of Dress. Clothes and Society 1500-1914*. London: National Trust, 1996.

Baird, Charles W. *History of the Huguenot Migration to America*. New York: Dodd, Mead & Co, 1885.

Bancroft, George. *History of the United States*. Boston: Little & Brown, 1834.

Barnard, Toby. *A New Anatomy of Ireland. The Irish Protestants, 1649-1770*. New Haven/CT, London: Yale University Press, 2003.

Beer, Esmond Samuel de. "The Revocation of the Edict of Nantes and English Public Opinion." *HSP (Proceedings of the Huguenot Society of Britain and Ireland)* 18.4 (1950): 292-310.

Birnstiel, Eckart. "'Dieu protège nos souverains.' Zur Gruppenidentität der Hugenotten in Brandenburg-Preußen." *Die Hugenotten und das Refuge. Deutschland und Europa. Beiträge zu einer Tagung*. Eds. Frédéric Hartweg and Stefi Jersch-Wenzel. Berlin: Colloquium, 1990. 107-28.

---. "La Naissance d'une "Nation." La Réorganisation Sociale dans le Refuge Huguenot." *Minorités et Construction Nationale, XVIIIᵉ-XXᵉ Siècles*. Ed. Michelle Bouix. Pessac: Maison des Sciences d'Acquitaine, 2004. 24-34.

---. "La France en Quête de ses Enfants Perdus. Mythe et Réalité du Retour au 'Pays des Ancêtres' des Huguenots du Refuge, de la Réforme à la Révolution." *Diasporas. Histoire et Sociétés* 8 (2006): 22-44.

Birnstiel, Eckart, and Andreas Reinke. "Hugenotten in Berlin." *Von Zuwanderern zu Einheimischen. Hugenotten, Juden, Böhmen, Polen in Berlin*. Eds. Stefi Jersch-Wenzel and Barbara John. Berlin: Nicolai, 1990. 16-152.

Butler, Jon. *The Huguenots in America. A Refugee People in New World Society*. Cambridge/Mass: Harvard University Press, 1983.

Centurier, François. "Die Hugenotten-Nachkommen und der Deutsche Hugenottenverein." *Die Hugenotten 1685-1985*. Eds. Rudolf von Thadden and Michelle Magdelaine. München: C.H. Beck, 1985. 213-20.

Chappell, Carolyn Lougee. "'The Pains I took to Save My/His Family.' Escape Accounts by a Huguenot Mother and Daughter after the Revocation of the Edict of Nantes." *French Historical Studies* 22.1 (1999): 1-64.

Cohen, Robin. *Global Diasporas. An Introduction*. Seattle: University of Washington Press, 1997.

Crouzet, François. *The Huguenots and the English Financial Revolution, in Britain, France and International Commerce. From Louis XIV to Victoria*. Cambridge/MA, London: Harvard University Press, 1996.

Diefendorf, Barbara B. "The Huguenot Psalter and the Faith of French Protestants in the Sixteenth Century." *Culture and Identity in Early Modern Europe (1500-1800). Essays in Honor of Natalie Zemon Davis*. Eds. Barbara B. Diefendorf and Carla Hesse. Ann Arbor: University of Michigan Press, 1993. 41-63.

François, Etienne. "Vom preußischen Patrioten zum besten Deutschen." *Die Hugenotten 1685-1985*. Eds. Rudolf von Thadden and Michelle Magdelaine. München: C.H. Beck, 1985. 198-212.

---. "La Mémoire Huguenote dans le Pays du Refuge." *Die Hugenotten und das Refuge. Deutschland und Europa. Beiträge zu einer Tagung*. Eds. Frédéric Hartweg and Stefi Jersch-Wenzel. Berlin: Colloquium, 1990. 233-9.

Glatzer, Ruth (ed.). *Berliner Leben 1648-1806*. Berlin (Ost): Rütten & Loening, 1956.

Goodfriend, Joyce D. "The Huguenots of Colonial New York City. A Demographic Profile." *Memory and Identity. The Huguenots in France and the Atlantic Diaspora*. Eds. Bertrand van Ruymbeke, and Randy J. Sparks. Columbia/SC: University of South Carolina Press, 2003. 241-54.

Gwynn, Robin D. "The Ecclesiastical Organization of French Protestants in England in the Later Seventeenth Century, with Special Reference to London." Ph.D. thesis University of London, 1976.

---. *Huguenot Heritage. The History and Contribution of the Huguenots in Britain*. Brighton, Portland: Sussex Academic Press, ²2001.

Hartweg, Frédéric. "Hugenotten(tum) und Preußen(tum)." *Hugenotten in Brandenburg-Preußen*. Ed. Ingrid Mittenzwei. Berlin: Akademie der Wissenschaften der DDR, 1987. 313-48.

---. "Die Hugenotten in Berlin: Eine Geschichte, die vor 300 Jahren begann..." *Die Hugenotten und das Refuge. Deutschland und Europa. Beiträge zu einer Tagung*. Eds. Frédéric Hartweg and Stefi Jersch-Wenzel. Berlin: Colloquium, 1990. 1-56.

Hoerder, Dirk. "Transcultural States, Nations, and People." *The Historical Practice of Diversity. Transcultural Interactions from the Early Modern Period to the Post-colonial World*. Eds. Dirk Hoerder, Christiane Harzig, and Adrian Shubert. New York, Oxford: Berghahn, 2003. 13-32.

Hunt Yungblut, Laura. *Strangers Settled Here Amongst Us. Policies, Perceptions and the Presence of Aliens in Elizabethan England*. London: Routledge, 1996.

Hylton, Raymond Pierre. *Ireland's Huguenots and their Refuge*. Brighton, Portland: Sussex Academix Press, 2005.

Jersch-Wenzel, Stefi. *Juden und "Franzosen" in der Wirtschaft des Raumes Berlin/ Brandenburg*. Berlin: Colloquium, 1978.

Joutard, Philippe. "1685 – Ende und neue Chance für den französischen Protestan-tismus." *Die Hugenotten 1685-1985*. Eds. Rudolf von Thadden, and Michelle Magdelaine. München: C.H. Beck, 1985. 12-3.

Keeble, Neil. *The Literary Culture of Nonconformity in Later Seventeenth-Century England*. Leicester: Leicester University Press, 1987.

---. *The Restoration. England in the 1660s*. Oxford and Malden: Blackwell, 2002.

Kidd, Colin. *British Identities before Nationalism. Ethnicity and Nationhood in the Atlantic World, 1600-1800*. Cambridge: Cambridge University Press, 1999.

Kotkin, Joel. *Tribes. How Race, Religion and Identity Determine Success in the New World Economy*. New York: Random House, 1992.

Lachenicht, Susanne. "Migration, Migrationspolitik und Integration. Hugenotten in Brandenburg-Preußen, Irland und Großbritannien: Ein Vergleich." *Hugenotten. Zwischen Migration und Integration. Neue Forschungen zum Refuge in Berlin und Brandenburg*. Eds. Manuela Böhm, Jens Häseler, and Robert Violet. Berlin: Metropol, 2005. 37-58.

---. "Differing Perceptions of the Refuge? Huguenots in Ireland and Great Britain and their Attitudes Towards the Governments' Religious Policy." *The Religious Cul-ture of the Huguenots from 1660 to 1789*. Ed. Anne Dunan-Page. Aldershot: Ashgate, 2006. 45-56.

---. "Huguenot Immigrants and the Formation of National Identities." *The Historical Journal* 50.2 (2007): 309-31.

---. *Hugenotten in Europa und Nordamerika. Immigrationspolitik und Integrationspro-zesse in der Frühen Neuzeit*. Forthcoming 2009.

Luu, Lien Bich. "Assimilation or Segregation. Colonies of Alien Craftsmen in Eliza-bethan London." *HSP* 26.2 (1995): 160-72.

Macaulay, Thomas Babington. *History of England from the Accession of James the Second*. Illustrated Edition ed. C.H. Firth. London: Longmans, Green, 1913-15.

MacDonagh, Oliver, W. F. Mandle, and Pauric Travers (eds.). *Irish Culture and Na-tionalism, 1750-1950*. Basingstoke et al.: Macmillan, 1983.

McClendon, Muriel, Joseph P. Ward, and Michael Macdonald (eds.). *Protestant Iden-tities. Religion, Society, and Self-Fashioning in Post-Reformation England*. Stan-ford/CA: Stanford University Press, 1999.

Mittenzwei, Ingrid. "Hugenotten und Manufakturkapitalismus. Zur Rolle der Hu-genotten in der gewerblichen Wirtschaft Brandenburg-Preußens." *Hugenotten in Brandenburg-Preußen*. Ed. Ingrid Mittenzwei. Berlin: Akademie der Wissen-schaften der DDR, 1987. 112-68.

Muret, Edouard. *Geschichte der Französischen Kolonie in Brandenburg-Preußen, unter besonderer Berücksichtigung der Berliner Gemeinde.* Berlin: W. Büchsenstein, 1885.

Murrin, John M. "Religion and Politics in America from the First Settelement to the Civil War." *Religion and American Politics. From the Colonial Period to the 1980s.* Ed. Mark A. Noll. New York: Oxford University Press, 1990. 19-43.

Racaut, Luc. "Religious Polemic and Huguenot Identity." *Society and Culture in the Huguenot World, 1559-1685.* Eds. Raymond A. Mentzer, and Andrew Spicer. Cambridge: CUP, 2000. 29-43.

Rosen-Prest, Viviane. "Historiographie et Intégration Culturelle. L'Exemple des 'Mémoires des Réfugiés' d'Erman et Reclam." *Les États Allemands et les Huguenots. Politique d'Immigration et Processus d'Intégration.* Eds. Guido Braun and Susanne Lachenicht. Munich: Oldenbourg 2007, 171-92.

Said, Edward. "Invention, Memory, and Place." *Critical Inquiry* 26.2 (2000): 175-92.

Thadden, Rudolf von. "Vom Glaubensflüchtling zum preußischen Patrioten." *Die Hugenotten 1685-1985.* Eds. Rudolf von Thadden, and Michelle Magdelaine. München: C.H. Beck, 1985. 186-97.

Thorp, Malcolm R. "The Anti-Huguenot Undercurrent in Late-Seventeenth-Century England." *HSP* 23.6 (1976): 565-80.

Tollin, Henri. *Geschichte der Französischen Colonie von Magdeburg.* 6 vols. Halle: Niemeyer, 1886-92.

Van Ruymbeke, Bertrand. "Minority Survival. The Huguenot Paradigm in France and the Diaspora." *Memory and identity. The Huguenots in France and the Atlantic Diaspora.* Eds. Bertrand van Ruymbeke, and Randy J. Sparks. Columbia/SC: University of South Carolina Press, 2003. 1-25.

---. *From New Babylon to Eden. The Huguenots and their Migration to Colonial South Carolina.* Columbia/SC: University of South Carolina Press, 2005.

Wheeler Carlo, Paula. *Huguenot Refugees in Colonial New York. Becoming American in the Hudson Valley.* Brighton, Portland: Sussex Academic Press, 2005.

Yardeni, Myriam. *Le Refuge Huguenot. Assimilation et Culture.* Paris: Honoré Champion, 2002.

CHAPTER FIVE

The Europeanization of the World. Colonial Discourses in the French Third Republic

BENEDIKT STUCHTEY

1

When Edmund Dene Morel saw the decline and fall of the West become a reality toward the end of the First World War, his warnings to his contemporaries over the previous decades proved to be justified. In his opinion the consequences of imperialism were rebounding on the colonial powers, and Europe had no reason to be proud of its history: "[...] the past thirty-five years, during which the political invasion of Africa by Europe has been consummated and practically the entire Continent divided up among sundry competing and hostile European powers, will rank as among the most disturbed in the modern history of Europe" ("The African Problem" 6).

What was Morel's motivation for criticizing the European expansion, and what signs are there of anticolonialism from the early modern period onward? Why did critics endeavor to realize a more humane and civilized world order, flying in the face of historical experiences? Despite the central relevance of colonialism for the history of globalization, critics of empire shared the common belief that colonial rule had mainly been accompanied and justified by force and violence. One of the most conscientious observers in the Victorian age, Charles Dilke, declared that colonial rule represented that form of political system, "where one man rules and the rest are slaves" (2: 367). Because of despotism and limited legitimacy colonialism always remained precarious, yet it was nonetheless a decisive motor of world history. By investigating some discourses on the Europeanization of the world, and in consequence the colonial debates that took place in the 'metropolis,' this essay concentrates on those scholarly critics of expansionism in the age of Empire whose work can be defined as part of a larger *cultural* encounter with the non-European world. The criticism of imperialism was usually much more precise than its justification. But to what extent were debates in Europe relevant given that the day-to-day business of running the empires lay mainly with the 'men on the spot' who had to find solutions to colonial problems? This was certainly a weakness on the part of critics who had never personally experienced the colonial periphery. The more radical their arguments, one could say, the less experience they had gained on a daily colonial basis. Therefore, the social and cultural background of the public moralists is particularly interesting if we are to understand them as intellectuals who negotiated a social contract with the public. This is especially revealing for genuine imperial powers such as France or Britain. French intellectuals in the Third Republic were particularly active in this, such as, for example, the geographer Elisée Reclus, who is hardly known today but played a major role within the French and international scholarly discourse. Five theses are proposed as a background to this investigation:

1. The public moralists – a term coined by the English intellectual historian Stefan Collini – did not accept the accusation with which many intellectuals were charged, that they had stayed remote in their ivory towers. Instead, it was claimed, they threw light upon crises of imperialism in order to rectify them. Here the semantics of crisis is of eminent importance, as illuminated by the shipwreck metaphor used by the German philosopher Hans Blumenberg, where the spectators cannot stand by idly but feel called upon to fight against the catastrophe. Anyone who becomes active, even if only verbally, demands change and does not accept scandals, even though they happen in the colonial periphery. Because scandals can be calculated, they can be averted. Though products of historical chance, they were nonetheless predictable given that colonial scandals had always happened as long as colonial expansion into the non-European world was taking place. One could say: no colonialism without scandal or crisis, and no crisis without the means to overcome it.

2. Colonial crises touched social, political, and ideological norms, they violated the established and cultivated image of colonial rule as a core element of the so-called civilizing mission with all its positive connotations. To study the critics of empire thus also means to question the continuity and exclusiveness of an imperial philosophy of history without, however, being able to dismantle it completely. Therefore, critics argued against the interpretation of colonial expansionism as the exclusive history of international relations.

3. The critics were no less eccentric individuals than the colonial enthusiasts. But in contrast to the latter the colonial world was not necessarily part of the critics' world. They relied on information brought from the peripheries to the metropolitan centers. The compensation for the lack of empirical knowledge was the intellectual alternative of tolerance, which was necessary to separate individual cases from general constants. As a consequence, criticism could easily arouse the suspicion that it was corroding the idea of imperialism because it dissected it into many single aspects.

4. The critics shared, to a certain extent, an antimodern conditioning insofar as colonial expansion was a phenomenon of modernity. They also shared a contempt for the enthusiasm for conquering the world. Their aim was unconventional, but they took a conventional path to achieve it. Referring to the historical model of Rome, they reconstructed the message of ancient colonialism, which had proved that overstretching empire advanced its decline.

5. The critics of empire were deeply embedded in the political and social processes they described. They did not always have a mandate that allowed direct involvement in politics, but as a rule they were not so detached as to forego social and political communication. Because of their integration into the public sphere they were capable of civic commitment.

2

Looking at France one finds a specific form of colonial criticism, inspired by Catholicism and divided from Socialism, which tried to function as the voice of the nation. For a long time it had been a widely accepted interpretation that the French Catholics favored the enlargement of the empire because they saw this as an advantage for the missionary societies (Perkins). Anticolonialism was usually the concern of the Left, moving to the extremes the more pressing colonial problems became. All in all the political and religious factions were at odds with each other to such an extent that French imperialism in the Third Republic only intensified this picture. Individual Catholics, whether they were Bonapartists, Orleanists, or Legitimists, were unanimous in their opposition to colonial expansionism in Tunisia, Egypt, and Madagascar (Ageron), while the official church and her missionary societies were ambivalent, as will be shown later in this essay. In a continuous recourse to the military weakness manifested in the Franco-Prussian War of 1870-71, the defeat was taken as a pretext for seeking neither military revenge nor colonial contest overseas. Instead priorities were to be set in the social and economic consolidation of the state. In an age when the Germans and French were again observing each other with hostility and reviving aversions rooted in the French Revolution and its aftermath, Ernest Renan exclaimed his famous 'Vae Victoribus' to his neighbors on the opposite bank of the Rhein. The scholar warned the enemy for his own good against the dangers of unlimited power politics (Jeismann 238).

For victory was a bad advisor. What became clear to the loser was invisible to the winner in the flashy light of success. The Christian dogma of the enhancement of the abjected also meant that victory was possibly Pyrrhic if antagonisms were consolidated at the borders. Eighteenth-century critics had already seen the outcome of the Seven Years' War as England's entrance into industrialization and systematic colonial expansion. The conclusion they drew was that English society would lose its balance as a consequence of these new economic developments and non-European interests. Following this interpretation the warning voices of 1870-71 claimed that Prussia would become a militaristic and despotic empire (Valette). In the age of nationalism, historical conflicts had culminated in quasi-religious, hereditary enmity. Definitions of the self and the other (which were fundamentally entangled) thus became reduced to symbolic formulas. According to these, the victor was only interested in the establishment of political unity and the loser in the defense of civilization, understood as a universally conceived concept, but tailored to France. Prussia's victory was contrasted with France's glory. In this way a peculiar transformation took place from the emphatic, libertarian stance of early nineteenth-century nationalism to the paranoid alignment with racism and imperialism in the age of Empire. While an interrelated construction of identity through enmity was taking shape, stereotypes and collective symbols were confirmed that charged the other side with degenerating toward an obsessive notion of war and conquest.

Following the arguments of the theorists of imperialism, the image of the colonial other replaced the construction of an internal enemy – a problem which Benjamin Disraeli had already addressed in his Two-England metaphor, thereby showing the tension of the nation-state, in this case the early republic (Taithe). The Victorian perspective had resulted in the rather pragmatic answer that this challenge should be met by economic adjustment, military reorganization and constitutional reorientation. In sum, both concepts adopted the defensive argument of the lessons of history with a special appeal for the nation whose interests should not be sacrificed to the interests of colonial expansion. The French Prime Minister Jules Ferry had argued that France's inner conflict would be overcome by colonial ventures. By contrast, the parliamentary opposition led by Duc Broglie declared that the French expeditions to Tunisia and Indochina were merely compensation for the loss of Alsace-Lorraine. The case of Tunisia in the early 1880s could, from the viewpoint of the radical opposition, even lead to the conclusion that colonial policy was nothing less than treason enacted to avoid any revenge of the French nation against Germany (Guétant).

However, the question remains as to whether this argument underestimated the military, economic, scientific, and missionary forces in favor of imperialism. Compensation for the defeat against Germany was one issue, the other was regeneration and the attempt to gain new perspectives. In the rhetoric of regeneration, reminiscent in many ways of the American frontier myth, aspects of a religiously elevated land were intertwined with the psychologically loaded myth of the colonial space that was regarded as a space for the hardening of male virtues. For quite a long time, probably until 1911 and the Franco-German confrontation in Morocco, the question of Alsace-Lorraine was excluded from public debate, only to return with even more explosive force when colonial and world policy were closely connected before the Great War (Wilsberg 44-57).

3

The global integrative power claimed by Catholicism predestined the church to be separated from other European cases. Elisée Reclus (1830-1905), probably the most important historically minded geographer in the second half of the nineteenth century (Osterhammel 265), even believed in the idea of a unity of mankind that he termed "immense Internationale," a collectivity of ideas, an ecumenism in language and ethnic descent. This corresponded with the ideal of a religiously anarchic, yet ethical canon of values:

> Des alliances de travail se font entre gens de toute race et de toute langue: d'un bout du monde à l'autre se forme une immense Internationale, – et j'entends ce mot dans son acception la plus large, – une immense Internationale professant les mêmes idées. Nous pouvons reprendre ici l'ancienne comparaison de la Bible qui nous montre la vérité s'élevant sans cesse comme une marée et recouvrant la terre entière ainsi que les eaux d'un océan. Nous progressions toujours, et bien que l'ère de la civilisation européenne ait commencé pour le Nouveau Monde, elle ne s'est point achevée pour l'Ancien. (Reclus, *Hégémonie* 13)

Reclus addressed the problem of colonialism repeatedly in his most important works, the *Nouvelle Géographie Universelle. La Terre et les Hommes* (1876-1894) in nineteen volumes, and *L'Homme et la Terre* (1905-1908) in six volumes. Whether it be Brazil, China, or other case studies, he was continuously occupied with aspects of European colonial rule (Reclus, "Le Brasil"; "L'Internationale"; *La Chine*). Reclus was among the first to coin a term that was translated into English as "social geography" (Dunbar). Along with Alexander von Humboldt's *Kosmos*, his *Nouvelle Géographie Universelle* is probably among the most influential geographical works that lend themselves to historical analysis.

As a moderate anarchist Reclus interfered in daily politics, and was thus not an armchair intellectual, although he did not possess the polemic acuity that was characteristic of later colonial critics such as Victor Augagneur, Jean Carol, and Paul Louis. The philosophical scientist feared nothing so much as ruthless, and, in his eyes, fanatical thinking. He, who appreciated inconsequential action, understood it as a source of tolerance: against human estrangement, economic exploitation, nationalistic narrow-mindedness, religious obscurantism, theological dogma, and overall human deficiencies. Consequently Reclus, who turned seventy around 1900, was assigned the role of a moral authority when he wrote pamphlets against the French policy in Madagascar such as, for example, *Guerre, Militarisme* (1902) and *Patriotisme, Colonisation* (1903) (Fleming).

How Reclus formulated a program of a social geography can easily be seen from the foreword to *L'Homme et la Terre*. He asserted that his time was shaped by crises that deeply affected society so that only the study of history could mediate major ideas and laws. The susceptibility to crises could be explained, according to Reclus, by three different historical stages displayed by social geography. As if a current event had occurred just to prove this theory, Reclus gave a speech shortly after the Russian Revolution broke out in 1905. He reminded his listeners of the end of the Commune and compared the revolutionary St. Petersburg with Paris. He expressed the hope that the Russian empire would grant freedom to the different nationalities under its rule. From the experience of revolution the geographer drew the conclusion that no heterogenous imperial power could continuously expand its frontiers without violating the political, social, and cultural entities in its interior. While all great powers supposedly sought to guarantee universal peace through conquest and territorial annexations, imperialism, according to Reclus, simply followed the law of power: "D'un côté, ils mangent, de l'autre, ils sont mangés" (Quoted from Chardak 415).

Reclus' perception of the problems caused by imperialism for the European balance of power was documented in his small booklet *Hégémonie de l'Europe* (1894). As in his major works he asked questions about the different types of colonial rule and which of them tended to cause crises, grievances, and scandals. He remained quite ambivalent on this point and only differentiated between 'les colonies d'exploitation' and 'les colonies de peuplement,' without, however, following the popular argument of the opposition between industrialized imperial powers on the one hand and oppressed peoples on the other. Thus, Reclus' judgment of settlement colonies was not entirely negative as long as they fit into the criteria of 'mise en valeur.' A generation later the governor of Indochina, Albert Sarraut, would define the criterion of 'mise en valeur' in two striking volumes as one of the most important motives for French colonial expansion since its early beginnings (Sarraut, *Mise en Valeur*; *Grandeurs*). In Reclus' eyes Algeria was therefore no 'colonie de conquête' but an extra-territorial part of a Greater France, or a 'France africaine.' The phenomenon of imperial rule was thus based on the different national, regional, and local levels.

This theory is astonishingly close to what John Robert Seeley and Charles Dilke wrote in their respective books about British imperialism. Their influence on French intellectual contemporaries was described early on by the French colonial theorist Paul Louis ("L'Imperialisme Anglo-Saxon" 257; "La Colonisation" 28). Reclus could be classified as an advocate of a cautious form of a 'république coloniale' (Bancel). The discrepancy inherent in the concept of a Republican nation-state that engages in colonial imperialism could be resolved by the insight that even colonial power was not unlimited and free from mythical configurations. Finally, in Reclus' eyes, it would be an impossible task to protect the mother country, be it republic or monarchy, from the negative effects of colonial rule. In all its forms, not least in the negative ones, colonial expansion could become part of the national heritage. It was a site of memory beyond the colonial space (Mouralis 12-7).

In this respect Reclus belonged to a group of scholars and intellectuals who did not possess institutionalized political power to fight against imperialism in parliament or other forums, but who expressed their resentment in literary and academic discourses. Thus narrowed down, they can be understood as representatives of an age when public moralists tried to withdraw from any collective attributes. A clearer definition can be attempted by summarizing Reclus' position with respect to what he termed 'colonies d'exploitation.' Unlike most geographers working historically in the late nineteenth century, he did not investigate the continuities but the changes that resulted from European colonial rule in the non-Western world. More precisely, he was interested in the colonial space as a space where 'civilization' met 'barbarism.' In fact, he used this terminology without valuation, but with the aim of sharpening the contrasts which, in his eyes, resulted from the contradictions of expansionism. The conflicts were marked both by economic globalization – a result of imperialism – and the ruthless pace at which colonies were established, thereby destroying indigenous societies and inflicting hitherto unknown famines (Bouche 2: 161-75).

The dialectics of colonialism and progress were interrelated. The pauperization, displacement, and exploitation of autochthonous peoples as one outcome of imperialism was most obvious to contemporaries. Often they criticized the starvation wages that led to famines and epidemics. In general, a scandalous colonial administration was to be made responsible for dramatic demographic changes in the colonies. In order to be able to sell their products to India, Reclus argued in *Hégémonie de l'Europe*, textile industries in Lancashire and Yorkshire made Indian import trade dependent upon the English economy. The wealth of the factory owners in Manchester was created by the hard work of both English and colonial laborers. In sum, Elisée Reclus is only one of many scholars who thought about European expansionism and the entanglements that world politics and the world economy were producing in global dimensions. He did not deny or ignore the possible positive, even pacifist results of this. But in his opinion the historical geography of a 'conquête coloniale' allowed neither the monopolizing precedence of a single country (naturally, in his time, the British Empire), nor the Europeanization of the world. He observed both tendencies with great unease, yet, in his words, "Le monde entier s'européanise: on peut même dire qu'il est européanisé déjà" (Reclus, *Hégémonie de l'Europe* 11).

4

Since France had opened the door to Africa shortly after the July Revolution of 1830 it seemed natural to pursue a colonial policy beyond the Mediterranean area. For a contemporary commentator of the 1880s like Paul Gaffarel Africa symbolized compensation for the loss of Alsace-Lorraine, but also an alternative to the Atlantic option, which had been lost in the Anglo-French rivalry for power in the New World. While the Rhine frontier and the Atlantic frontier were closed, the imperial future lay, according to Gaffarel, in the North of Africa where the French 'mission civilisatrice' encountered frontier colonialism similar to what white settlers had once found on the American continent: "Nous avions dans ce pays un Far West à découvrir, une Californie à exploiter" (Gaffarel 562; Schivelbusch 211 ff.). Furthermore, with the territorial integration of Algeria into the French state, a form of expansionism was espoused that was different from Pierre-Joseph Proudhon's idea of a moderate agrarian colonialism or Etienne Cabet's attempt to found a socialist commune in Algeria. Early French socialists before the Revolution of 1848, like Louis Blanc, had, as a matter of principle, regarded imperialism as ambivalent. They condemned the alleged obligation to colonial expansionism and world policy, but they also understood themselves as heirs to Jacobin Socialism, whose missionary zeal and cosmopolitan patriotism called upon the French nation to liberate mankind. Some especially enduring elements of world political thinking from the nineteenth century survived well into the time of the French Third Republic: one was criticism of capitalism as a preliminary stage to criticism of militant and nationalist colonialism, another the plea for a humanitarian and civilizatory colonization (understood as the West's moral duty).

For many colonial theorists the discovery of this positively connotated continuity represented a yardstick for the political and civilizatory modernization of the country (Lehning, Hazareesingh, Charle). By contrast, some critics argued that by rejecting the colonial policy of the past, they were fighting against the contemporary expansionism. Some went as far as the author Raboisson in his book *Études sur les Colonies* (1877). He thought colonial expansion was a rudimentary phenomenon regarded by the broader public with disinterest and indifference. The lack of enthusiasm for the colonial project was explained with its accidental outcome. Unlike British imperialism, the French counterpart did not constitute a genuine aspect of the nation but was merely a mirror of the republic's obsession with increasing national prestige in order to compensate for the military defeat of 1870-71. This was Raboisson's interpretation. French state imperialism geared toward gaining international prestige was contrasted with British private imperialism geared toward gaining economic profits. In consequence, France's lack of interest in the export market and in opening up new markets for its industrial production in general was seen as less aggressively motivated and less orientated toward social Darwinist concepts because it was less existential than in Britain or Germany (Raboisson). From this it could be deduced that the scant interest in an expansionist industrial culture, and therefore France's economic backwardness in the late nineteenth century, could be attributed to antimodernist prejudices and a distrust of global market mechanisms that were deeply rooted in French society (Bourguignon, Caron).

These theses of contemporary critics of colonialism are partly confirmed by modern research (Baumgart 69ff., 114ff., 127ff.), but nonetheless they need to be questioned. They can be summarized as follows: French colonial expansionism in the age of Empire did not have the aggressive character of the German ideology of *Lebensraum*. According to Linda Clark, social Darwinist ideas had no appeal in the French Third Republic since global expansion as an alternative to a failed European policy had only compensatory aims (Clark 108). To a certain extent Bismarck's calculation had worked out. The German chancellor had encouraged French imperial ambitions in order to reignite the rivalry between France and Britain, and at the same time to defuse the problem of Alsace-Lorraine. However, this strategy eventually failed in the first Morocco crisis of 1905, and equally importantly it signaled Bismarck's relative indifference to German colonialism, for which he was heavily criticized in parliament (Goldberg).

'La France africaine' had pointed the way from the narrow confines of Europe to the vast expanses of the overseas world. John Robert Seeley's concept of a 'Greater Britain' had equally promoted extending the achievements of the European cultural nations to the colonial periphery. The projection of cultural imperialism marked by the recovery of the nation since 1890 reflected the victory of the 'Parti colonial' even over the most irreconcilable anticolonialists from the political camp of the Boulangists (Grupp). From the end of the nineteenth-century resistance to imperialism became less vocal, while the 'idée coloniale,' according to Girardet's main thesis, helped the nation to regenerate, released it from its medium-term orientation to the Rhine, and, most importantly, created the myth of a chosen people. Just as the French Revolution had brought freedom to the people of Europe, the Europeanization of the world would bring freedom to the people of North Africa who were suffering under Arabic despotism.

The civilizing mission was an important argument for the proponents of empire, i.e., the propagandists of the 'Parti colonial,' because they did not interpret colonialism as a contradiction to 'liberté,' 'egalité,' and 'fraternité' but as their realization. One of the most influential journalists of his time, Paul Leroy-Beaulieu, expressed the opinion that Europe had dominated French politics for too long and distracted from France's real interests in Africa and Asia (Leroy-Beaulieu). In a political process in which the fundamental opposition to the system of the republic as well as to colonial expansion lost both its social and its political significance, French critics of empire became less relevant in the public discourse (Murphy 140). Equally, they themselves could become the focus of criticism when their affinity with anti-Semitism was revealed: some had argued that gentlemanly capitalism and overseas interests served Jewish financial power politics. Several of these points are valid. The fact that individual European anticolonialists had anti-Semitic tendencies had already been a significant problem in the context of the debate about Benjamin Disraeli's colonial policy in Victorian England. In his struggle against British high finance during and after the South African War of 1899-1902, John Hobson illustrated the strength of his arguments against Jewish businessmen by making their financial circles responsible for the sins of imperialism (Cain, 92-3, 96, 110). And after all, France had been shaken quite substantially by the Dreyfus Affair. Nationalism, anti-Semitism, even racism on the one hand, and anticolonialism on the other were not entirely contradictory. Indeed, the problematic publication *La France Juive* (1886) by Edouard Drumonts showed that they complemented each other in so far as they reacted to the same popular instincts and preventive mechanisms (Drumont).

However, the critics of French imperialism, in Girardet's words the "adversaries," did not completely disappear from the "grandes controverses des années 1880" (Girardet 66). Although they were not prominent, and attempts were made to relegate them to the political background, these intellectuals nonetheless succeeded in keeping resentment of expansionism alive. Perhaps it was their most important short-term achievement to have prevented the colonial question from disappearing from the public debate. For French society was certainly not indifferent to the colonial empire (Brunschwig, "Vigné d'Octon and Anti-Colonialism" 140-71),[1] but while political, social, and religious controversies competed for attention the relevance of the colonial empire can ultimately be deduced from how it reverberated on the great national debates.

The economist Yves Guyot already knew that the cultural-political debates of his time could hardly be understood outside the colonial-political zeitgeist. Describing himself as a patriot in harmony with the ideals of the French Revolution, and attracting attention during the last years of the Kaiserreich as a journalist for radical-republican papers before he became a member of Parliament in Paris for the 'radicaux,' the Breton had published a book under the title *Lettres sur la Politique Colonial* (1885). The 'letters,' which had been printed a year earlier in the journal *La Laterne*, were quite special because here Guyot polemicized unreservedly against all aspects of French colonial expansion. While the majority of critics did not really attack colonialism as such but only methods of colonial rule, and while they were not calling for immediate decolonization, Yves Guyot tried to combine all points in one. He was angered by the concept of the 'mission civilisatrice' and condemned a term such as the French 'race.'

Reflections on the civilizing mission had been lurking in French minds at least since Auguste Comte's *Système de Philosophie Positive* (1851-54). Comte regarded this mission as a European project under French guidance that other European nations should join in a hierarchical order. In this context, he even suggested that a committee of Western positivists invite representatives from Africa and Asia to become members after its foundation, supposedly for their own cultural advancement (Taguieff, Cohen). Elements of a racist terminology were concurrently invented that were refined by theorists like Gobineau, Le Bon, and Lapouge. This is where contemporary refutations by Quatrefages and Novicow set in, which Guyot endorsed and initiated in order to move from the general, yet Eurocentric level of racial theories, to the concrete, yet globally applicable question of colonialism and imperialism.

Guyot's thought processes can hardly be esteemed highly enough. They laid bare the contradictions of French imperialism, and at the core they defeated the 'idée coloniale' as an idea with which France betrayed the values of the Revolution of 1789. French historical research proceeds unanimously from the assumption that imperial France as represented by Jules Ferry during the Third Republic followed the basic idea of universalism. Beyond the aim of universal brotherhood the colonized peoples were to be renamed French citizens. However, were they also prepared to embrace the achievements of 'liberté' and 'egalité' apart from 'fraternité'?

1   "The French people – the 'average Frenchman' – were not interested in the colonies" (168).

Without doubt liberty and equality are even more important than fraternity. This had been the viewpoint of numerous parliamentarians since 1871 who, in contrast to the civilizatory claim of the colonial project, welcomed the representatives of Algeria and Martinique, of Guadeloupe and Senegal – but they welcomed the representatives of colonial rule, not those of the indigenous populations. When people talked about assimilation, which was ratified in the constitution of 1875, this did not mean a renunciation of anthropological racism that never accepted physical and cultural equality. The term 'mission civilisatrice' already implied the devaluation of other, non-Western civilizations and cultures (Adas 199-270). Scientific racism had made possible the marginalization of humanism and universalism in the age of high imperialism. Chauvinist nationalism and solid economic interests contributed to the fact that imperialism did not stand for modernity, progressiveness, or even altruism as claimed by its advocates, but represented violence, subordination, and contempt for the 'other' as criticized by its enemies. Accordingly, even 'fraternité' was self-deception. Guyot unmasked this ideology by using the family metaphor: the bad habits of the child by no means justify the brutality of the parents. Seventy years after Guyot, the poet and politician from Martinique, Aimé Césaire, took up this play on words. In *Discours sur le Colonialisme* (1955) he invented the word 'fraternalisme,' an allegory for the double-dealing of colonialism, which manifestly betrayed the idea of 'fraternité.'

In sum, colonial expansion in the early Third Republic constituted an intense field of political struggle similar, for example, to that of religion. Its critics therefore played a significant role in the daily public debate. On the other hand, it would attach too much weight to anticolonialism to describe it as identity-forming for the radical opposition of the republic, given that its nature was pragmatic rather than a matter of principle, and it could not therefore exert decisive influence on political decisions (Guillen 110 ff.; Meyer [ed.] 1: 640 ff.). According to Dominique Lejeune, no fundamental philosophical difference existed between radical and republican intellectuals as long as they could direct their attention toward the common enemy, the boulangists and monarchists: "[...] les deux courants du parti républicain partageaient une même culture et une même tradition politique qui leur permetaient de se rassembler sans trop de problèmes chaque fois que la conjoncture politique – voire le 'danger monarchiste' – l'exigeait" (Lejeune 52).

5

The colonial-political debates were less concerned with *whether* colonies should be acquired at all than with *how* the methods of expansion and colonial rule should be executed. Critics of empire targeted the behavior of politicians such as Jules Ferry who tried to avoid colonial debates in parliament or obtained legitimation for his actions from parliamentarians once *faits accomplis* at the colonial periphery had been established. Arguments did not disappear completely from the public sphere once colonial rule had been integrated into the supposedly trouble-free business of everyday politics. In order to counterbalance any such specula-tion, critics of empire again made themselves prominent after the establishment of French colonial rule in Tunisia and Indochina.

When the physician Paul Vigné d'Octon published his report on the deploy-ment of the French military in Tunisia (1911), he brought a painful subject to the attention of the nation once again. *La Sueur du Burnous. Les Crimes Coloni-aux de la IIIe République* and the pamphlet *La Terreur en Afrique du Nord* were directed both at the colonial administration and the French political elite by ac-cusing them of not taking the problems caused by colonialism seriously enough (Vigné d'Octon 181 ff.: "Les Méfaits de la Grande Colonisation"). However, the way in which the pragmatists dealt with everyday problems at the periphery, that is, whether administrators, missionaries, scientists, physicians, soldiers, and teach-ers were actually influenced by debates in the metropoles of power is quite anoth-er story. From a manual published shortly before the outbreak of the First World War it becomes clear how colonial work was practiced on a daily basis (Viénot). The global perspective of anticolonialism was hardly compatible with the local one in the colonies themselves (Rébérioux and Haupt). In moments of colonial crises different forms of anticolonial thinking could manifest themselves parallel to each other. In the French Third Republic they were, to a certain extent, rem-iniscent of the philosophical and moral intensity that debates had reached in the second half of the eighteenth century.

A further important example of the Europeanization of the world is Madagas-car. Its colonial development had begun in the sixteenth century with the Portu-guese, to be followed by French coastal bases beginning in 1642. In 1885 the is-land then became a protectorate and was populated by settlers until formal French colonial rule was established in 1896. After that, numerous rebellions broke out in the province of Farafangana to be suppressed only in 1903 by the then general governor J. S. Gallieni. To describe these events French historiography has used the term 'pacification' (Lebon; Bouche 83; see also Deschamps). The revolts had been caused by social and economic factors. The religious question of whether French Catholicism or English Methodism should be predominant also produced some tension, especially because, according to a contemporary report, the Cath-olic church of France and its official organ, *Le Français*, were very interested in asserting their influence in the colonies (Lecanuet 250 ff.).

In 1905 the socialist, journalist and writer Paul Louis published his observa-tions of these and other global events under the plain title *Le Colonialisme*. It led the French historian Henri Brunschwig to argue that the term 'colonialism' was not in use before 1905. Accordingly, he believed that French anticolonialism did not exist before the turn of the century (Brunschwig). Paul Louis' publications, however, qualified this thesis, although the *Grand Larousse* defined colonialism until the 1930s as a mere "colonisation capitaliste" and as a phenomenon against which critics of empire fought as "une forme d'impérialisme issue du mécanisme capitaliste" (Quoted from Biondi 75). But when in 1900 he turned his studies of British capitalism to the question of whether the economic process or power-political, ideological, or national motives were of prime importance for imperialism – and as a Marxist theorist he favored global mechanisms and their inevitabilities as the driving forces behind Europe's colonial expansion – Louis had introduced the terminology of colonialism into the French theoretical debate.

Paul Louis mainly wrote for the journals *Revue Bleue* und *La Revue Socialiste* – similar to the German Eduard Bernstein, who presented colonial-political topics on a regular basis in the *Sozialistische Monatshefte* (Louis, *La Guerre Economique*; *Le Colonialisme*). As a critical analyst of the British empire, Louis put his findings into a comparative perspective with the colonial policy of the Third Republic as well as of the United States and the German Kaiserreich (Louis, "L'Imperialisme Anglo-Saxon"; "La Politique Extérieure"; "La Grandeur des Etats Unis"; "La plus Grande Allemagne"). He was a meticulous observer of the trouble spots of his time and was concerned with China, the Philippines, and South Africa ("La Partage de la Chine"; "A propos de la Guerre Hispano-Américaine"; "La Question Sud-Africaine"). From the cases he investigated he concluded that economic, social, and legal aspects must certainly not be underestimated. But against the background of the rising number of colonial scandals and crises, he believed that the moral argument had equal weight ("La Colonisation" 29 ff.).

This claim was as important as it was up to date. In order to lead France out of an atmosphere molded by ideas of decadence and materialism, the author Romain Rolland had, since 1904, been preparing a cyclical novel with the title *Jean Christophe*, by which he wanted to show moral greatness and a sense of justice, humanitarian ideals and a pacifist understanding between the peoples. The biographer of Beethoven and Gandhi, Rolland was, in the words of Stefan Zweig, a fighter for an idea who like the characters in his novels tested his opportunities in the light of resistance (Zweig 121; see also Francis 64-89). Rolland's literary skepticism was the skepticism of the intellectual facing the moral dangers of power. He rejected in principle any form of violence, including the mental one, and set skepticism and critique, as tokens of individuality, against the collectivism of chauvinist and imperialist passion.

Few represented such an ethical ideal as vividly as Rolland or, as another example, Anatole France, who in his novel *Sur la Pierre Blanche* (1905) combined his aestheticism with an irony reminiscent of Montaigne and Diderot, subtly treating the topic of colonialism as a topic of the past that needed to be overcome (Gier, esp. 481 ff.). As a political intellectual he can be considered along with Paul Louis. Their works constantly revolved around the same central problem: why colonial expansion could not be reconciled with the ideals of socialism, and why in the end imperialism produced and promoted absolute and militaristic structures of power (Louis, "Le Socialisme"; "Impérialisme – Absolutisme – Militarisme"). Since, according to Hannah Arendt, the origins of totalitarianism went back to imperial systems, Louis was convinced that they could be confronted by antiimperial arguments that resulted directly from actual colonial situations. In order to strengthen the arguments it was helpful to instrumentalize moral indignation at a colonial scandal. Therefore, it seems just to assess Paul Louis in terms of having provided the French colonial debate around 1900 with an authoritative and theoretical basis on which colonial practicioners could count.

There were two quite different colonial practitioners among the many who felt competent to express their opinion about French rule over Madagascar: Jean Carol and Victor Augagneur. Carol published his studies as *Chez les Hova. Au Pays Rouge* in 1898 when the revolts and their suppression by the French troops were entering their most violent phase. Augagneur approached the public only twenty-nine years later, shortly before his death, with a publication that left little room for misunderstanding: *Erreurs et Brutalités Coloniales* (1927). Both had been active as colonial administrators, which qualified them to judge the mechanisms of power between the center in Paris and Madagascar from the perspective of an insider. Carol, who had worked as a journalist and whose name was actually Gabriel Laffaille, had come to Madagascar toward the end of 1895 where he worked as a secretary for General Laroche (Paillard 5-34). He soon became intrigued by the indigenous population, the 'Hova,' observing them through the eyes of the ethnologist and with a fascination for their allegedly natural life, which he wanted to protect against Europeanization. He wrote articles for the Parisian newspaper *Temps*, which finally resulted in a book in 1898. The purpose of this book was first of all to arouse sympathy for the way of life of the indigenous population on the island, which came close to a call for greater understanding of their struggle against French colonial rule. When Gallieni's troops marched in, the French public reacted with patriotic pride, as could have been predicted, and not with protest as Carol had hoped. Indignation was only expressed by the anticolonialists. At the heart of their argument was Carol's description of the 'civilisation originale,' for which he promoted respect.

Victor Augagneur's book belonged to a different category. As in British or German history, one finds numerous examples of reports from French colonial administrators whose experience stemmed from different stages of the empires. They reflected on them partly to justify their administrative work, but also partly to find explanations for why it was possible to transfer techniques of rule from one colony to the other in some cases, but not in others. In the case of Madagascar there were several administrators who kept what they called "journals" (For example Talvas). In this sense Augagneur conceived his book mainly as a stock-taking of the rebellions on Farafangana. His perspective was not anticolonial in principle, but rather intended to reflect on ways of improving the colonial administration for which he had worked since 1905 after the revolt had calmed down. The facts he noted were distressing: the population of Madagascar had been reduced by 1.3 million as a consequence of colonial warfare (Augagneur).

In the preface to the book Augagneur argued that he was less interested in the political, economic, and legal aspects of his subject than in the moral ones.

This critic of civilization, who had waited twenty-five years before publishing his work, out of consideration for the rights of the political activists of his time, did not fear a controversy arising from colonial enthusiasts in Paris. Rather, he declared that he was not criticizing colonial expansion as such but its methods, the "procédés de violence, les méthodes tyranniques." For this reason he pleaded for a "bonne politique indigene" (Augagneur, 199-200). Only if imperialism represented the interests of the nation and not of individuals, Augagneur explained, would he be prepared to see himself as a "partisan determiné." In that case he was a "Partisan de la colonisation pratiquée dans l'interêt de la Nation tout entière et non pour le plus grand avantage de quelques-uns [...]. Mais la première condition d'une colonisation intelligente et productive, c'est d'avoir avec soi la population indigène" (Augagneur VII).

6

To sum up, even those well-disposed to humanitarian ideas defended the 'discursive hegemony,' while in general a kind of occidental blindness was at work. As famously, but not uncontroversially, stated by Edward Said, only a few Europeans were able to avoid justifying colonial expansionism by way of transcultural self-denial (*Orientalism*). However, this minority was neither as small as sometimes suggested, nor could its political and philosophical contribution to colonial and imperial theories be dismissed as of no relevance. By contrast this essay has aimed to show that critics of the imperial idea accompanied the history of cultural, military, economic, and missionary expansionism from its beginnings, disputing the legitimacy of the whole undertaking, and pointing to the unwanted consequences of its realization. As regards intellectual history, the anticolonial voices were rhetorically fascinating and historically rewarding – in fact they were predominantly the voices of scholars, scientists, intellectuals, writers, and men and women who had originally been in imperial service as administrators, missionaries, and teachers, or had served in other functions and had then returned home disillusioned.

Their critical attitudes toward imperialism reflected political and ethical positions within society that were naturally not popular at times when territorial expansion was a question of national prestige. But when, in the age of decolonization, indigenous elites revolted against their foreign powers, many of the anticolonial arguments that had been used by European public moralists from the fifteenth century to the 1950s were reinvented. In short: both transnational scholarly discourses and global cultural encounters could result in a different perception of colonial expansionism. The focus of this essay has been on how they influenced national debates on empire and formed new counterhegemonic points of view, and how the arguments were developed in the incongruent context of intellectual scope on the one hand, and restricted room for limited political maneuvers on the other. It is therefore helpful to point to occasional crises at the imperial periphery and a normative disposition of criticism of colonialism to social and political dissidence. Both phenomena also relate to the sometimes difficult relationship between rhetorical commonplaces and a strong policy of morally based intervention, both of which were characteristic of the critics of empire. After all, the criticism of imperialism and of colonial methods for establishing hierarchical power, the game of obtaining imperial objects, the close connection between national or domestic forces and imperial crises in which fundamental positions on political morality, racism, and the legitimacy of power crystallized, intensified in this age when colonial discourse gained an unparalleled density and an almost global range.

References

Adas, Michael. *Machines as the Measure of Men. Science, Technology and Ideologies of Western Dominance*. Ithaca and London: Cornell University Press, 1989.

Ageron, Charles-Robert. *L'Anticolonialisme en France de 1871 à 1914*. Paris: Presses Univ. de France, 1973.

Augagneur, Jean Victor. *Erreurs et Brutalités Coloniales*. Paris: Éd. Montaigne, 1927.

Bancel, Nicolas, Pascal Blanchard, and Françoise Vergès. *La République Coloniale. Essai Sur une Utopie*. Paris: Michel, 2003.

Baumgart, Winfried. *Imperialism. The Idea and Reality of British and French Colonial Expansion, 1880-1914*. Oxford: Oxford University Press, 1982.

Biondi, Jean-Pierre. *Les Anticolonialistes (1881-1962)*. Paris: Laffont, 1992.

Bouche, Denise. *Histoire de la Colonisation Française*. Vol. 2 (*Flux et Reflux, 1815-1962*). Paris: Fayard, 1998.

Bourguignon, François, and Maurice Lévy-Leboyer. *The French Economy in the Nineteenth Century. An Essay in Economic Analysis*. Cambridge: Cambridge University Press, 1990.

Brunschwig, Henri. "Colonisation – Decolonisation. Essai Sur le Vocabulaire Usuel de la Politique Coloniale." *Cahiers d'Etudes Africaines* 1 (1960): 44-54.

---. "Vigné d'Octon and Anti-Colonialism under the Third Republic". *European Imperialism and the Partition of Africa*. Ed. E.F. Penrose. London: F. Cass, 1975.

Cain, Peter J. *Hobson and Imperialism. Radicalism, New Liberalism, and Finance 1887-1938*. Oxford/New York: Oxford University Press, 2002.

Carol, Jean. *Chez les Hova. Au Pays Rouge*. Paris: Ollendorff, 1898.

Caron, François. *Histoire Économique de la France XIXe-XXe Siècles*. Paris: Armand Colin, 1981.

Chardak, Henriette. *Elisée Reclus, une Vie. L'Homme Qui Aimat la Terre*. Paris: Stock, 1997.

Charle, Christophe. *Les Elites de la République 1880-1900*. Paris: Fayard, 1987.

Clark, Linda. *Social Darwinism in France*. Alabama: University of Alabama Press, 1984.

Cohen, William B. *The French Encounter with Africans*. Bloomington, Ind.: Indiana University Press, 1980.

Comte, Auguste. *Système de Philosophie Positive ou Traité de Sociologie Instituant le Religion de l'Humanité*. 4 vols. Paris: L. Mathias, Carilian-Goeury et Vor Dalmont, 1851-54.

Deschamps, Hubert. *Histoire de Madagascar*. Paris: Berger-Levrault, 1965.

Dilke, Charles Wentworth. *Greater Britain. A Record of Travel in English-Speaking Countries During 1866 and 1867*. 2 vols. London: Macmillan, 1868.

Drumont, Edouard. *La France Juive Devant l'Opinion*. Paris: Flammarion, 1886.

Dunbar, Gary S. "Some Early Occurrences of the Term 'Social Geography'". *Scottish Geographical Magazine* 93 (1977): 15-20.

Fleming, Marie. *The Anarchist Way to Socialism. Elisée Reclus and Nineteenth-Century European Anarchism*. London: Croom Helm, 1979.

Francis, R. A. *Romain Rolland*. Oxford: Berg, 1999.

Gaffarel, Paul. *L'Algérie. Histoire, Conquête et Colonisation*. Paris: Firmin Didot, 1883.

Gier, Albert. *Der Skeptiker im Gespräch mit dem Leser. Studien zum Werk von Anatole France und zu seiner Rezeption in der französischen Presse 1879-1905*. Tübingen: Niemeyer, 1985.

Girardet, Raoul. *L'Idée Coloniale en France de 1871 à 1962*. Paris: Hachette Littératures, 1978.

Gobineau, Arthur de. *Essai Sur l'Inégalité des Races Humaines*. Paris: Firmin-Didot, 1853-55.

Goldberg, Hans-Peter. *Bismarck und seine Gegner. Die politische Rhetorik im kaiserlichen Reichstag*. Düsseldorf: Droste, 1998.

Grupp, Peter. *Deutschland, Frankreich und die Kolonien. Der französische "Parti colonial" und Deutschland von 1890 bis 1914*. Tübingen: Moor, 1980.

Guétant, Louis. *La Politique d'Extension Coloniale et les Principes Républicains: Lettre d'un Travailleur à M. Jules Ferry*. Lyon: s.n., 1885.

Guillen, Pierre. *L'Expansion, 1881-1898*. Paris: Imprimerie Nationale, 1984.

Guyot, Yves. *Lettres Sur la Politique Coloniale*. Paris: C. Reinwald, 1885.

Hazareesingh, Sudhir. *Intellectual Founders of the Republic. Five Studies in Nineteenth-Century French Political Thought*. Oxford and London: Oxford University Press, 2002.

Jeismann, Michael. *Das Vaterland der Feinde. Studien zum nationalen Feindbegriff und Selbstverständnis in Deutschland und Frankreich 1792-1918*. Stuttgart: Klett-Cotta, 1992.

Lapouge, Georges Vacher de. *Race et Milieu Social. Essais d'Anthroposociologie*. Paris: M. Rivière, 1909.

Le Bon, Gustave. *Lois Psychologiques de l'Évolution des Peuples*. Paris: Alcan, 1889.

Lebon, André. *La Pacification de Madagascar, 1896-1898*, Paris, 1928.

Lecanuet, Emile. *L'Eglise de France sous la Troisième République*. 3 vols. Paris: Ancienne Libraire Poussielgue, 1907-30.

Lehning, James R. *To Be a Citizen. The Political Culture of the Early French Third Republic*. Ithaca and London: Cornell University Press, 2003.

Lejeune, Dominique. *La France des Débuts de la IIIe République, 1870-1896*. Paris: Colin, 1994.

Leroy-Beaulieu, Paul. *De la Colonisation Chez les Peuples Modernes*. Paris: Guillaumin et cie, 1874.

Louis, Paul. "A propos de la Guerre Hispano-Américaine". *Revue Socialiste* 27.161 (1898): 604-19.

---. "Impérialisme – Absolutisme – Militarisme." *Revue Socialiste* 32.191 (1900): 586-91.

---. "La Colonisation Sous la Troisième République." *Revue Socialiste* 25 (January 1897): 24-38.

---. "La Grandeur des Etats-Unis." *Revue Socialiste* 30.176 (1899): 181-99.

---. "La Plus Grande Allemagne." *Revue Socialiste* 31.181 (1900): 96-101.

---. "La Politique Extérieure de la Troisième République." *Revue Socialiste* 26.152 (1897): 129-53.

---. "La Question Sud-Africaine." *Revue Socialiste* 30.175 (1899): 59-63.

---. "Le Partage de la Chine." *Revue Socialiste* 27.160 (1898): 385-96.

---. "Le Socialisme et l'Expansion Coloniale Contemporaine." *Revue Socialiste* 29.173 (1899): 553-72.

---. "L'Impérialisme Anglo-Saxon." *Revue Socialiste* 29.171 (1899): 257-74.

---. *La Guerre Économique*. Paris: La Revue Blanche, 1900.

---. *Le Colonialisme*. Paris: Soc. nouv. de libr. & d'éd., 1905.

Meyer, Jean (ed.). *Histoire de la France Coloniale*. Vol. 1 (*Des Origines à 1914*). Paris: Colin, 1990.

Morel, Edmund Dene. *The African Problem and the Peace Settlement*, Union of Democratic Control Pamphlet No. 22a (1917), 6, London School of Economics, Morel Papers F 13/5/2 (6).

Mouralis, Bernard. *République et Colonies. Entre Histoire et Mémoire: la République Française et l'Afrique*. Paris: Présence Africaine, 1999.

Murphy, Agnes. *The Ideology of French Imperialism*. Washington/DC: Catholic University of America Press, 1968.

Novicow, Jacques. *L'Avenir de la Race Blanche. Critique du Pessimisme Contemporain*. Paris: Alcan, 1897.

Osterhammel, Jürgen. "Geschichte, Geographie, Geohistorie." *Geschichtsdiskurs*. Vol. 3. Ed. Wolfgang Küttler, Jörn Rüsen, and Ernst Schulin. Frankfurt/Main: Fischer, 1997. 257-71.

Paillard, Yvan-Georges (ed.). *Les Incertitudes du Colonialisme. Jean Carol à Madagascar*, Paris: L'Harmattan, 1990.

Perkins, Alfred. "From Uncertainty to Opposition: French Catholic Liberals and Imperial Expansion, 1880-1885." *The Catholic Historical Review* 82 (1996): 204-24.

Quatrefages, Armand de. *Histoire Générale des Races Humaines*. Paris: Hennuyer, 1855.

Raboisson, Pierre. *Études Sur les Colonies et la Colonisation au Regard de la France*. Paris: Challamel Ainé, 1877.

Rébérioux, M., and G. Haupt. "Le Socialisme et la Question Coloniale Avant 1914. L'Attitude Internationale." *Le Mouvement Social* 45 (1963): 7-37.

Reclus, Elisée. "Le Brasil et la Colonisation." *La Revue des Deux Mondes* 39 (15 June 1862): 930-59.

---. "L'Internationale et les Chinois." *Le Travailleur* 2.3 (March/April 1878): 22-31.

---. *Hégémonie de l'Europe* (Edition de la Société nouvelle). Bruxelles: s.n., 1894.

---. *La Chine et la Diplomatie Européenne*. Paris: Éd. de l'Humanité Nouv., 1900.

---. *L'Homme et la Terre*. Ed. Béatrice Giblin. 2 vols. Paris: F. Maspero, 1982.

Said, Edward W. *Orientalism. Western Conceptions of the Orient* (1978). London: Penguin Books, 1995.

Sarraut, Albert. *Grandeurs et Servitudes Coloniales*. Paris: Editions du sagittaire, 1931.

---. *La Mise en Valeur des Colonies Françaises*. Paris: Payot, 1923.

Schivelbusch, Wolfgang. *Die Kultur der Niederlage. Der Amerikanische Süden 1865, Frankreich 1871, Deutschland 1918*. Berlin: Fest, 2001.

Taguieff, Pierre-André. *La Couleur et le Sang. Doctrines Racistes à la Française*. Paris: Ed. Mille et une Nuit, 1998.

Taithe, Bertrand. *Citizenship and Wars. France in Turmoil 1870-1871*. London: Routledge, 2001.

Talvas, Georges. *Madagascar Depuis l'Occupation Française. Journal d'un Administrateur*. Paris: Grandes Éditions de Paris, 1939.

Valette, Jacques. "Note Sur l'Idée Coloniale Vers 1871." *Revue d'Histoire Moderne et Contemporaine* 14 (1967): 158-72.

Viénot, Alfred. *Personnels des Gouverneurs, des Secrétariats Généraux des Administrateurs des Affaires Indigènes et des Services Civils des Colonies*. Paris: Berget-Levrault, 1913.

Vigné d'Octon, Paul. *La Sueur du Burnous. Les Crimes Coloniaux de la IIIe République* (1911). Ed. Maurice Rajsfus. Paris: Nuits rouges, 2001.

Wilsberg, Klaus. *"Terrible Ami – Aimable Ennemi." Kooperation und Konflikt in den deutsch-französischen Beziehungen 1911-1914*. Bonn: Bouvier, 1998.

Zweig, Stefan. *Europäisches Erbe*. Ed. Richard Friedenthal. Frankfurt/Main: Fischer, 1987.

CHAPTER SIX

The European Impact on Christian-Muslim Relations in the Middle East During the Nineteenth Century. The Ethiopian Example

SAMUEL RUBENSON

In a much quoted circular letter to all the prominent European powers written in April 1891, Emperor Minilik of Ethiopia describes his country as a "Christian island surrounded by a sea of pagans" (Sven Rubenson, *Survival* 393; Caulk 227). The letter, in which the emperor demarcates the boundaries of his empire and emphasizes its independence, is primarily directed against the Italian ambitions to make Ethiopia an Italian protectorate. The reference to an isolated Christianity is, no doubt, part of his strategy to gain European support for his people and country. That Ethiopia was encircled by non-Christians and was thus vulnerable was apparently an argument considered so obvious that it could be adduced even in a letter complaining about colonial ambitions! It might strike us as rather odd that the emperor refers to Christian vulnerability when the real enemy is a European state, but his reference is actually just mirroring the ideas of his addressees about a fundamental conflict between Christians and non-Christians. The claim to be a Christian nation was a claim for respect in opposition to being made the target of colonial or missionary ambition. By referring to his own nation as Christian and his enemies as pagans Minilik hoped to direct European ambitions to the conversion and colonialization of neighboring nations.

All images have their history and purpose, including that of Ethiopia as a Christian island surrounded by a threatening sea of pagans. The aim of this paper is to look into the background and the purpose of this image and more specifically the role of colonialism in its promotion. I will do this by presenting material from the other side, from the people the Europeans pretended to speak for. I will also try to show that an image such as this one, although created for one purpose, could be used for a very different one. I have chosen Ethiopia, since this example enables us to see how, when, and hopefully why authors in the Middle East make use of a framework consisting of a fundamental conflict between Christians and Muslims. For although Minilik writes generally about "pagans," his letter was read against the background of an old European notion of Ethiopia being a Christian nation surrounded by Islam. Even if today many do not consider Ethiopia as part of the Middle East at all, the consensus was very different up to the nineteenth century, when Ethiopia was strongly tied to Egypt and the Arabian peninsula with regard to its politics, economy, and religion.

The perception of Ethiopia as isolated, surrounded, and threatened by forces antagonistic to its heritage pervades much of European literature on the history and culture of Ethiopia. From a European perspective, Ethiopia's isolation was an isolation from Europe that was created by the presence of the Islamic powers of the Middle East, and thus threatening. In modern European studies on Ethiopia and its history, beginning with Edward Ullendorff's classical study, *The Ethiopians. An Introduction to Country and People* (1965), Ethiopia is the Christian mountain fortress stemming the flood of advancing Islam. This view is all pervasive in the more recent and detailed studies of Ethiopia's relations to the Middle East by Haggai Erlich, *Ethiopia and the Middle East* (1994) and *The Cross and the River* (2002).

There are, however, good reasons to question this perception of Ethiopia and its history and to ask if the Ethiopians themselves have looked upon their country in these terms. Did, for instance, Minilik, who knew that a considerable number of his subjects, as well as some of his most important governors, were Muslims, and who nurtured good relations with his Muslim neighbors, think of Muslims when mentioning pagans? And if so, did he have any special reasons for using the image of an isolated and threatened Christian island?

In spite of the fact that the Islamic conquest of Palestine, Syria, and Egypt in the mid-seventh century A.D. cut the Ethiopian Christian kingdom of Aksum off from its previously close and culturally decisive relations with the Christian Roman Empire and its center in Constantinople, there is no reason to see Ethiopia in itself as isolated or threatened by its Islamic neighbors throughout its history. There were no attempts by the Islamic rulers of the early Islamic centuries to conquer Ethiopia, or even to take advantage of the isolation of the Christian rulers of Ethiopia from Byzantium. Ethiopian contacts with the Christian centers in Egypt and Palestine continued through the Middle Ages, including the regular appointment of the Head of the Ethiopian Church by the Coptic Patriarch under the control of the Muslim rulers of Egypt. Ethiopian monks were allowed by the Muslim rulers to take advantage of the expulsion of the crusaders from Jerusalem and establish themselves in the ruined Crusader monastery at the Church of the Holy Sepulchre. Representatives of the Ethiopian Church went to Rome and took part in the ecumenical councils of Florence in 1439-43. The strong revival of the Ethiopian kingdom in the fourteenth and fifteenth centuries would not have been possible without major interaction with Christians in the Eastern Mediterranean, a sort of interaction that depended on good relations with the Muslim rulers along the Red Sea as well as in Egypt and Palestine. It was during these centuries that the decisive texts for the Ethiopian Church and the Ethiopian kingdom were translated into the classical Ethiopian language, Gi'iz, from Arabic texts originating among the Christians in Egypt.

The conquests of Ahmad Ibrahim, nicknamed "Gragn," lasting for little more than a decade, did not seriously change the relations between the Ethiopian kingdom and the Muslim rulers of the Eastern Mediterranean. Although Ottoman-Portuguese rivalry in the Red Sea and Ottoman support for the campaign into the Christian highlands were important, there was no real attempt by the Ottomans to conquer Ethiopia and the war did not result in any isolation of the kingdom and its Christian rulers by the leading Islamic powers. More important was the steady growth of Islam in Ethiopia and the growing influence of Ethiopian Muslims among the political and commercial elite of the country. There is, however, little evidence for any serious or lasting conflicts between Muslim and Christian Ethiopians coming out of the wars of the sixteenth century. Even when Muslim participation in the rule of the country reached a climax in the late eighteenth and early nineteenth century, there is no real evidence that the internal tension and conflicts that plagued the country were primarily shaped by a division between Muslims and Christians. In spite of this, not only Erlich, but also Trimingham in his classical study on Islam in Ethiopia (Trimingham 1952), as well as Abir in his work on the period (Abir 1968), presuppose a basic Christian-Muslim conflict. This ethnocentric European perspective is, moreover, highlighted in Ahmad Hussein's brief study of the historiography of Islam in Ethiopia (Ahmad 1992). In fact, there seems to have been little reason for Ethiopians in general, as well as for their rulers in the early nineteenth century, to regard their country as a Christian island threatened by Islam.

Developments in Ethiopian foreign relations during the nineteenth century challenged the relations between Christianity and Islam in Ethiopia. The wars with Egypt and Sudan and the impact of European intervention in Ethiopian affairs, both of which were part of the European colonial enterprise, are probably the most important developments. Due to the expansionist policy of Egypt under Muhammad Ali and his successors in the Sudan as well as along the Red Sea, Ethiopia was for the first time in history confronted with a major foreign Islamic enemy. In the 1820s as well as in the 1840s, Egyptian pressure on the western borders of the country led to a series of conflicts with Christian and Muslim rulers opposing each other. In the 1870s Egypt, sponsored by the European powers, tried to take advantage of and foster Muslim opposition to Christian rulers and succeeded in occupying areas both in the North and the East. This finally resulted in the war of 1875-76 in which Egypt was decisively defeated by the Ethiopian army. Although it is evident that the war was by no means a religious war, it could easily be presented as such when necessary. Ethiopia, led by a Christian king, was attacked by Egypt, ruled by a Muslim *khedive* under the authority of the Great Sultan of Istanbul, the *khalifa* of the Prophet.

By contrast, the European adventurers, colonialists, consuls, and missionaries were Christians, fellow religionists of the Ethiopian rulers. For them an emphasis on a clear division between Christianity and Islam meant that they could claim to be the supporters and even protectors of Ethiopia against its enemies. A stress on a common Christian ground was regarded both as a key to the heart of the Ethiopians and a legitimate reason to establish a foothold in the country. With an emphasis on being co-religionists of the Ethiopians the European missionaries arriving in the mid-nineteenth century could claim a right to be accepted and even welcomed as reformers of the Ethiopian Church and thus of Ethiopian culture. An interpretation of the position of Ethiopia in terms of a fundamental Muslim-Christian conflict thus served their interests well. There is, however, little evidence that European missionaries actually encountered Muslim opposition or sided with Orthodox Ethiopians against Muslims. Their real conflict was with the Orthodox Church (Samuel Rubenson, "Interaction" 71-3).

We first have to ask, however, to what degree the European perspective was shared by the contemporary Ethiopians, and secondly, if a shared perspective can be found, to what degree it can be said to be the result of European influence. To be able to answer these questions, we need the voice of the Ethiopians. The publication of the series *Acta Aethiopica* has made readily available most of the letters written by Ethiopian rulers and notables between 1800 and 1880. We are thus in a unique position to see how the relationship between Christianity and Islam is presented not only by the Europeans, but by the Ethiopians themselves, and in what context they refer to an antagonism between Christianity and Islam and a proposed vulnerability of the Christian state as a basic model of interpretation.

The Correspondence

The Ethiopian letters from the first half of the nineteenth century contain few references to Christianity and Islam at all and even fewer to any Christian-Muslim conflict. References to a common Christian identity uniting Ethiopians and Europeans and to Muslim hostility can always be traced back to European initiatives, usually the requests by European commercial agents, adventurers, and missionaries for letters to take back to Europe to foster their own ambitions. Moreover, a closer look at many of these letters reveals that they are not only dictated by Europeans, but are often just plain forgeries made to dupe the European officials at home. In several cases no original version is preserved and the Amharic copies are clearly composed by a European, who in his own correspondence reveals his own strong involvement. Even where there is no reason to suspect a forgery, it is clear that the purpose on the Ethiopian side has little to do with any Christian-Muslim rivalry or any request for European assistance against Muslims (*Acta* I docs. 2, 23, 28, 29, 32, 39, 88, 120, 121 with notes).

It is obvious that throughout this period, it is the European influence that creates the image of Christian Ethiopian rulers needing the help of European Christians against a strong enemy identified as Muslim. Within Ethiopia, as well as in relation to powers outside Ethiopia, the conflicts are identified as conflicts between regions and their rulers, including the Turks and the Sultan, and there is nothing to indicate that the Ethiopian rulers saw their land as 'a Christian island.' Only in connection with the Europeans are these conflicts identified as being between Christians and Muslims. In all cases where there are references to a Christian-Muslim conflict, the initiators behind and mostly even the actual composers of the letters are European agents in Ethiopia and the addressees are the European rulers.

The above mentioned letters can be compared with the letters written by Ethiopian rulers and dignitaries to representatives of Egypt and the Ottoman empire. Here, any European influence is either almost or completely absent. In the letters from the political and commercial elite (Christian as well as Muslim) written in Gonder in 1844, we find almost identical Muslim greeting formulae and several other markers of Muslim identity in spite of the fact that some of the authors are Christians (*Acta* I, docs. 75-81). Even more revealing are the letters by *Shaykh* Kasa Haylu, the future emperor Tewodros, who writes in Arabic and includes Muslim terminology, but signs the letters with a cross (*Acta* I, docs. 93, 94, 96 and 100). In contrast to *Ras Ali* and *Itege* Menen, Kasa Haylu seems to have regarded it as essential to mark his Christian identity. Not only do we have the crosses in two letters, but the author also omits the prophet's name and refers blessing and peace to "the best of all men." One letter even lacks the traditional Muslim greeting in the beginning and in the last letter it has been added by another hand. The letters clearly betray a self-confident author who proudly maintains his Christian identity in spite of the fact that he writes in an Islamic tradition and language to Muslim colleagues.

In spite of this, and even though the letters deal with Kasa's own conflicts with Muslim enemies, there is not the slightest hint that religion plays any part in the conflicts. It rather seems as if the author deliberately tries to keep an ambiguous language with the kind of references to God and to swearing on the Book that are acceptable to both Muslims and Christians. It is obvious that it is the use of the Arabic language that carries with itself an Arabic epistolographic tradition, including Muslim phrases of greeting, safe-conduct, and blessing. A specifically Christian Arabic epistolographic style is first introduced by the Coptic secretaries of the emperors after 1855. Thus, neither Muslim terminology nor the use of Christian signs should be taken as manifestations of an emphasis on religion. On the contrary, the contents of the letters prove that the distinction between Muslim and Christian was of no relevance to the political issues discussed. There is no sign that any of the authors of these letters regarded themselves as living on a religiously isolated and threatened island.

The coronation of Tewodros as emperor in 1855, and the subsequent efforts to centralize the Ethiopian state, led to more prominent demonstrations of Christian identity. Instead of the traditional phrase "Praise be to God alone" used by both Christians and Muslims before, as well as the invocation "In the Name of God the benevolent and merciful," used by the Head of the Ethiopian Church in most of his Arabic letters, we find the invocation of the Trinity at the opening of imperial letters from 1861 on. But again there is good evidence that this was a result of European initiatives, as it first occurs in treaties drafted by European agents and letters from Protestant converts. The invocation of the name of the Trinity, of Father, Son, and Holy Ghost, appears first in the French draft of a treaty presented to both emperor Tewodros and his rival Niguse in 1859, a text manifestly composed by the Italian Catholic missionary Leon des Avanchers (*Acta* II, doc. 43), and the only place outside Tewodros' letters where the same invocation appears before the late 1860s is in a letter of 1862 from the Christian Felasha community established by Protestant missionaries (*Acta* II, doc. 103). Although used by both King Minilik and Emperor Yohannis in the 1860s and early 1870s, the invocation of the Trinity disappears almost totally from imperial letters after 1872.

It should also be noted that when Tewodros in his letters to European rulers regularly emphasizes his Christian identity, thus signaling a common identity with his European correspondents, he does so to stress that he is in no need of missionaries, and that he is equal to his European royal correspondents (*Acta* II, docs. 4, 24, 89). Reading the references as signs of a request for a united anti-Islamic front only reflects what Europeans wished to find. In his dealings with Muslim rulers Tewodros is eager to stress his impartiality and the equality between Muslims, Christians and Jews, both in his own country and in Egypt (*Acta* II, docs. 22, 23, 89, 90, 91). When he writes about instances of Muslim oppression of the Christians and the need for common solidarity, the enemies are clearly identified as the "Galla and the Turks" and the letters betray a certain disappointment with the Europeans for not assisting him in gaining better communication through the Turkish lines (*Acta* II, docs. 117, 118). Isolation is a problem, albeit not for the survival of a threatened Christian nation, but for communication with Europe. The only genuine request for the help of a Christian king against an "infidel" enemy "destroying Christians," a letter to Napoleon III dated 9 June 1856, is actually an appeal by an Ethiopian rebel for assistance against the Christian emperor (*Acta* II, doc. 14)!

As already mentioned, we only begin to find strong anti-Muslim language in letters not drafted by Europeans and clear references to the idea of Ethiopia needing the assistance of fellow Christians against their Muslim neighbors during the Ethiopian-Egyptian war of 1872-76 (*Acta* III, docs. 88-93, 107, 108, 110, 111, 113, 138, 158, 220, 221). Suddenly we encounter expressions about "the wickedness of the Muslims" and requests for help from fellow Christians against Muslims. When Emperor Yohannis mentions the campaigns of Ahmad Gragn in the sixteenth century in a letter to Queen Victoria, it is obvious that he wants to convey the picture of a conflict between Islam and Christianity, but it is evident here as well as in other letters that he expresses his disappointment with the British acceptance or even support of the Egyptian invasion of Ethiopia (*Acta* III, doc. 88). The problem of Egyptian attempts to strangle Ethiopia and cut off all lines of communication is present, but so is the feeling that the Europeans have betrayed their fellow Christians. But still the conflict is not primarily between Islam and Christianity but between Yohannis' country and the expansionist policies of the Egyptian rulers. This is also evident in the letters written by the governors directly involved in the conflict with Egypt. Nowhere is there any reference to the conflict as a conflict between Islam and Christianity (*Acta* II, docs. 223, 224; *Acta* III, docs. 19, 115, 144, 145, 150-2, 157, 178, 181-4, 196, 200, 201, 223). Moreover, the Ethio-Egyptian war was clearly not a Christian-Muslim conflict at all. The Egyptian forces were led by European Christians and supported by European powers, and the Ethiopian forces included both Christians and Muslims. Even among those Ethiopians who decided to join the Egyptian invasion force we find both Christian and Muslim notables. There was no need to become a Muslim in order to defect to the Egyptian side, and no need to become a Christian in order to join the emperor.

In the numerous letters from prominent Muslim leaders on the Red Sea coast there is not a word about Islam and Christianity being opposed to each other. On the contrary, it seems as if the Muslim *shaykhs* tried their utmost to cooperate with Ethiopian as well as European Christians whenever it was to their own benefit. Caught between the Egyptians ruling the sea and the Ethiopians ruling the highlands, in their attempts to defend their own interests and positions, the shaykks never refer to a Christian-Muslim conflict. When the pressure from the Egyptians, acting on behalf of the Ottoman sultan, became too strong in mid-1863, they were happy to ask for French support. Later on they sought the help of the British against the French, and when discerning that the British were cooperating with the Egyptians, they solicited Italian support against both the British and the French. Only when writing to their Muslim overlords did they use religious bonds as an argument – although not directed against Ethiopian Christians but against the inroads of the Europeans (*Acta* III, doc. 45). The presentation of the situation as that of a Christian island surrounded by hostile Muslims was one addressed to the European rulers, who were apt to see it as such anyway, and who, it was probably believed, would react favorably to such a view.

Even in the letters of Emperor Yohannis, who is often depicted in both European and Arab sources as an Orthodox Christian fanatic, the clear anti-Muslim phraseology occurs primarily in letters written to European rulers. In his other preserved letters, written during the same years to Europeans as well as Egyptians, there is no reference to an overall Christian-Muslim conflict. In his often harsh letters to Egyptian officials as well as to the Egyptian *khedive*, Yohannis refrains from anti-Muslim slogans, and in letters to other Europeans does not mention Islam as opposed to Christianity. His letter to the patriarch of the Coptic Church, Kirillus V, even contains a long and very interesting statement on religious freedom granted Muslims in his territory.

> As for what is mentioned in the letter of Your fatherliness about the Muslims, who reside in the kingdom of the *nigus* and its subordinate districts, and your admonition to us to treat them gently, to deal with

them in kindness, to facilitate for them the practice of the rites of their religion, I bring to your noble knowledge that we did not proclaim anything that might disturb their mind. Far be it for us to wrong any creature of God. They farm, eat, trade, make profit and prosper in every district in which they settle. We do not claim poll tax (*jizya*) from them, command them to go to war or force them to become Christians, since the pure Gospel does not order us [to engage in] any such coercive actions, but to give the people freedom. (*Acta* III, doc. 218)

The many letters from Church officials and Ethiopian Christian noblemen included in the volumes of *Acta Aethiopica* confirm the general image presented above. In matters of religion, there are numerous references to conflicts between Christians, mainly between the Catholics with their European backing and the Orthodox with their Coptic affiliation, but also conflicts between fractions within the Ethiopian Church. But I have not been able to detect a single reference to an overall competition or conflict between Christianity and Islam. This is true for letters from court officials as well as collaborators with the Catholics. Neither do we find any traces of a conflict between Christians and Muslims in the letters of representatives of the Orthodox Church, or in those from Ethiopian Catholic clergy or prominent converts. Not even in the texts by Ethiopians working with the Protestant missionaries is it possible to find any anti-Muslim rhetoric. Muslims are only mentioned once in a letter by Mahdere Qal to the French consul: he complains that the missionaries very soon lose interest in the Muslims and concentrate on attempting to change the religion of the Ethiopian Christians (*Acta* III, doc. 217). This claim is, moreover, corroborated by several letters of Protestants and Catholics complaining about persecution by the rulers simply because of their new Christian faith (for example *Acta* III, doc. 129).

Conclusion

The analysis of the Ethiopian material clearly shows that the idea of Ethiopia as an isolated Christian country surrounded by Muslims posing a threat to them was primarily a European idea. This does not mean that the Ethiopians were not aware of the fact that Ethiopia preserved and protected a Christian heritage in a Muslim surrounding. But they were equally aware of the fact that Muslims and Christians had coexisted in the country for centuries and that Ethiopia had always depended on good relations with its Muslim neighbors along the Red Sea. There is little evidence that the Christian rulers of Ethiopia regarded Islam as a threat in the nineteenth century. It was from a European perspective that Ethiopian Christianity was threatened and in need of protection by the Europeans. All early letters that refer to a need for assistance are written to European rulers and can be traced back to European initiatives, and often even to European forgeries. They appear as part of the European eagerness to have the Ethiopians ask for European help and seem to have the simple purpose of convincing European rulers, and perhaps the European public, that support should be given to Ethiopia through the missionaries, consuls, and colonialists. In letters to others, Europeans as well as Egyptians, references to Islamic-Christian relations are very few, and usually positive. It seems as if the Ethiopian Christians and Muslims were reluctant to make use of anti-Muslim and anti-Christian propaganda even when they were in direct conflict with each other.

To the authors of the letters analyzed here, the Ethiopians were not living on a Christian island set apart from the surrounding pagans and Muslims. The struggle against Egyptian inroads was not conceived as a struggle against Islam. In general, the Christian rulers in Ethiopia were uninterested and reluctant to believe in the promised support of their fellow Christians from Europe, and were most often proved right in their skepticism. However, they slowly adapted to European conventions in their letters to European rulers and were not unwilling to take the advice of the European consuls and missionaries in how to present their case. Some of them even realized that the European image of Ethiopia as an isolated Christian island in a hostile Islamic sea could be useful in gaining European support. But for most of them, the Europeans turned out to be more of a problem than a solution to internal or external struggles.

Epilogue

Against the background of the Ethiopian material we have to ask if it is possible to detect a similar development in other parts of the Middle East, especially in Egypt and Syria. Did European commercial, political, military, and ecclesiastical agents promote the perception of a basic conflict between Christianity and Islam in Christian and Muslim communities who did not themselves regard the difference as being politically, economically, or culturally decisive? Did Christians in the Middle East in general begin to see Islam as a threat in the nineteenth century, and if so, was this an idea introduced by Europeans? Is it possible, contrary to what could be expected, that secular European involvement tended to emphasize the importance of religious difference in traditionally more religiously tolerant societies? Are modern nation-states, with their emphasis on ethnic, secular, and rational equality and unity, less prone to accept religious differences and tolerance than multinational states where a variety of ethnic and religious identities are regarded as integral to a shared geographical entity and a common history?

In order not to take for granted images presented to us on the basis of European material, as has often been done, I think more research on material produced by Egyptians and Syrians themselves is necessary. We should also be sensitive to the contexts and purposes of their writings. I would also argue that views of the Christians in the Middle East are of particular interest since they were often targeted by the Europeans as sharing the same religion. Lacking studies and even the kind of collected evidence conveniently presented in the *Acta Aethiopica*, it is necessary to accumulate data on how Christians in the Middle East in the nineteenth century identified their own position vis-à-vis Islam, and to what extent their views changed due to European influence. In this endeavor, one should start with the official correspondence of the heads of the various Christian communities, especially the Coptic Orthodox and the Syrian Orthodox churches.

References

Abir, Mordechai. *Ethiopia: The Era of the Princes*. London: Longmans, 1968.

Acta Aethiopica vol. I. Getatchew Haile, John Hunwick and, Sven Rubenson (eds.). *Correspondence and Treaties 1800-1854*. Evanston, Ill.: Northwestern University Press/Addis Abeba: Addis Ababa University Press 1987.

Acta Aethiopica vol. II. Sven Rubenson (ed.) and Amsalu Aklilu, Merid Wolde Aregay, Samuel Rubenson (co-eds.). *Tewodros and His Contemporaries 1855-1868*. Addis Abeba: Addis Ababa University Press/ Lund: Lund University Press, 1994.

Acta Aethiopica vol. III. Sven Rubenson (ed.) and Amsalu Aklilu, Merid Wolde Aregay, Samuel Rubenson (co-eds.). *Internal Rivalries and Foreign Threats 1869-1879*. Addis Abeba: Addis Ababa University Press/New Brunswick: Transactions Publishers, 2000.

Ahmad, Hussein. "The Historiography of Islam in Ethiopia." *Journal of Islamic Studies* 3.1 (1992): 15-46.

Caulk, Richard. *Between the Jaws of Hyenas. A Diplomatic History of Ethiopia (1879-1896)*. Wiesbaden: Harrassowitz Verlag, 2002.

Erlich, Haggai. *Ethiopia and the Middle East*. Boulder, Colo./ London: Lynne Rienner, 1994.

---. *The Cross and the River. Ethiopia, Egypt and the Nile*. Boulder, Colo./ London: Lynne Rienner, 2002.

Rubenson, Samuel. "The Interaction Between the Missionaries and the Orthodox: The Case of Abune Selama." Getatchew Haile, Aasulv Lande and Samuel Rubenson (eds.). *The Missionary Factor in Ethiopia. Papers from a Symposium on the Impact of European Missions on Ethiopian Society*. Frankfurt am Main etc.: Lang, 1998. 71-84.

Rubenson, Sven. *The Survival of Ethiopian Independence*. London: Heinemann Educational Books, 1976.

Trimingham, John Spencer. *Islam in Ethiopia*. London: Oxford University Press, 1952.

Ullendorff, Edward. *The Ethiopians. An Introduction to Country and People*. London: Oxford University Press 1960.

CHAPTER SEVEN

Restoring Mesopotamia to Iraq. Archaeological Monuments and the Nation-State

STEFAN ALTEKAMP

Babylon

After many centuries of continuous decay the city of Babylon had nearly passed from site to mere memory when an initial period of vigorous excavations (1899-1917) uncovered much of her surviving material fabric. The physical delicacy of the newly exposed mud brick structures, however, threatened to condemn the relics to final disintegration. Visitors to the place found reason to complain about the lack of impressiveness and generally desperate appearance. Babylon became the subject of different cures to improve this situation, culminating in the *Archaeological Revival of Babylon Project*. Launched in 1978, it was inaugurated by two international conferences held in Baghdad and conceptionally radicalized by the Iraqi government in the 1980s. The most prominent foreign proposal for the development of the site as a whole was presented by Italian archaeologists. They suggested an archaeological park, abundant landscaping, and other visual pointers to indicate horizontal and vertical lines of bygone architectural spaces (Gullini; Parapetti, "Planning proposals"; Parapetti, "Southern palace"). The Iraqi officials at first held an ambivalent position on how far to proceed with straightforward reconstruction work, but later presented schemes for filling the site with 1:1 archaeological replicas of several landmark buildings of the city, including a megalomaniacal project to reerect *Etemenanki*, the famous Tower of Babylon (Damerji, Mahdi, Bakir, "Archaeological Revival"). The European recommendation echoed the somewhat dated but theoretically established principle of never reconstructing diminished historic fabric. The Iraqi proposal refrained from adopting this philosophy and argued in favor of the value of a city silhouette mirroring as closely as possible a historical setting rather than the story of its temporal transformations and reductions.

It is easy to dismiss the Iraqi project of reerecting parts of the physical setting of ancient Babylon as dictatorial misuse of history in order to impress the national and international public. It is easy to delegitimize the realized Babylon scheme since it actually was dramatically oversized and utterly superficial at the same time. But there is more to it. To demonize the Babylon project – hailed under the slogan *From Nebukadnezar to Saddam Hussein, Babylon/Iraq is rising again* – as an outflow of the late Baath regime's propaganda is to overlook a long established Iraqi tradition of dealing with historic monuments that had a clear-cut rational basis and eventually culminated in the excessive Baath party project. To follow the evolution of the project, we have to look back more than half a century – and to add a few remarks on archaeological practice in general.

Premises

Whereas it is not uncommon to expect archaeology to produce written narratives, its exclusive product is not the text but the exposition and arrangement of matter, of physical leftovers from the past. Contrary to a generally held view, this vital part of archaeological praxis – transforming material relics into images of past environments – is anything but uniform; it depends on material preconditions as well as on deliberate cultural choices. Three examples will help to illustrate this point:

1. Classical antiquity in the Mediterranean appears in noble ruins such as the Temple of Athena in Priene, modern Turkey (Fig. 1). The past is irrevocably passed and represented predominantly by specimens of fine architecture. The ruins produce an aura of distance and respect.

Fig. 1: Priene (Turkey), Temple of Athena, partly reconstructed. Stefan Altekamp (1981)

2. European pre- and protohistory, for example, in the archaeological park of Berlin-Düppel, Germany (Fig. 2) comes along as physical resurrection of everyday environments, often accompanied by reenactment programs. The past seems to be mentally close and physically palpable.

Fig. 2: Berlin-Düppel (Germany), house, reconstructed. Stefan Altekamp (2005)

3. East Asian archaeology tends to produce 1:1 replicas of vanished structures like the halls of the Buddhist Yakushi-ji at Nara, Japan (Fig. 3). They highlight the timeless relevance of historical models and contemporary respect for the integrity of historical aesthetic solutions.

These results are strongly predetermined by material conditions: in Mediterranean antiquity, stone architecture is ubiquitous. Constructional wood and unfired brick tend to disappear, but stone building elements remain in conspicuous quantities. Surviving heaps of worked stone easily lend themselves to partial reelevations of columns, entablatures, and walls. At the same time, partial *Anastelosis* comes close to a monument type that is familiar in all places where stone architecture prevails: the ruin.

Construction in European prehistory and in traditional East Asian architecture is based on wood as the main building material. In abandoned structures, little or nothing remains above ground. To give an intelligible picture of the past situation,

Fig. 3: Nara (Japan), Yakushi-ji, reconstructed. Stefan Altekamp (2004)

physical surrogates are needed. The replica seems to be a natural solution, where-as a partial reconstruction appears as culturally implausible.

It is obvious that the different results shown so far are not exhaustively explained by material factors alone; they additionally and finally follow decisions on how we want the past to reemerge: as obviously gone or tentatively present, as tradition or experience, as noble or humble, as ever-new or as worn and used?

Ancient Mesopotamia and Modern Iraq

The primordial constructive base of ancient Near Eastern architecture is mud brick. Without maintenance mud brick structures eventually devolve into a quasi-natural physical state. In the nineteenth century, archaeology had virtually recreated ancient Near Eastern monuments, but sharply separated the results from their physical settings: ideally and materially. The ancient Near East was regarded as part of Western tradition. Its image reappeared in the books of Western academia and in the exhibition halls of European museums in Paris, London, and later Berlin (Bohrer).

The ancient Near East was not regarded as a cultural foundation of the Islamic Middle East and the growing knowledge of its material culture was not reintroduced to the cultural landscape of Mesopotamia.[1] Moreover, because of the decaying processes of mud brick, it was regarded as impossible to preserve the remains of excavated structures *in situ*, i.e., at their place of creation: monument conservation would be unworkable under these circumstances, Friedrich Sarre concluded in 1919 (Sarre 192). Monument conservation, it should be added, following the evolving European perspective of the problem, which regarded historic substance as main conservation target, excluded alternative ways of representation using surrogate materials.

My essay will show that heritage management in Iraq, an independent nation, reversed this situation of the archaeology drain and implemented tangible results of the growing archaeological knowledge in the region itself. It will further highlight the fact that Iraqi politics dismissed European theories which restricted practice to inaction. Its decisions were embedded in a larger framework that neatly repulsed Western principles, which were regarded as instruments to 'internationalize,' i.e., patronize Iraqi affairs, thus obstructing the nation's full autarchy.

The use of history and archaeology to construct various elaborations of a state ideology for Iraq have been intensively commented upon (Bahrani; Baram, *Culture*; Baram, "Identity"; Baram, "Ideology"; Baram, "Mesopotamian Identity"; Baram, "Nationalism"; Bernhardsson; Davis; Simon). This paper focuses on the practical choices by which archaeology was made instrumental in serving the needs of nation building in a situation of cultural encounter and antagonism.

Gertrude Bell and Sati al-Husari

For the first years of Iraq's independence, this development is epitomized in the personal relationship between two intellectual founding figures of independent Iraq who also became political rivals over diverging visions of Iraq's direction: Gertrude Bell from the outgoing British semi-colonial regime, and Sati al-Husari as representative of a new nationalist Arab bureaucratic elite. Gertrude Bell (1868-1926) was a leading British expert in "Arab affairs" and played a key role

---

1 The land of Euphrates and Tigris was called "Mesopotamia" (Greek for: Land between the Rivers) in classical antiquity. This geographical name remained in use until the early twentieth century, when the area consisted of three Turkish provinces. "Iraq" is an Arab geographical name for the central area of "Mesopotamia" and was made the name of the nation state evolving after the First World War on "Mesopotamian" soil. Since then "Mesopotamia" has gained a predominantly historical meaning. The "Ancient Near East" covers what today is called "Middle East" in political terms and refers to a succession of early city states and monarchies (for example Sumer, Akkad, Babylon, Assur). From the fourth century BC to the seventh century AD "Mesopotamia" successively belonged to Hellenistic, Roman, Parthian and Sassanian Empires, until it was incorporated into the Arab Empire. The second Islamic dynasty, the Abbasids, moved their capital from Damascus to "Mesopotamian" Baghdad. In the sixteenth century AD "Mesopotamia" passes under Turkish (Ottoman) rule. Occupied by British forces in the First World War, "Mesopotamia," then "Iraq" became a British mandate of the League of Nations in 1921. The country gained formal independence in 1932.

first in conceiving the British mandate of Iraq, and second in designing Iraq as an independent Arab state. She was also a devoted archaeologist, acting as first head of the Directorate of Antiquities, founding the Iraq Museum (1923), and drafting Iraq's first antiquities law (1924). Her work is widely known through her letters, available in different publications, and several biographies (Burgoyne; *Gertrude Bell Archive*; Howell XI-XIII. 442-7; *Letters*; Lukitz 3-5, 224-9; Sommer; Winstone 389-90, 398, 404-9, 415). The thinking of Sati al-Husari (1882-1968) was fundamental for early Arab nationalism and pan-Arabism. In Iraq he held different official positions in education – and in archaeology. In 1934 he became the country's first non-European Director of Antiquities. A supporter of the 1941 philonazi *coup d'état*, he had to flee the country after the putsch's breakdown. The wide impact of his work is generally acknowledged by scholars of political history and the history of ideas (Baram, "Identity"; Dawisha 49-74; Tibi). His archaeological activities are much less known, and a major source of material about his public life in Iraq, a two-volume biography (al-Husari), has not yet been translated into a Western language.[2] Controversies developed along the lines of sovereignty, autarchy, and the use of history for the sake of nation building. While these issues partly exceed the realm of heritage management, they nevertheless describe the conceptual framework for the main decisions that determine Iraqi heritage policy.

While the nation was striving to overcome its status as a semi-independent British mandate (1921-32), its 1924 antiquity legislation guaranteed substantial privileges to foreign archaeological institutions and missions digging in Iraq, assigning generous shares of finds to participating foreign countries. By the early twentieth century, the international division of archaeological finds had begun to decrease, whereas the practice of leaving finds in their country of origin had clearly begun to prevail. In this respect, Gertrude Bell's 1924 law was already somewhat outdated. The fact that it was enacted at all clearly reflected the relative weakness of Iraq as a sovereign nation, unable to buck the established tradition in which portable valuables from the Mesopotamian past were taken from the country headed for destinations in Western centers of learning and places of display. al-Husari, as permanent secretary of education, had protested the scheme, hinting at its incompatibility with contemporary international trends. Within ten days of having presented the not yet approved draft law, Bell, however, succeeded in outflanking al-Husari's authority by transferring the responsibility for the Directorate of Antiquities (her office at the time) from the Ministry of Education to that of Planning and Transport, which agreed to the bill (al-Husari 1: 177-81; cf. Burgoyne 290, 316, 324; *The Gertrude Bell Archive* 25.6.1924; *Letters* 645, 658).

Generally, the British officials argued for cooperation and shared rights and duties according to given competences (meaning the superior competence on the European side). The Iraqis opted for autarchy, again based on sovereignty as

2 I owe a copy of this important text to Tom Stern (Essen) and the translation of selected passages to Nabil Ezzeldin (Berlin).

paramount principle. Iraq in its early years was not able to perform professional archaeological services, an administrative phenomenon fully in the European tradition and guided by criteria developed through European scholarship and legislation. Even so, it reclaimed sole responsibility. Thus archaeology in Iraq gradually became nationalized. As already noted, in 1934 none other than al-Husari (as a nonexpert in the field) became the first Iraqi national to head the Directorate of Antiquities. Among his initiatives (apart from designing a new antiquities law) was a reform of the Directorate's technical services that would enable the department to perform its restoration work at a higher level, both qualitatively and quantitatively, so that fewer of the fragile archaeological objects would have to be sent abroad in order to be restored. For Gertrude Bell this "loaning" of antiquities to the west had seemed a service to the young nation, but 15,000 objects "on loan" outside the country in 1934 were too many for al-Husari to tolerate (al-Husari 2: 409). Again the question of place came up: where could the archaeological vision of Iraq's past materialize itself?

It would be unjustified to ignore Gertrude Bell's complex loyalties – including those toward the land she devoted much of her work to and ended her life in. "I am an Iraqi official," she wrote in a letter to England in March 1924, after she had put her hand on a very prominent object from Ur, which, against the expressed opposition of the British excavator, was to enrich the collections of the Iraq Museum, which Bell headed (*Letters* 687). In principle, however, she held an intermediate position, with a strong allegiance to British interests. Her action followed a model of continuing British patronage, which for Iraq became increasingly unacceptable.

It is to Gertrude Bell that Iraq owes the institution of the Iraq Museum, and on the basis of the legal dispositions she designed, she worked hard to augment its collections. In fact, however, these collections overwhelmingly referred to the Mesopotamian past, with the Islamic past remaining nearly unrepresented until the mid 1930s. Again a gap was constructed between a culturally separated, distant past and a present with seemingly no roots in this past. al-Husari recalled a foreign scholar visiting the museum in 1934 who could not believe that the former capital of the Abbasid empire was not represented by objects in the national museum. As a result, al-Husari claimed to have decided to change this situation within a two-year period (al-Husari 2: 409-10; cf. *Letters* 756, 767, 772).

al-Husari's activities and strategies describe the general matrix of a genuine Iraqi history policy, out of which a policy of the archaeological monument could evolve. The antagonistic relationship between Bell and al-Husari allows us to highlight key issues of this matrix. Beyond the anecdotal flavor added by a personalized debate, the structural essence of Iraq's evolving management of the historic or archaeological monument became clearly visible.

Iraqi monument policy materialized itself in Iraqi hands and in Iraqi lands. The European practice had separated the country from the experience of the distant history of its lands – locally and conceptually. The Iraqi state reintroduced the results of growing archaeological knowledge into the country's cultural land-scape. By trying to make them visible, on-site management under Iraqi control was introduced.

The history of the land was conceived as the history of a population indig-enous to a territorial unit, a population that was regarded as an essentially sta-ble ethnic entity with a stable identity. al-Husari emphasized the ethnic continu-ity against religious discontinuity (the advent of Islam). As far back as tradition or scholarship could trace, history was regarded as Arab history. Arabism, not re-ligion, played the key role. However, Arabism, or more precisely Pan-Arabism, was faced with the political realities that only allowed for Arab independence to develop in a few fragmented nation-states, among them Iraq. The longer these states existed the more they needed a cultural *raison d'être* that justified their existence within the established boundaries. Separate national narratives supple-mented Pan-Arabism. As the official responsible for public education, al-Husa-ri was eager to foster national consciousness in this narrow sense by pointing at historical achievements of the Arab nation in general and of Arabs in Iraqi lands in particular. On the school level, he favored the emotional approach, strongly based on an intimate acquaintance with the tangible heritage (al-Husari 1: 215-6; 2: 281-2). Producing appealing and intelligible archaeological sites was part of this strategy.

The Emergence of the Islamic Past

While European interest had concentrated on pre-Islamic history, for Arab na-tionalism the Islamic past became an important point of reference. According-ly, historicizing the cultural landscape started with the period after the Arab con-quest. The first excavations undertaken by the Directorate itself (instead of for-eign teams) were devoted to the early Islamic sites of Samarra, Kufa, Wasit, and Ukhaidir (al-Husari 2: 442-4).

These excavations at crucial sites of the conquest and the Abbasid caliphate period not only sought to produce knowledge, but also to (re)gain or visual-ly improve formerly impressive monuments. The instruments used to establish these monuments were restoration and reconstruction programs. Samarra, north of Baghdad, for example, was the caliph's residence in the ninth century AD. UNESCO regards the area as the most extended archaeological site in the world. Whereas aerial views reveal the dimensions and the importance of the site up to the present day, the elevation of most ruins is insignificant. Samarra's major land-marks are two former mosques: the Great Mosque and the Mosque of Abu Dulaf. At both buildings restoration and reconstruction started already in the 1930s.

Restoration and Reconstruction Principles

The principles of restoration had been a major battleground for European heritage experts for more than a century. In the early twentieth century the moderate position, preferring consolidation instead of massive changes, had won – in theory. Mere consolidation is a desperate strategy for many Mesopotamian sites, given their material conditions. In this situation, only a few sites have the 'natural' potential to gain the status of cultural symbols, for which, according to Georg Simmel, a critical quantity of matter and an aesthetically intelligible form is required to stimulate the imagination (Simmel). While the preservation dilemma is not uncommon for archaeology in general (for Iraqi sites it is typical), the theory of heritage management, which takes "buildings," not "sites" as its starting point, never provided an adequate answer.

Therefore, in Iraq, massive intervention was preferred. While international guidelines for the management of historic monuments suggested a reduced introduction of new material, the Iraqi way soon turned to extensive rebuilding. Partial rebuilding instead of consolidation helped to avoid two specific modes of conceiving the past: history as a shattered and therefore unimpressive relic; and history in a state of ruin (even of noble ruin) and therefore sealed off as definitively passed. To put it positively: in contrast to what had been advocated by Western scholarship, the archaeological heritage in Iraq was liberated from the doctrine of material authenticity and turned into replicas of what their 'genuine' outer appearance had been.

Purity of the Reconstructed Monument

In 1934, a former Turkish citadel in the city center of Baghdad, incorporating the remains of an Abbasid school, was cleaned, the remainder of the school exposed, and foundations of lost sections excavated. The operation was initiated by al-Husari, who eagerly ordered the most ancient remains to be isolated and the results of following transformations (including an Ottoman bath complex) to be removed (al-Husari 2, 428-33; *Remains*). The former school, which had been organized around a courtyard, did not survive entirely; two of the original four wings had disappeared over the centuries (Fig. 4). Within a very short time the facades of the two remaining sections were reconstructed and the building renovated for use both as a museum of Islamic architecture and a memorial for the first King of Iraq, Faisal I.

Fig. 4: Baghdad, "Abbasid Palace": Directorate of Antiquities. *Remains of the Abbasid Palace in the Baghdad Citadel*. Baghdad: Government Press, 1935. pl.40

Fig. 5: Baghdad, "Abbasid Palace". Stefan Altekamp (1990)

In a reconstruction scheme that ultimately lasted for half a century, the foundations of the lost sections of the school were excavated and the exterior components of the original Abbasid structure eventually recreated. In the course of this reconstruction the Turkish citadel completely disappeared. The result was impressive, complete (without any indication that it had been a ruin) and was purely 'Abbasid' (Fig. 5). It tells a story of Baghdad as the caliphate and not its own story as a monument, which had lasted for centuries and reflected the vicissitudes of the city's history.

Western heritage policy had started to teach the integrity of monuments as testimonies not only to genius and creativity, but also to time as process and a force of constant revision. This concept did not enter the Iraqi practice. Instead, restored and rebuilt monuments amounted to a selection of idealized representations of crucial historical periods.

The Emergence of the Mesopotamian Past

The foregrounding of these idealized periods had initially marginalized the pre-Islamic past. This attitude mirrors the older European concept, which reclaimed the ancient Near Eastern civilizations as part of the European tradition. Fading Pan-Arabism and rising Iraqi nationalism led to a new perception of the ancient Mesopotamian past as an integral part of the history of the people – a perception already maintained by al-Husari and now entering the policy of monuments.

A more and more essentialist view of Iraq and an Iraqi people as timeless entities tied to the lands between the two rivers became widespread. "Mesopotamianism" became the keystone to a genuine Iraqi policy of archaeological monuments as a result of an antagonistic dialogue with Western principles.

The incorporation of the ancient Near East began with a highly symbolic act. In the nineteenth and early twentieth century the public image of archaeology in Mesopotamia was dominated by vigorous action and the performance of superior organizational and technical skills. Nothing could better illustrate the ability and strength of Western genius than the successful transport of gigantic Assyrian sculptures (half bull, half human) from the ruins of Assyrian palaces, over land and over seas, into European and North American exhibition spaces (Bohrer; Larsen). By chance most of these conspicuous sculptures came from a single place: the palace of Khorsabad close to ancient Niniveh (modern Mossul). As late as 1929 a gigantic bull left Khorsabad for Chicago, but this practice changed when the export of two additional bull sculptures, discovered in 1934, was denied. These two bulls were transported to Baghdad in 1939 and used as the only original parts of a (somewhat fanciful) replica of an Assyrian gate on a plot reserved by al-Husari for a new building of the Iraq Museum (Fig. 6). Ancient Mesopotamia had made its entry into the country's capital.

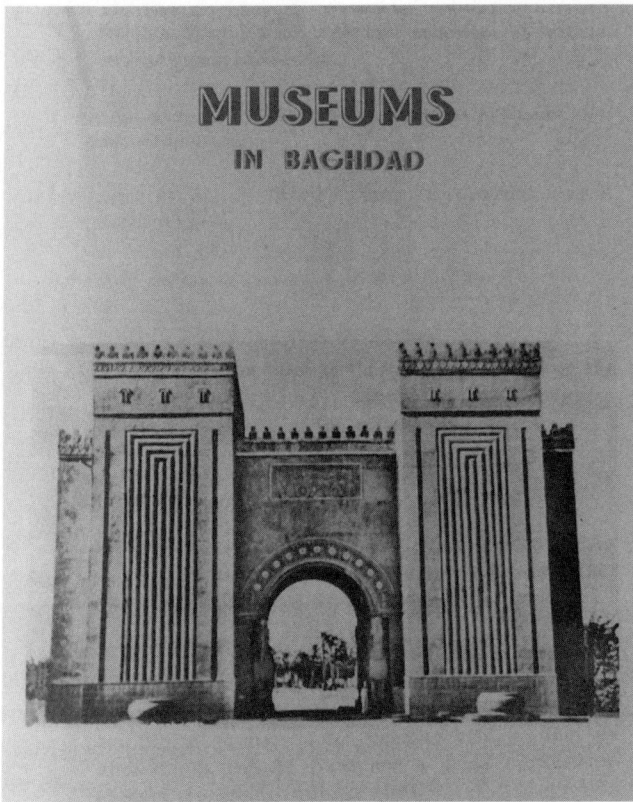

Fig. 6: Baghdad, Assyrian Gate. *Iraq – A Guide Book*. Baghdad: Summer Resorts and Tourism Service, 1961. 119

The Canonical Past: From Remote History to the Present

Since the 1950s and 1960s, long-term reconstruction programs operated at selected archaeological sites from different periods, visualizing the evolutionary path of Iraqi history from remote times to the present. The historical base of the "ancient" Near East was mainly represented by Ur of Chaldea (Fig. 7), Dur-Kurigalzu (Aqr Quf) (Fig. 8), and Babylon. The period of the late pre-Islamic local culture was portrayed by the site of Hatra, the early Islamic era by the palace-fortress of Ukhaidir (Fig. 9), and the capital Samarra. In the last years of the Baath regime this approach was systematized by concentrating large sums on large reconstruction schemes at three paradigmatic sites: Babylon – for the ancient pre-Islamic civilizations (Fig. 10), Hatra – for an early Arabic, still pre-Islamic period (Fig. 11), and Samarra – for the splendor of the Abbasid caliphate (Fig. 12). It could be argued that architectural allusions to historic Mesopotamian/Iraqi monuments built by the Baath party's regime crowned all the earlier heydays of the nation's history (Fig. 13).

Fig. 7: Ur, Ziggurat. Stefan Altekamp (1990)

Fig. 8: Aqr Quf, Ziggurat. Stefan Altekamp (1990)

Fig. 9: Ukhaidir, Palace-Fortress. Stefan Altekamp (1990)

Fig. 10: Babylon. Stefan Altekamp (1990)

Fig. 11: Hatra. Stefan Altekamp (1990)

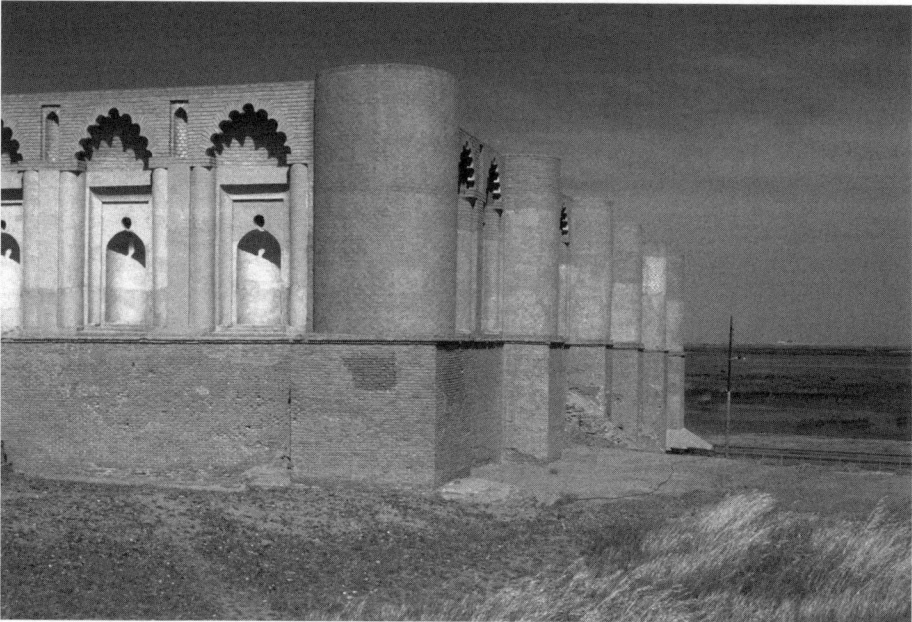

Fig. 12: Samarra, Qasr al-Ashiq. Stefan Altekamp (1990)

Fig. 13: Baghdad, Monument
to Unknown Soldier.
Stefan Altekamp (1990)

Conclusion

Work at the historic sites was executed under increasingly unfavorable economic conditions and was left unconsolidated at the time of the invasion in 2003. The
partly disastrous state of the sites can easily lead to too hastily connecting these
projects with the hypertrophic program of a final stage tyrannic regime. What I
hope to have shown is that core elements of this program form part of a rationale
leading back to Iraq's early years as a nation-state.

The main components of the Iraqi practice can be summed up as follows:

1. It tried to avoid any notion of the ruin. Even if projects only replicate the exterior appearance or parts of monuments, they keep well away from the broken,
fragmented, or hybrid form. The past lives on in the present.

2. Reconstruction is concentrated on symbols of power (government, central cult).
Everyday life is not reconstructed but the history of empires, dynasties, peoples
as protagonists of history, linked to each other by ethnic descent.

3. Accordingly, most projects do not introduce new practical functions to the reconstructions. The replicas are empty monuments to look at.

To a considerable extent the practice of archaeological site management corresponds with a fundamentally essentialist vision of Iraq as a nation, a vision which, up to 2003, demanded that state ideology play a key role. After 2003 the agenda was again reduced to the problem of sheer protection. Future Iraqi heritage management will probably further redefine this path.

References

"Archaeological revival of Babylon." *Sumer* 45 (1987/88): 85-6.

Bahrani, Zainab. "Conjuring Mesopotamia. Imaginative Geography and a World Past." *Archaeology Under fire. Nationalism, Politics and Heritage in the Eastern Mediterranean and Middle East.* Ed. Lynn Meskell. London: Routledge, 1998. 159-74.

Bakir, Taha. "The Ziggurat of Babylon and the Problems Involved in Its Reconstruction." *Sumer* 35 (1979): 248A-248D.

Baram, Amatzia. "Mesopotamian Identity in Ba'thi Iraq." *Middle Eastern Studies* 19 (1983): 426-55.

---. "Culture in the Service of *wataniyya*: The Treatment of Mesopotamian-inspired Art in Ba'thi Iraq." *Asian and African Studies* 17 (1983): 265-313.

---. *Culture, History and Ideology in the Formation of Ba'thist Iraq 1968-1989.* Basingstoke: Macmillan, 1991.

---. "A Case of Imported Identity: The Modernizing Secular Ruling Elites of Iraq and the Concept of Mesopotamian-inspired Territorial Nationalism, 1922-1992." *Poetics Today* 15 (1994): 279-319.

---. "Re-inventing nationalism in Ba'athi Iraq 1968-1994: Supra-territorial and Territorial Identities and what Lies Below." *Princeton Papers. Interdisciplinary Journal of Middle Eastern Studies* 5 (1996): 29-56.

Bernhardsson, Magnus T. *Reclaiming a plundered past. Archaeology and Nation Building in Modern Iraq.* Austin: University of Texas Press, 2005.

Bohrer, Frederick N. *Orientalism and Visual Culture. Imagining Mesopotamia in Nineteenth-century Europe.* Cambridge: Cambridge UP, 2003.

Burgoyne, Elizabeth. *Gertrude Bell from her Personal Papers.* Vol. 2. London: Benn, 1961.

Damerji, Muayad Said. "On the Dimensions of the Archaeological Revival of Babylon Project." *Sumer* 35 (1979): 40-4.

Davis, Eric. *Memories of State. Politics, History, and Collective Identity in Modern Iraq.* Berkeley: University of California Press, 2005.

Dawisha, Adeed. *Arab Nationalism in the Twentieth Century. From Triumph to Despair.* Princeton: Princeton UP, 2003.

The Gertrude Bell Archive [http://www.gerty.ncl.ac.uk/]

Gullini, Giorgio. "Babylon as cultural heritage." *Sumer* 35 (1979): 187-93.

Howell, Georgina. *Daughter of the Desert. The Remarkable Life of Gertrude Bell.* London: Macmillan, 2006.

al-Husari, Abu al-Khaldun Sati'. *Mudhakkarati fi-l-'Iraq 1921-1941 [My Iraqi memoirs 1921-1941].* 2 vols. Beirut: Dar al-Tali'a, 1967/68.

Larsen, Mogens Trolle. *The Conquest of Assyria. Excavations in an Antique Land 1840-1860*. London: Routledge, 1996.

The Letters of Gertrude Bell. Ed. Lady Bell. Vol. 2. London: Benn, 1927

Lukitz, Liora. *A Quest in the Middle East. Gertrude Bell and the Making of Modern Iraq*. London: Tauris, 2006.

Mahdi, Ali Mohammed. "Reality of Babylon and the Main Plan for its Archaeological Revival." *Sumer* 35 (1979): 57-60.

Parapetti, Roberto. "Babylon: Town Planning Proposals. Protection of Cultural Heritage: Ideology." *Sumer* 35 (1979): 215-9.

---. "The Southern Palace of Babylon: a Restoration Proposal." *Sumer* 41 (1985): 55-7.

Remains of the Abbasid Palace in the Baghdad Citadel. Ed. Directorate of Antiquities. Baghdad: Government Press, 1935.

Sarre, Friedrich. "Kunstwissenschaftliche Arbeit während des Weltkrieges in Mesopotamien, Ost-Anatolien, Persien und Afghanistan." *Kunstschutz im Kriege. Berichte über den Zustand der Kunstdenkmäler auf den verschiedenen Kriegsschauplätzen und über die deutschen und österreichischen Maßnahmen zu ihrer Erhaltung, Rettung, Erforschung*. Ed. Paul Clemen. Vol. 2. Leipzig: Seemann, 1919. 191-202.

Simmel, Georg. "The ruin." *Essays on Sociology, Philosophy and Aesthetics*. Ed. Kurt H. Wolff. New York: Harper and Row, 1965.

Simon, Reeva S. *Iraq Between the Two World Wars. The Creation and Implementation of a Nationalist Ideology*. New York: Columbia UP, 1986.

Sommer, Michael. "'The Oriental is like a very old child' – Die Orientreisende Gertrude Bell." *Reisen in den Orient vom 13. bis zum 19. Jahrhundert*. Stendal: Winckelmann-Gesellschaft, 2007. 233-41.

Tibi, Bassam. *Arab Nationalism between Islam and the Nation-state*. 3rd ed. Basingstoke: Macmillan, 1997.

Winstone, H.V.F. *Gertrude Bell*. Rev. ed. London: Barzan, 2004.

CHAPTER EIGHT

"Mistaken Readings" – Gayatri Spivak's Deconstruction of Hegel and the *Bhagavadgītā*

ANDREAS NEHRING

For centuries India has been the prime object of colonial desire. If we listen to Hegel, it is India's destiny to be the land of desire for conquest. In 1822 and in the following years Hegel read his lectures on the Philosophy of History in which he gives India a place in the early phase of world history. Even more, he depicts India as a culture that remained unable to enter the process of world history. Hegel writes:

> India [...] is a phenomenon antique as well as modern; one which has remained stationary and fixed, and has received a most perfect home-sprung development. It has always been the land of imaginative aspiration, and appears to us still as a Fairy region, an enchanted world. [....] The dreaming Indian is therefore all that we call finite and individual; and at the same time, as infinitely universal and unlimited, a something intrinsically divine. (Hegel, *Philosophy of History* 156, 158)

As an "enchanted world," itself unable to act politically, India, according to Hegel, remains in the initial stages of world history, and any synchronism with the West is denied. Our knowledge of India, its history, its religions, and its society, is largely a product of the colonial past. Colonial interests, missionary concerns, but also inner-European political motives have colored information about India down to seemingly incontrovertible facts, as they occur in reports, translations, and comprehensive books on Hinduism and Indian social structure. Eighteenth and nineteenth-century cultural values, religious concepts, and religious convictions have formed the European view of India.

In the wake of recent debates on Orientalism within colonial discourse studies and postcolonial cultural studies, this hitherto dominant image of India has been criticized from various positions. Indologists like Ronald Inden, historians like Nicholas Dirks, and numerous Indian scholars, among them the by now famous "Subaltern Studies Group," have exposed the hegemonic character of these Western images.

One of the most influential theoretical interventions comes from Gayatri Spivak, a Bengali-born literary critic teaching at Columbia University in New

York, who throughout her work has focused on India and Indian themes. Spivak has even offered a deconstructive reading of Hegel's commentaries on the *Bhagavadgītā*, which are scattered in his *Philosophy of History*, his *Lectures on the Aesthetics*, and his *Lectures on the History of Philosophy*.

As a religious studies scholar I am interested in the role Indian texts play in scholarly discourses, and a symposium on 'Cultural Encounters and the Discourses of Scholarship' offers an opportunity to raise some questions regarding the theoretical implications of this cultural encounter. This is even more relevant since the *Bhagavadgītā*, written somewhere between 200 BC and AD 200, has acquired the status of a "cultural text," to use Aleida Assmann's term (Assmann 232), a text that is crucially significant for large parts of Hindu society. It is one of the most important and widely distributed and read Hindu texts in India today.

Nonviolence activists like Mahatma Gandhi have frequently referred to what is commonly called 'the *Gītā*' as a foundational text of India's cultural pluralism and lived tolerance. And the text has just as often been used (and continues to be used) since the early nineteenth century by Hindu nationalists and religiously intolerant radicals who interpret the *Gītā* as a national text of Hindu exclusivism. The distinctive role of the *Bhagavadgītā* in modern Hindu society is nevertheless heavily determined by colonial readings of this text.

Charles Wilkins' translation of *Bhagavadgītā* (1785) was received with enthusiasm by the Romantic authors in Germany as well as in Britain (Drew 80; Halbfass 78-9; Sharpe 15-6). Johann Gottfried Herder (1744-1803) was one of the first Germans who had certainly read the *Gītā* by the late 1780s. He mentions the book and quotes from it in his *Ideen zur Philosophie der Geschichte*. But Herder never gave the *Gītā* the prominence it gained in later European discourses on India and in the discourses on Indian cultural identity among reformers of Hinduism in India. For Herder the *Gītā* was one of many relevant Indian texts, nevertheless he strongly promoted the idea that although traces of degeneration like the caste system and the idea of reincarnation can be found in India, India had also acquired the deepest wisdom, which could be of value even for Europeans. He found evidence for this deeply rooted wisdom and virtue in India's scriptural sources. Forty years later, the knowledge about India and Indian religions had grown enormously. The foundation of the Asiatic Society (1784) in Bengal and the introduction of Indology to European universities enabled more in-depth studies of Indian texts in the original language. In 1825, August Wilhelm Schlegel (1767-1845) translated the *Gītā* into German, and in that same year Wilhelm von Humboldt gave a long lecture on the *Gītā*, which he considered to be a "Naturdichtung," an excellent example of philosophical poetry and not a religious text (Humboldt, quoted in Sharpe 19). According to Humboldt, the importance of the *Gītā*, not only for India but for the whole of humanity, is to be found in its emphasis on the immutable *dharma*, the eternal law and code of conduct, in combination with individual piety as expressed in *bhakti* devotion. Since the mid-nineteenth century the text of the *Gītā* has been translated into several languages and has gained a status as one of the deepest spiritual texts of humanity among theosophical as well as other India-enthusiastic authors.

Hegel published two long review articles on Humboldt's commentaries on the *Gītā* in which he critically investigates the Romantic conviction that Indian wisdom, being rooted in the oldest historical tradition, has to be esteemed as a corrective of Western enlightened rationality. Hegel's interest in India, as Wilhelm Halbfass has pointed out, was interwoven with his critique of the Romantic enthusiasm for origins (Halbfass 116). By the time Hegel published his first review article in 1826, Henry Thomas Colebrooke had given a first detailed account of the systems of Indian philosophy, which initially appeared in the *Transactions of the Royal Asiatic Society* and was compiled in his *Miscellaneous Essays* ten years later. Hegel was an avid reader of the latest Indological research of his time and his knowledge of Indian philosophy was mainly informed by these contemporary accounts. In his reflections on Indian philosophy he admits that these representations of Indian thought are still limited and that no overall account of an Indian philosophical doctrine can be gained from the Western texts at hand. Only the command of ancient Indian languages would enable the Western philosopher to read Indian philosophical texts and to gain access to all philosophical and mythological systems in order to compare them with one another (Hegel, "Bhagavad-Gita" 1: 133). Hegel assumes that the *Gītā* is a text that is particularly suitable for giving a clear impression of the peak of Indian philosophy (Hegel, "Bhagavad-Gita" 1: 134).

However, in her reading of Hegel, Gayatri Spivak does not focus so much on these two review articles but on Hegel's *Lectures on the Aesthetics*.

> As a literary critic by training, I will concentrate on a couple of paragraphs from the *Lectures on the Aesthetics*. Because I am Indian and was born a Hindu, I will also attempt to satisfy the increasing, and on occasion somewhat dubious, demand that ethnics speak for themselves, by focusing on a bit in Hegel on Indian poetry. (Spivak, *Critique* 40)

It is this "dubious demand" to speak for oneself as a native that Spivak is addressing in her opus magnum *A Critique of Postcolonial Reason*, in which she is tracking "the figure of the Native Informant through the various practices: philosophy, literature, history, culture" (Spivak, *Critique* ix). I will follow her on this track as a student of religion who is especially interested, first, in the role of theory in criticizing cultural encounters with the "Other," respectively Western representations of, it; secondly, in Spivak's deconstructive reading of Hegel and the *Gītā;* and, thirdly, in Indian reactions to Western readings of the *Gītā* and the Indian appropriation of this text as a cultural monument.

The Role of Theory in Criticizing Cultural Encounters

> Some of the most radical criticism coming out of the West today is the result of an interested desire to conserve the subject of the West, or the West as Subject.
>
> Gayatri Spivak, "Can the Subaltern Speak?"

Until today, this famous opening of Spivak's widely discussed essay, written twenty years ago, raises questions of whether and how our 'Discourses of Scholarship' on cultural encounters are involved in Eurocentric or neocolonial hegemonic thought structures. Spivak analyzes a discussion between Michel Foucault and Gilles Deleuze about the production of theory as action and the impossibility of distinguishing between representation as theoretical reflection and action as theoretical practice. Theory, in other words, is always involved in the question of power. Spivak nevertheless criticizes in Deleuze and Foucault that in their activist concern for "Chinese Maoism" and the "Workers' Struggle" they implement a sovereign subject position by pretending that the subject has no geopolitical determinations. While the Western intellectual "must attempt to disclose and know the discourse of society's other" and can be named and differentiated, the "other," i.e., "Maoism" and "Workers' Struggle," remain anonymous ciphers in a discourse that "symptomatically renders the Other transparent." Spivak acknowledges the importance of the theoretical production of this "new Philosophy" and yet accuses it of ignoring "the question of ideology and their own implication in intellectual and economic history" (Spivak, *Critique* 248-9).

What then can be the critical role of theory in reading magisterial texts from the Western philosophical tradition? The problem of saying something new today, as Roland Barthes already pointed out in an interview in 1974, is that a historical shift of objects has taken place. He argues:

> Today the avant-garde object is essentially theoretical: the double pressure of politics and intellectuals ensures that it is now theoretical positions (and their exposition) which are avant-garde and not necessarily creative works themselves. (Barthes 191)

Gayatri Spivak's *A Critique of Postcolonial Reason*, a book of 350 pages published in 1999, is certainly not avant-garde in its overall structure or in the topics she deals with. In four long chapters, *A Critique of Postcolonial Reason* looks at the general topics of philosophy, literature, history, and culture, using a transdisciplinary approach that Spivak in an interview with Jason Boog refers to as a "literature trade" (Boog 25). She engages with the traditional canon of philosophy by reading Kant, Hegel, and Marx. She then focuses on Charlotte Brontë's *Jane Eyre,* Mary Shelley's *Frankenstein*, and Coetzee's *Foe,* as well as on various documents from the colonial archives. Throughout her book she stresses the inaccessibility of the cultural "Other," and this emphasis is accompanied by metacritical reflections influenced by Marxism, feminism, and poststructuralist deconstruction. What makes her approach a specifically challenging one is Spivak's concern that her theoretical interventions relate to culturally and historically specific contexts. As Henry Staten points out, "there is always too much history, too much human reality beyond what language can adequately represent" (Staten 111).

How can we identify a new or even an avant-garde theoretical position in such readings? Roland Barthes again gives a first opening. "Theory," he says, "which is the decisive practice of the avant-garde, has no progressive role in itself – its active role is to reveal as past that what we still believe to be present: theory mortifies, and that is what makes it avant-garde" (Barthes 191).

If, as Barthes puts it, theory "mortifies" by taking a position in the present and if it critiques what is believed to organize the present, it constantly has to (re)invent itself in order not after all to mortify itself. Theory as action has to invent "theoretical positions," and since this invention has no proper domain of objects, it must be seen as an instance of catachresis, a term Spivak likes to use for pointing out contradictions in reading positions. Spivak takes a theoretical position by referring to her readings of canonical texts of the Western philosophical tradition as "Mistaken Readings." This involves two aspects on which I would like to comment:

1. that these texts must be read from an angle or a perspective which differs from the disciplinary conventions of the Western philosophical traditions;
2. that a mistaken reading involves "mistaken significations," deferred naming, and improper metaphors in order to open re-significations and reinscriptions of a seemingly fixed philosophical terminology.

Catachresis, in Spivak's use of the term, is a figurative and performative strategy that indicates the unsettling capacity of linguistic representations of the world. Spivak not only questions the idea of a stable and comprehensible relation between language and the world; she goes beyond other theoretical positions in the poststructuralist field by always relating her reflections on the relation between language and world to a culturally and historically specific context. She focuses specifically on the use of language in colonial discourses. In her reading, the comprehension model of the relation between language and reality employed in colonial discourses appears to be a hegemonic one through which the West was able to constitute a stable and controllable reality as the object of knowledge. In this knowledge formation, the "Others" not only have no voice, they are even foreclosed from the production of knowledge in order to render this production pure. Spivak uses the term 'foreclosure' by referring to the psychoanalysis of Jacques Lacan and Laplanche/Pontalis (166-9) in order to read the "pre-emergence of narrative as ethical instantiation" (Spivak, *Critique* 4).

Spivak argues that postcolonial studies are in danger of relating to colonialism or the problem of Western dominance only diachronically by focusing predominantly on the representation of the colonized in Western texts. Postcolonial studies in this line of analysis, she argues, collaborate with the hegemonic Western project to constitute an intending subject behind a seemingly transparent text. Her own theoretical move is a deconstructive reading whose aim is to show that this claimed purity or transparency is a fiction and never existed in any consistent fashion. "Knowledge of the other subject," she claims, "is theoretically impossible" (Spivak, *Critique* 283). Of course this statement also applies to all other subjects, but Spivak focuses on specifically cultured subjects, namely, those who are foreclosed from dominant discourses: the subaltern. Her book can be read as an attempt to track the trace of this other subject of Western discourses in dominant Western texts. Since knowledge of this other subject is theoretically impossible, the "other" always remains an "(im)possible perspective" (Spivak, *Critique* 9). Spivak does not join those voices that critically advise the producers of neocolonial knowledge to admit "'that one cannot know the cultures of other places, other times' and then proceed to diagnose hegemonic readings" (Spivak, *Critique* 50). Her own approach could rather be called an 'interventionist deconstruction.'

That which has been effaced from the "symbolic order" (Lacan) of the dominant discourse in order to make it appear pure, leaves a trace, which, if taken up and followed, leads beyond the transparency of language. What has been foreclosed from the symbolic order Spivak calls the "Native Informant," "a name for that mark of expulsion from the name of Man" (Spivak, *Critique* 6) – "Man," with capital "M," used as a synonym for Western humanism and rationalism. Her aim is to track the figure of the "Native Informant" through the various disciplinary practices she touches on in her book. The term "Native Informant" has been borrowed from Ethnology. The 'Writing Culture' debate during the late 1980s expounded the problem of the production of ethnographic texts and criticized that in this enterprise the native voice disappears behind the objectifying representation of another culture. The then new approach to ethnography struggled with two related problems, namely, that the attempt to know the cultural other would have to treat him or her as an object of knowledge, and thereby deny him/her subjectivity, and that the attempt to present a "thick description" of the "other" would offer a mirror image of one's own culture. By referring to this critical self-reflection of ethnology Spivak identifies this "other," whom she calls "Native Informant," as a blank space, inscribed in classical Western ethnographic, philosophical, literary, and cultural texts.

But she goes a step further by establishing the "Native Informant" as a theoretical position that "mortifies" (Barthes) in order to invent itself. Spivak is naming her/him "a mark crossing out the impossibility of the ethical relation" (Spivak, *Critique* 6). I take this paradoxical phrase to say that the impossibility of an ethical relation cannot be annihilated. It can only be crossed out, that is, the impossibility of an ethical relation is put "*sous rature*," or as Spivak calls it in her translator's introduction to Derrida's *Of Grammatology*, it is put "under erasure" (Spivak, "Translator's Preface" xiv). The purpose of this visible act of deletion is to show "that our own language is twisted and bent even as it guides us. Writing 'under erasure' is the mark of this contortion" (Spivak, "Translator's Preface" xiv).

The "Native Informant" is neither a position that can transform the impossibility of an ethical relation into a positive possibility, nor a position of absolute difference that can render the impossibility of that ethical relation absolute. Spivak criticizes that too often the position of the native informant is uncritically and unconsciously taken over by those who claim a subject-position in the postcolonial field by positioning themselves as representative native informants from the South or as representatives for diasporic identities. Spivak calls them benevolent cultural nativists who instrumentalize cultural identity positions in order to represent themselves to the dominant culture (Spivak, *Critique* 6).

For Spivak the "Native Informant" is less a subject-position that can be be traced, outlined, and identified, than a particular reading strategy or strategic perspective, "a kind of deconstructive lever through which questions of radical alterity, responsibility, and persistent critique can be constantly re-posed" (Rai, "Review" 1). In that sense it is a theoretical perspective of action, a perspective that mortifies by constantly deferring reading positions. By this strategic move Spivak tries to draw the reader into a process of responsibility and accountability, a process she once called in an interview an "ethical semiosis" (Sanders, "Interview" 110-1). By ethical semiosis she has in mind a multilayered process, a responsibility and accountability that is at the same time an act of translation in which the ego is put together. This translational act is not merely a speech act: Spivak throughout her work relates the ethical semiosis to the inaccessible fullness of time and context within which subjectivity can and must be located. Spivak's concern with specific contexts is what makes her postcolonial theoretical approach appear so radical. As Henry Staten has pointed out, it is this experience of the impossible perspective of the "Other" in a specific context that Spivak calls the perspective of the "Native Informant" (Staten, "Tracking" 111). In an appendix to her book, called "The Setting to Work of Deconstruction," Spivak refers to Derrida who in his later, rather "affirmative" phase addressed *différance* by using the concept-metaphor of "the experience of the impossible": "If radical alterity was earlier conceived of as a methodologically necessary presupposition that is effaced in being named, now the category of presupposition is deliberately blurred and made more vulnerable as 'experience'" (Spivak, *Critique* 426).

Gayatri Spivak's Deconstructive Reading of Hegel and the *Gītā*

We will see how Spivak is employing this theoretical premise in her deconstructive reading of Hegel and the *Gītā*. This reading she calls 'mistaken,' "for it attempts to transform into a reading-position the site of the "Native Informant" in anthropology, a site that can only be read, by definition, for the production of definitive descriptions" (Spivak, *Critique* 49). The experience of an impossible perspective of the "other" requires a differentiation between various contextual figurations of the "Native Informant." Spivak urges her readers to contextualize the anthropological figure of the "Native Informant" by

> investigating the difference in the opposition of the Australian Aborigine and groups like the Fuegans [Spivak identified them as foreclosed 'Native Informants' in Kant's *Critique of Judgement*; A. N.] and the production of the dominant Hindu colonial subject, rather than positing a unified "third world," lost, or more dubiously, found lodged exclusively in the ethnic minorities in the First. (Spivak, *Critique* 49)

Hegel, as has already been pointed out, does not give India a prominent position on the epistemograph of history, the graph on which "the Spirit acts out the scenario of Self-knowledge" (Spivak, *Critique* 40). On the chronograph of the Hegelian Spirit, India is a static moment in the beginning, and it remains there, unable to push into history. In his *Lectures on the Aesthetics* Hegel argues that India has to remain in a static position because neither Indian art nor Indian philosophy permits a dialectical process. The Indians, according to Hegel, remain fixed in their determinatedness by sticking to endlessly reiterated concepts (Spivak, *Critique* 40). Even Indian art is nothing more but a permanent repetition of the same. The essence of Indian art is that it restlessly moves back and forth. As Hegel writes:

> From one side it is driven into the opposite one, and out of this is pushed back again into the first; without rest it is just thrown hither and thither, and in the oscillation and fermentation of this striving for a solution thinks it has already found appeasement. (Hegel, *Aesthetics* 1: 333-4)

In a similar way, Indian literature, and especially the *Bhagavadgītā*, is, according to Hegel, repetitive by bringing "before our eyes [...] always one and the same thing over again" (Spivak, *Critique* 44).

Before I go into Spivak's reading, I will briefly sketch out the content of the *Gītā*. The *Bhagavadgītā* (Song of God) is a Sanskrit text. While for Hegel the *Gītā* is not a document of history, it is possible to read this differently. The *Gītā* must be situated within the great epic called *Mahābhārata*, of which it is a small albeit important part. The *Bhagavad Gītā* is considered and revered as sacred by many Hindu traditions, especially by followers of Krishna. To read this text today implies the necessity of working oneself through different layers of Indological, orientalist, and Romanticist interpretations as well as interpretations from neo-Hindu movements and from popular culture in India today, television series as well as movies, that take this text as their basis.

The content of the *Gītā* is a conversation between Krishna and Arjuna that took place on a battlefield called Kurukshetra on the eve of the great battle between the Pandavas and the Kauravas, two clans that descended from the same ancestors. Arjuna, one of the warriors, is facing the moral dilemma of whether he should fight in the battle and run the risk of killing some of his relatives or whether he should renounce violence and become a *sanmyasin*, spending the rest of his life meditating and begging for alms. Krishna, Arjuna's charioteer, is now responding to Arjuna's confusion and moral dilemma, and he explains to Arjuna his duties as a warrior and Prince and elaborates on a number of different philosophical positions and *margas* (paths) to liberation like *karma-marga* (the path of action), *bhakti-marga* (the path of devotion), and *jnana-marga* (the path of knowledge), using examples and analogies. During the discourse, Krishna reveals his identity to Arjuna as the Supreme Being (Bhagavan). In search of traces of the "Native Informant," Spivak's intention is not to critique the Hegelian orientalist representation of this Eastern text by establishing an argument of the socio-political relevance of Arjuna's discourse with Krishna for the history of India, although she refers to the Indian historian Romila Tapar's reflections on the *Gītā* as a passage text that leads from an earlier semiotic field of lineage to an emerging one of the developing state. Neither does Spivak imagine a "Native Informant" contemporary with Hegel. She rather aims at a deconstructive reading of the difference or even opposition between Hegel and the *Gītā*. Spivak sees a structural complicity between Hegel's argument and the *Gītā* in that both manipulate time. Spivak's reading, which she calls "mistaken," focuses on the "play of law and history" in the *Gītā* (Spivak, *Critique* 47). It is not the historical quest that is of relevance here, not the problem of the historicity of the text or the events narrated in the *Gītā*, but how the question of history is raised and performed within the narrative. With this focus Spivak elaborates an enormously relevant point for a discursive reading of modern interpretations and commentators of the *Gītā* in the nineteenth and twentieth centuries. A mere critique of Western orientalist representations of Indian texts, which is still prominent in much of postcolonial studies, appears for Spivak to be after all "a legitimation-by-reversal of the colonial attitude itself" (Spivak, *Critique* 39). It is the complicity of both, Hegel and the *Gītā*, that has contributed to turning the *Gītā* from text into scripture in modern Hindu discourse.

Hegel as well as the *Gītā* deal with the question of history and both offer a concept of "Time as Law." Spivak focuses on one moment in the discourse of Arjuna and Krishna in which the question of history comes up. After Krishna, in the third canto of the *Gītā*, expounds to Arjuna age-old Yoga teachings, which he obviously had already taught to the sun (*sūrya*), Arjuna in the opening of the fourth canto asks Krishna about the legitimation of his historical authority: "Your birth was later and the birth of the sun was earlier. How should I know that you said all this first?" To this Krishna gives three kinds of answers:

1. We come and go many times. I know the times and you do not.
2. I become by inhabiting my own nature through my own phenomenal possibility. I am above all beings.
3. I can incarnate whenever it is necessary, or when the dharma is in decline. (Spivak, *Critique* 51-2).

Spivak now brings up the question of history and she reads the exhortation of Krishna as a negation and sublation of history. Krishna contains all history within his true self, only revealing this to Arjuna by special dispensation. Krishna is unborn and imperishable, and manifests whenever the law is in decline, but was already there at the beginning. Human time is a lesser time here (Spivak, *Critique* 53). Historical timing is overridden into a cosmological and ontological order of time, which is ruled by Krishna. By revealing the cosmic order of his being, Krishna presents himself as the best of an infinite number of historical possibilities. It is this presentation of excellence that Hegel criticizes as repetitive. (Hegel, *Aesthetics* 1: 333). Spivak's reading aims, as mentioned earlier, at a deconstruction of the opposition of Hegel and the *Gītā*. Her intention is to show "that 'Hegel' and the 'Gita' can be read as two rather different versions of the manipulation of the question of history in a political interest, for the apparent disclosure of the Law" (Spivak, *Critique* 58). These two different versions nevertheless inform modern interpretations of the *Gītā*. The "Native Informant" is "inscribed as evidence in the production of the scientific or disciplinary European knowledge of the culture of the others" (Spivak, *Critique* 66-7). This knowledge has been disseminated in colonial India. The search for history and the origin of culture has become a prime enterprise in the anticolonial nationalist movement during the nineteenth and early twentieth centuries. "Timing" (the lived time) in this movement has been subordinated to "Time" (the graph of the Law).

Some Remarks on Indian Reactions to the Western Readings of the *Gītā*

The perspective of the "Native Informant" that Spivak constructs in the *Gītā* is, however, an (im)possible perspective. Neither the colonial subject nor the postcolonial subject can adopt or inhabit this perspective completely. Western views are refracted into the colonial subject.

Of course the ideological use of the *Gītā* as authoritative text is also a practice in India – the Brahmanical tradition can and has used the *Bhagavadgītā* as a convenient vehicle for spreading its doctrine. The *Gītā* can be read as a legitimization of central concepts of Brahmanical Hinduism like karma and caste. Even a critical reading of the *Gītā* is possible in that Krishna induces Arjuna into what is now revealed as conservative or even fundamentalist Hindu ideology, as promoted by political parties like the Bharatiya Jananta Party (BJP), militant religious organizations like the Rashtriya Svayamsevak Sangh (RSS), and by the globally operating Hindu Organization Vishwa Hindu Parishad (VHP).

But the Neo-Hindu readings, although often claiming to represent an authoritative view, are never instantaneous nor pure. Spivak shows that nationalist as well as spiritualist commentaries on the *Gītā* by Sri Aurobindo and Servapalli Radhakrishnan at the beginning of the twentieth century are more or less a displacement or reversed legitimation of earlier Western readings of the text. Sri Aurobindo, one of the outstanding Indian nationalists during the time of India's struggle for independence, wrote a commentary on the *Gītā* in 1916 in which he depicts the *Gītā* as the key text for the evolution of mankind. Itself a monument of universal truth for Aurobindo, the *Gītā* is seen by him as a document that shows the way of the evolution of all beings as the "Becoming of the Absolute": "This is the Zeitgeist, this is the purpose that runs through the process of the centuries, the changes of the suns, this is that which makes evolution possible and provides it with a way, means and a goal" (Aurobindo, quoted in Minor, 74). Aurobindo aims at a spiritual progress of a developing humanity, and he elaborates the practical concept of 'Integral Yoga' to achieve the ultimate state for all beings. The *Gītā* appears to be a key text of the integral yoga that Aurobindo promotes. Spivak now argues that this concept is neither the pure theological concept of the *Gītā*, nor the graphic linear image of Hegel, but a mixture of both (Spivak, *Critique* 63).

In a similar way, the Indian Nationalist Bal Gangadhar Tilak, who lived in Maharashtra (1856-1920), wrote a commentary on the *Gītā* while he was in a British jail in 1910. Tilak emphasizes the aspect of *karma marga* in the *Gītā* and claims that the *Gītā* is first of all a text for action and political progress toward *swarāj*, self-rule. He is trying to universalize the *Gītā* in order to demonstrate that the concept of *svadharma*, one's own law, which according to him transcends limited caste rules of Hindu society and therefore is best applied to all nations that are seeking independence and self-determination, can best be understood not as social determining rule but as "one's own religion" (Stevenson 59).

The philosopher cum statesman Servapalli Radhakrishnan, who in all his comparative work on philosophy tries to show various parallels of historical developments between Indian and Western culture, and even draws analogies in the development from Judaism to Christianity and the pre-Arian religion to Aryan Hinduism, refers to Hegel in an essay of 1911. He quotes Hegel's devastating analysis of the developments in India: "No morality, no determination of freedom, no rights, no duties have any place here; so that the people of India are sunk in complete immorality" (Radhakrishnan 467). By taking Hegel seriously, Radhakrishnan generates an apologetic argument that the *Gītā* can help to develop the spiritual foundings of India as universal values, which after all are by far more profound than Western rationality, which has contributed to a materialistic and egotistic society.

Theory mortifies, Roland Barthes has argued, by taking a position in the present and critiquing what is believed to organize the present. Spivak's "mistaken readings" of Hegel and the *Bhagavadgītā* appear more as a reading of mistakes and lay open that even today's encounters with the *Bhagavadgītā* by Indians and others are embedded in discursive formations that are genealogically linked to colonial representations of Indian culture, Hegelian ones among them. Spivak implicitly questions nationalist and nativist adoptions of the Indian text for constructing a pure or real Indian mind and restoring a lost "historical India"

(Spivak, *Critique* 65). In current debates about Indian identity, which are often communalistic or even fundamentalist, Spivak's interventions appear to be a radical critique of all temptations to establish a pure or authentic position of identity. "If as literary critics and teachers, we could have taught ourselves and our students the way to informed figurations of that 'lost' perspective," she writes, "then the geopolitical postcolonial situation could have served as something like a paradigm for the thought of history itself as figuration, figuring something out with 'chunks of the real'" (Spivak, *Critique* 65).

References

Assmann, Aleida. "Was sind kulturelle Texte?" *Literaturkanon – Medienereignis – Kultureller Text. Formen interkultureller Kommunikation und Übersetzung.* Göttinger Beiträge zur Internationalen Übersetzungsforschung 10. Ed. A. Poltermann. Berlin: Schmidt, 1995. 232-44.

Barthes, Roland. *The Grain of the Voice. Interviews 1962-1980.* Trans. Linda Coverdale. New York: Hill and Wang, 1985.

The Bhagavadgītā in the Mahābhārata. Trans. and ed. J.A.B. van Buitenen. Chicago: University of Chicago Press, 1981.

Boog, Jason. "No Deconstruction Before Marriage? Reading Philosophy with Gayatri Chakravorty Spivak." http://*www.meteoritejournal.com*/pdfs/3.Spivak.Interview.pdf [26.08.2007].

Colebrooke, Henry Thomas. *Miscellaneous Essays.* Vol. 1. London: s.n., 1837.

Drew, John. *India and the Romantic Imagination.* Delhi: Oxford University Press, 1987.

Halbfass, Wilhelm. *Indien und Europa. Perspektiven ihrer geistigen Begegnung.* Basel/Stuttgart: Schwabe und Coag, 1981.

Hegel, Georg Friedrich Wilhelm. *Aesthetics. Lectures on Fine Art*, Trans. T.M. Knox. 2 vols. Oxford: Clarendon Press, 1975.

---. "Über die unter dem Namen Bhagavad-Gita bekannte Episode der Mahabharata von Wilhelm von Humboldt." *Berliner Schriften 1818-1831* (*Werke in zwanzig Bänden.* Vol. 11), Frankfurt a. M.: Suhrkamp, 1970. 131-204.

---. *Philosophy of History.* Trans. J. Sibree. Ontario: Kitchner, 2001.

Humboldt, Wilhelm von. "Über die unter dem Namen Bhagavad-Gitā bekannte Episode des Mahā-Bhārata." Berlin: Druckerei der Königlichen Akademie der Wissenschaften zu Berlin, 1826.

Laplanche, Jean, and Jean-Bertrand Pontalis. *Das Vokabular der Psychoanalyse.* Frankfurt/M.: Suhrkamp, 1991.

Minor, Robert (ed.). *Modern Indian Interpreters of the Bhagavadgita.* Albany: State University of New York Press, 1986.

Radhakrishnan, Servapalli. "The Ethics of the Bhagavadgita and Kant." *International Journal of Ethics* 21/4, (1911): 465-82.

Rai, Amit S. "*A Critique of Postcolonial Reason*: Toward a History of the Vanishing Present." Book review. http://findarticles.com/p/articles/mi_m2220/is_1_42/ai_63819094/pg_1 [27.08.2007].

Sanders, Mark. "Interview with Gayatri Chakravorty Spivak." *Gayatri Chakravoty Spivak. Live Theory.* Ed. Mark Sanders. London/New York: Continuum, 2006.

Sharpe, Eric. *The Universal Gītā. Western Images of the Bhagavad Gītā, a Bicentenary Survey.* La Salle: Open Court Publishing, 1985.

Spivak, Gayatri Chakravorty. *A Critique of Postcolonial Reason. Toward a History of the Vanishing Present.* Cambridge/London: Harvard University Press, 1999.

---. "Can the Subaltern Speak?" *Colonial Discourse and Post-Colonial Theory. A Reader.* Eds. Patrick Williams and Laura Chrisman. New York: Columbia University Press, 1994. 66-111.

---. "Translator's Preface." Jacques Derrida. *Of Grammatology.* Trans. Gayatri Spivak. Baltimore: Johns Hopkins University Press, 1974. ix-1xxxvii.

Staten, Henry. "Tracking the 'Native Informant:' Cultural Translation and the Horizon of Literary Translation." *Nation, Language, and the Ethics of Translation.* Eds. Sandra Bermann and Michael Wood. Princeton/Oxford: Princeton University Press, 2005. 111-26.

Stevenson, Robert W. "Tilak and the Bhagavadgita's Doctrine of Karmayoga." *Modern Indian Interpreters of the Bhagavadgita.* Ed. Robert Minor. Albany: State University of New York Press, 1986. 44-60.

CHAPTER NINE

The Concept of Microtonality and the Construction of Indian Music in Nineteenth and Twentieth-Century Europe

LARS-CHRISTIAN KOCH

Music historians are not the only ones faced with the task of describing musical phenomena in a historical framework, evaluating them, and creating a basis for a deeper understanding. Ethnomusicologists face this challenge, too. We are confronted with the often unconscious fact that our work has to be done from a certain point of view, which reflects our own personal involvement. The question of the perspective of the observer, researcher, and author is particularly important if foreign musical cultures in which we do not ourselves participate are the subject of research.

In this respect, the music of India in the nineteenth and early twentieth century is a good example: we have comparatively early sources both from India and Europe, and since it was not thought necessary at that time to become practically involved in foreign music cultures, two different perspectives can be considered. My thesis is that the results of any music historiography depend on the contexts of their respective authors. Most European music historiography has been significantly Eurocentric. With the methods and approaches of interpretative ethnology, it is possible to reevaluate non-Western music historiography.

This can be done with the help of indigenous sources (including oral ones) – and non-indigenous sources should be analyzed in the same way, that is, with the context of the authors in mind. Here the concepts of historical musicology and applied methods, as well as the approaches of ethnomusicology, have to be considered. In particular, the methods of music ethnology, anthropology, or, more precisely, cultural anthropology play a decisive role with regard to the potential for new and effective links between the two subdisciplines.

In this context, the term *music culture* plays a crucial role, so let me just explain my understanding of this peculiar term. Along with James Peoples and Garrick Bailey (17), I understand *culture* as socially transmitted knowledge and behavior that is shared by a group of individuals. *Music* I understand – like Marcia Herndon and Norma McLeod – as culture. Music is regarded as an integral part of culture in this way, rather than being seen in relation to culture. Music is subjected to a dynamic that is determined by human actions, which in turn are a crucial factor for the conception of culture. Drawing on the above definition of culture, music is thus the shared, socially transmitted knowledge and behavior of a group of individuals in relation to acoustically defined systems[1] of expression and communication that are perceived as such.[2] In this way it is possible to establish a broad approach regarding the consideration of music, musical norms and values, classifications and structures in music, the integration of music into space and time perceptions, and of course the connection between music and religion. This approach mainly concerns cultural knowledge and behavior as well as the construction of culture and cultural concepts.

Thus, music in itself is neither spiritual nor transcendent. A culture must give meaning to sounds and connect them to the cultural reality. Here I agree with Clifford Geertz (9) that man gives meaning to the surrounding world by acting, which in turn affects the acting of others in the process of interpretation. He compares the work of the anthropologist to the reading of texts that are divided into subordinated texts containing symbols in two different forms:

1. Sensuous form: material culture, language, sound, social relations, body behavior
2. Nonsensuous form: meaning

Meaning only exists in connection with sensuous phenomena. The anthropologist wants to establish readings of human behavior. The world should be decoded out of the context of speaking, behaving and acting. Symbols provide information about the world, as well as rules to live by. They create cultural relationships and their parts are connected to each other like the threads in a piece of fabric. The ethnomusicologist is part of this whole process because the interpretation cannot be one-sided – knowledge about any foreign reality is necessarily limited and biased.[3] Partners from different cultures meet here in a process of understanding.

This approach seems at first glance to be ideally suited to the study of contemporary phenomena, but I would like to show that it is equally applicable to historical phenomena in different cultures. In this context I understand *history* as the changing process of human society as a whole or of individuals in all their cultural forms and temporal implications. History is also the process of acquisition of these forms and implications by a particular people. Transferring this to non-Western music historiography will lead us to work with historical sources in which all the parties understand the process of their particular space-time relationships[4]. History will be split into several histories, all connecting the past in a logical relationship to the present. This in turn leads to several distinct perspec-

---

1 For Nettl, "system" means a distinguishing from other cultural expressions with signal character (24).
2 The "singing" or rather recital of the Quran is not considered as music.
3 In postmodern cultural anthropology, the subjectivity and authority of the anthropologist is an integral part of research.
4 This means in the past, present, and future as long as there are clear concepts about this kind of time structure.

tives on the same phenomenon. To illustrate this, I will give a brief outline of one characteristic aspect in the music of the Indian subcontinent: the well-known phenomenon of microtones, the so called srutis.[5]

According to the ancient theorists, a sruti is the barely perceptible, smallest pitch change. Based on the different evaluations of the meaning of the sruti phenomenon by Indian and European authors, I will demonstrate that interpretive methods and the inclusion of contemporary music practice clearly indicate different perspectives on the same subject and also allow an assessment of historical sources. The vigorous research of the sruti phenomenon by Western musicologists could even today lead to the assumption that these microtones play a crucial role in contemporary music performances. A detailed examination reveals, however, that compared to the old written sources, a completely different concept of microtones is currently in use.

I will show that for Indian authors, the phenomenon is an important part of their music history, whereas European authors, although they see the historicity of this phenomenon, idealize it, and in their analysis (which is not performance oriented) continue to assume that srutis are a constant part of Indian music in the same way they used to be.

The first presentation of the srutis was made by Bharata in his *Natyasastra*, written approximately 2,000 years ago, and still the most important classical Indian work on drama and music from ancient times. Although it is mainly concerned with the theory of drama, music is dealt with in a separate chapter that established the fundamentals of Indian music theory. Bharata divides the octave into seven notes (svara). By the number of srutis he defines the size of the intervals. The svaras remain the basis of the Indian tone system, and are still widely used.

In music practice and theory the tones have names, with their initials used for solmization.

sadja	→	Sa	→	S
rishab	→	Re	→	R
gandhar	→	Ga	→	G
madhyama	→	Ma	→	M
pancama	→	Pa	→	P
dhaivat	→	Dha	→	D
nishad	→	Ni	→	N

The term svara means the sound itself, as well as the interval between the svara and the underlying tone. The size of this interval is measured in srutis.

After discussing the phenomena of consonance and dissonance, Bharata explains the development of different scale models by using the srutis. Since Bharata, Indian theorists have divided the octave into twenty-two srutis. Bharata primarily used the srutis as a constituent element for the formation of the basic scales of the system, the grama (which literally means village or community). These are

5   Sanskrit *sru* – to hear.

heptatonic octave scales, which are mentioned in the *Natyasastra* in two forms, both divided by the twenty-two srutis. Dividing an octave into twenty-two srutis – this comes close to twenty-two quarter tones (one quarter tone equals 50 cents; one sruti is equal to 54.5 cents[6]) – means in the two cases mentioned in the *Natyasastra* (XXVIII 23-8) that scales are constituted by the size of quarter tones, developing subtle differences. In the *Natyasastra*, Bharata says that to get the madhyamagrama – one of the two mentioned cases – the interval Ma-Pa should be reduced by one sruti, which leads to a scale structure defined by sruti:

$$4 - 3 - 2 - 4 - 4 - 3 - 2 \quad \text{(sadjagrama)}$$
$$4 - 3 - 2 - 4 - 3 - 4 - 2 \quad \text{(madhyamagrama)}$$

Sa   Re   Ga   Ma   Pa   Dha   Ni

Transposing Ma to Sa we get:

$$4 - 3 - 4 - 2 - 4 - 3 - 2$$

  Ma   Pa   Dha   Ni   Sa   Re   Ga

(transposed)   Sa   Re   Ga   Ma   Pa   Dha   Ni

The only, but essential, difference is the third.

Sadjagrama:

1 2 3 4 5 6 7 8 9 10 11 12 13 14 15 16 17 18 19 20 21 22

    | | | | | | |

    Sa   Re   Ga   Ma   Pa   Dha Ni

Madhyamagrama:

1 2 3 4 5 6 7 8 9 10 11 12 13 14 15 16 17 18 19 20 21 22

    | | | | | | |

    Sa   Re   Ga   Ma   Pa   Dha Ni

(see Kuckertz 85)

The grama are named after their fundamental tone, sadja → sadjagrama → sa-grama or and madhyama → madhyamagrama or → ma-grama.

In the madhyamagrama Ma practially equals Sa. If we take them as fundamentals, we get two scales comparable to the following scales from Western theory.

      Sa-grama: d e f g a h c d   (Dorian mode)

      Ma-grama: g a h c d e f g   (Mixolydian mode)

This only works if the srutis in their basic structure 4-3-2-4-4-3-2 lie beneath the svara. If they lie above, a scale with a strong similarity to a Western major scale evolves.

---

6   The cent system was established by Alexander J. Ellis, who defined a tempered tone with the ideal unit of 100 cents, independently of which cultural setting they are used in or which tuning system is followed. In this way it is possible to compare different tone systems.

1	2	3	4	5	6	7	8	9	10	11	12	13	14	15	16	17	18	19	20	21	22

| Sa | | Re | | Ga | | Ma | | | | | | | Pa | | | | Dha | | | Ni | |

This is how most authors understand the srutis; it is a scholarly consensus.

Beginning with the *Natyasastra*, the sruti system became part of all major works on Indian music and music theory. I will only briefly mention some of these works of the last two thousand years. Between the first and eighth century, the treatise *Dattilam* was written, which is clearly oriented toward the *Natyasastra*, but extends the concept of svara to some functional aspects (final, dominant, initial etc.).[7] In the *Bhrhadesi*, written in the ninth or tenth century, Matanga states that the number of srutis is endless. He reflects on the relationship of sruti and svara, concluding that the svara are constructed through the srutis. Sarngadeva wrote his *Sangitaratnakara* in the thirteenth century, and it is surely the most influential treatise on music after the *Natyasastra*. Of course he mentions the sruti, referring to the *Natyasastra*. He defines it as a barely perceptible difference in pitch. He regards a svara as an uninterrupted series of srutis in "harmonious" relationship. (Bake, "Music of India" 206) His evaluation of the srutis is identical with that of Bharata. Sarngadeva is the first author to mention the occurance of a gap between theory and practice in his own time. In the sixteenth century, the *Ragatarangini* (Locanan-Kavi) and *Sadragancandrodaya* were written. Here practical applications involve more recent systems. The first text describes the raga, the typical melody models or sound personalities in Indian music, as featuring twelve tones, the latter work attributes to them seven main tones (shuddha) and their seven variants (vikrta). In the *Sangitaparijata*, which Ahobala Pandit wrote in the late seventeenth century, we find for the first time a mathematical calculation of the srutis based on the division of a vibrating string.

The *Natyasastra* describes the often cited example of the two-bowed harps – the vinas of the time – where the srutis are achieved by detuning several open strings. The division of the strings by tapping on a fingerboard or on frets occured a thousand years later and subsequently became the popular musical practice.

Even Ahobala Pandit refers to the twenty-two srutis of Bharata. In his description he uses seven main notes and five alterations, as is common practice today. But by then, in practical terms, the music of the Middle East was already exerting a heavy influence on the music of the Indian subcontinent, and the sounds of the courtly music had little relation to the theoretical writings of ancient Indian music. The Indian music of the seventeenth, eighteenth, and nineteenth centuries changed significantly: new styles were created, such as the very ornamented vocal style Khyal and different instrumental styles. In the nineteenth century, increased mobility allowed a much wider reception of courtly music. The system of the twenty-two srutis, however, remained untouched and unquestioned. We still find the sruti system in the writings of Raja Sourindo Mohan Thakur (Tagore)

---

7   For the following descriptions see also Oesch 221, 234 ff., 254 ff.

at the end of the nineteenth century (1877 [1982]: 9 ff.). He devoted his work to the study of Indian music and its history, published more than thirty books on the topic, made staff notations of some raga compositions, and hoped in this way to show that Indian music is equal to Western music. Furthermore, he applied the knowledge he had gained in a practical way by creating musical instruments and later ordering full collections of them from special instrument makers. These collections – mostly decorative or hybrid research instruments – he sent to different courts and museums in Europe (Capwell, 1991). Collections of his instruments are now in Berlin, Brussels, Dresden, Copenhagen, Stockholm, Rome, and Vienna.

Finally, the great Indian music scholar Vishnu Narayan Bhatkhande was already writing about the sruti by the beginning of the twentieth century, and such discussions by Indian theorists continue today.

The discovery of Indian music by Western scholars[8] began with Sir William Jones's monograph, *On the Musical Modes of the Hindus* (1792), which was published in Erfurt under the title *Über die Musik der Indier* already in 1802, and was the first publication on Indian music in German. Jones arrived in Calcutta in 1783, where he became chief judge at the High Court for the East India Company, and where he eventually died in 1794. Jones had studied at Oxford and was a renowned linguist: he claimed to speak twenty-eight languages. A year after his arrival, he founded the Asiatic Society of Bengal in Calcutta. During his ten-year stay in India, he worked intensively on different aspects of Indian life. He translated Persian poetry, studied the philology of Sanskrit, and developed theories of Sanskrit's connection with the Indo-European language family, a project that made a crucial contribution to the development of comparative research on modern languages. The discovery of the connection between Sanskrit and several European languages made the study of non-Western cultures a respectable research field. In 1789, Jones translated into English the Indian poet Kalidasa's drama *Abhijñānaśākuntalam* (ca. 400 A.D.); Georg Forster translated it into German in 1791; the second edition of his translation contained a preface by Johann Gottfried Herder. Goethe was very excited about it, and it inspired his "Vorspiel auf dem Theater" in *Faust* – even the actors are similar to 'Sakuntala'.

Music was only one of Jones's many interests, regarding it as a branch of science, closely related to poetry. This is why he begins his monograph with a philosophical discourse on the nature of musical aesthetics and its relationship to the world. He adds Indian stories about the magical effects of music, remarking that he does not know whether they are true, but has access to an eyewitness. He then discusses similar effects in European music – we find ourselves in the time of Mozart and Haydn – and finally points out the relationship between Greek, Persian, and Indian music. About the srutis, Jones writes that there are twenty-two, and that they are third or quarter tones, dividing the octave into the fundamen-

---

8 See Tagore. For a selected list of authors see bibliography.

tal scale 4-3-2-4-4-3-2. He suggests that in this regard, the srutis are not exactly equidistant, but that they are taken as equidistant in theory.

Other European scholars soon followed Sir William Jones's writings, and almost all of them discussed the sruti phenomenon. Forty years later, Augustus Willard devoted at least five pages of his *Treatise on the Music of Hindoostan* (1834) to the srutis and their relationship to the different scales in Indian music. Other nineteenth-century European scholars writing on Indian music and the sruti in depth were:[9]

- Sir William Ouseley. *Anecdotes of Indian Music* (1875)
- J. D. Paterson. *On the Grámas or Musical Scales of the Hindus* (1875)
- William C. Stafford. *The Music of India or Hindustan* (n.d.)
- R. H. M. Bosanquet. *On the Hindu Division of the Octave, with some Additions to the Theory of Systems of the Higher Orders* (1877)

Among them, Bosanquet was the first to seek a mathematical definition of the sruti. In the view of European authors researching Indian music, determining the absolute size of the sruti remained the dominant problem, one to which Indian authors, by contrast, did not pay significant attention. Authors following the model of Bosanquet were C. R. Day (1891) and Arthur Fox-Strangways (1914), who dedicated more than thirty pages of his *The Music of Hindostan* to the sruti system. His writings are based on the hypothesis that the srutis are created by the combination of different intervals in perfect pitch, and are therefore not equidistant. Scholars like Alain Danielou more or less follow these theories, others expand them or come to new results, but they always try to measure the srutis mathematically. This approach continues up to the 1960s in the work of Heinrich Husmann (1961). In the twentieth century, a number of different authors tried to arrive at a mathematical definition of the sruti. But they did not strive to interpret the old treatises by their textual content. Instead, most writers sought to prove their own subjective notions of them. The system described by Bharata was combined and extended to elements of pythagorean tuning, perfect pitch, and modern concepts of acoustics. (Deva, Clements, Danielou).

Did or does the concept of the sruti exert any kind of influence in the course of performance? It would be presumptuous to claim that the existence of the twenty-two srutis is no longer relevant to today's music performances. It is still relevant – but not in the way most Western theorists think. In this context, Rabindralal Roy should be cited: "It is doubtful if any musician produces the same sruti twice [...] Different musicians again, may sing the same phrases with slightly different srutis and yet be effective [...] The mechanical calculation of srutis has no meaning in the world of the art of music" (Roy 92-3).

The importance of the srutis for today's practice was taught to me by my teacher, Dr. Trina Purohit-Roy. When I asked her how to play the sruti correctly, she explained: "Sruti are like lotus flowers, they are mounted on the ground, in

---

9   All these articles were collected and published in Thakur, *Hindu music*.

the same way as the svara is fixed. They move above the water surface, moving back and forth without ever losing contact to their roots." In practice, this means that the srutis cannot be classified in an acoustic-analytical pitch-distance scheme because they have a strong individual character with regard to their intonation.

Let us return to the nineteenth century. Considering the practice of courtly Indian music, we must bear in mind that musicians were then rarely able to read elaborated Sanskrit literature on music theory. The Indian education system is in fact based on the teacher-pupil relationship (*guru-shishya-parampara*) as an oral tradition. What was and is transferred from the teacher to the student is essential. This concept and practice are still valid today, and it may still happen that on being told that his interpretation does not entirely conform to the ancient writings (the sastra), a musician will answer: "I do not care about the sastras, I have learned this from my teacher." Even in the practice oriented writings of the late nineteenth century (Thakur), where the tone structure of the ragas is discussed in detail, srutis are hardly ever mentioned.

In today's practice, srutis are referred to in the sense of pitch qualities and intonation instructions to individual notes. Asking a musician about a certain note in a raga, you might get a reaction like "The komal-Dha must be played a sruti deeper in this raga." Another quality of these microtones is attributed to the general color of the tone played or sung in a peculiar way to put some life into it.

To discuss this, let me briefly explain a crucial element of Indian music: the raga. According to Matanga (800-900 A.D.), the author of the *Brhadesi*, a raga is "the peculiar melody which is defined through tones and their combination and which colors the minds of human beings, that melody is called a raga by the sages" (quoted by V. N. Bhatkhande, *Abhinavaragamanjar*). Trina Purohit-Roy defines a raga as: "a fixed combination of successive tones following certain rules, which follows an inner sentiment" (Purohit-Roy 286).[10]

The ragas Bhairava and Bhairavi are good examples, two ragas for morning time with komal Re (flat second) and komal Dha (flat sixth), they differ only in intonation, i.e., they are played with different srutis. In addition, Bhaivari has a flattened third and a flattened seventh (komal Ga and komal Ni).

Bhairava:

Arohi (upward movement):	S	R̲	G	M	P	D̲	N	Ṡ
Avarohi (downward movement):	Ṡ	N	D̲	P	M	G	R̲	S

Komal Re and komal Dha are intended to be intonated a sruti lower in connection with a strong vibrato.

---

10 "Eine durch besondere Regeln festgelegte Kombination aufeinanderfolgender Töne, die jeweils einer inneren Einstimmung entspricht."

Bhairavi:

Arohi:	S	R̲	G̲	M	P	D̲	N̲	Ṡ
Avarohi:	Ṡ	N̲	D̲	P	M	G̲	R̲	S

Here, komal Re and komal Dha are intended to be played without a sruti alteration. The following three-dimensional analytical graphs show the sound of the notes Re and Dha played on a sitar (plucked string instrument). The frequencies of the overtones are visible, while the sound of the plucked string fades away. Here, the quality of pitch change in the process of the embellishment *andolan* is clearly visible: it is not a fixed pitch at all.

Concerning this apparent irrelevance of the ancient sruti concept in practice, it

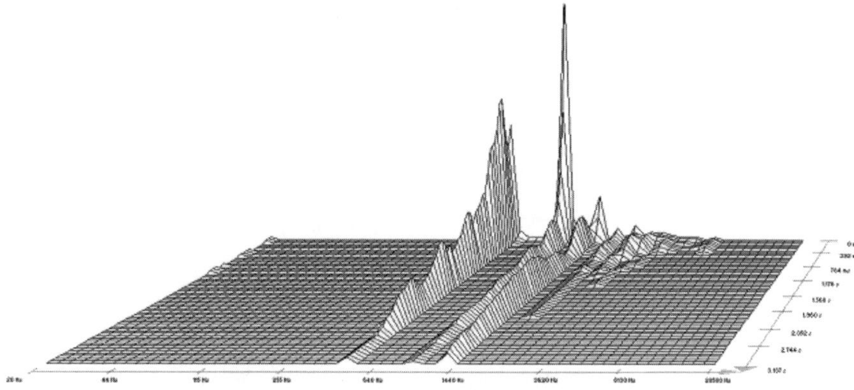

Fig. 1: Re in Bhairava / andolan, with sruti movements.

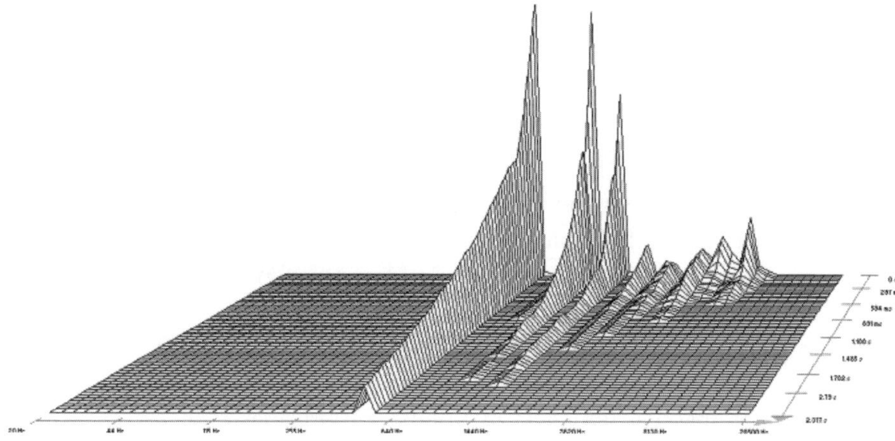

Fig. 2: Re in Bhairavi / no andolan, no sruti movements.

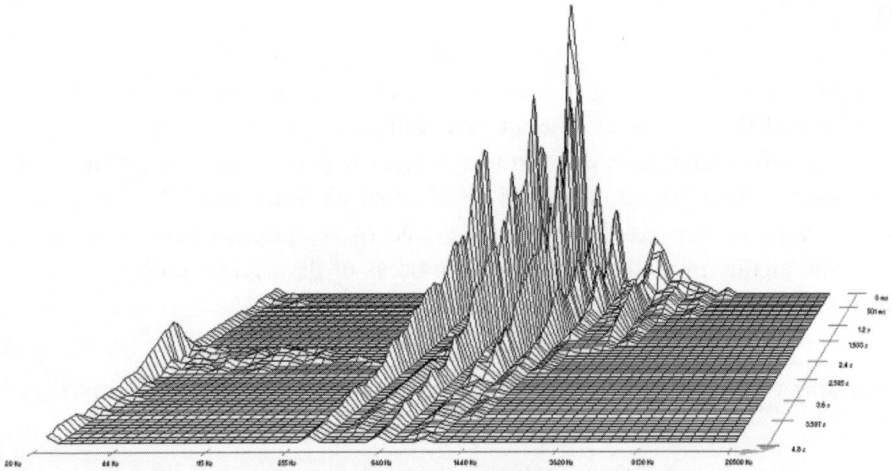

Fig. 3: Dha in Bhairava / andolan, with sruti movements.

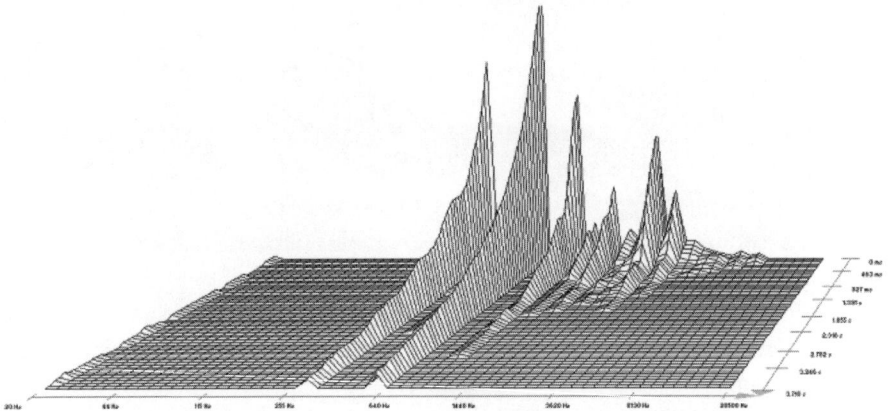

Fig. 4: Dha in Bhairavi / no andolan, no sruti movements.

seems surprising that the discourse on this phenomenon continued for such a long time, especially in Western literature. For different reasons, the sruti became a symbol of Indian music for both European and Indian musicologists. It has been accepted as a sign of the value of Indian music, although Indian and European authors attach different meanings to it.

As numerous sources on the musical life in eighteenth-century Calcutta testify, Sir William Jones knew the Indian music of his time well[11] – but he did not take into account the massive influence of Middle Eastern music on the changes in north-eastern Indian music cultures. He cites only ancient texts, which by his time were already more than one hundred and sixty years old. These texts show an attitude Charles Widdess characterizes as "archaic didactic intent" (Widdess cited

11 For music in eighteenth-century Kolkata see Woodfield.

after Farell 25). Jones only looked at a very small part of the Indian musical culture of his time, to which he attributed importance from his own perspective.

In the beginning, I defined the term music culture as music as well as culture in all their diversity – this is deliberately hidden by Jones: he draws a special, selective picture of Indian music. Of course there are reasons for this. Jones wrote at a time when it was regarded as most desirable to discover the "real" India. This was the India fixed in the old Sanskrit treatises, the India with a clear Hindu background, not the India – as Jones calls it – described in the "muddy streams of Muslim writers on India," but the "pure source of the Hindu scholarship." (Jones 136) This attitude toward Indian culture informs the entire range of the European humanities of this time and during the following decades. The European scholars regarded historical India as comparable to ancient Greece, which to them symbolized an advanced civilizational stage. The Indian culture of the eighteenth and nineteenth centuries was for most European scholars a culture in decline, which of course made it easy to find reasons for the massive presence of European nations on the subcontinent. For Western authors – as Jones had already shown – the parallels between Indian and ancient Greek culture were essential up to the first half of the twentieth century. These parallels demonstrated the high value attributed to Indian culture and music.

Regarding the perspective of nineteenth- and early twentieth-century scholars on Indian music, the critical position of interpretive or postmodern ethnology is that most cultures are represented as separate and outwardly completed systems. This causes not only physical distance but also distance in the perception of time. Numerous, and often long lasting influences are deliberately hidden in favor of pure and authentic, precolonial idealistic cultures. This results in a static, ahistoric image of those cultures that were characterized as traditional. This view lacked any consciousness of the difference of Indian history from that of the West.

For the Indian authors, the srutis were a confirmation of the existence of their own ancient music culture and its relative complexity, especially in comparison to European music. They were always faithful to their forefathers, documenting authority and truth through this historical consciousness. But simultaneously, in India, too, an elitist image of music was created regarding the sruti phenomenon, which in some cases had nothing to do with music in performance. The microtones here also serve as a symbol of the value of Indian music.

In Indian literature, music theory was only slowly connected to performance practice. One of the key personalities in this regard was V. N. Bhatkhande, who left behind a large number of publications dealing with the composition of several hundred ragas. Since then, the preoccupation with music theory in relation to performance practice has increased significantly. Only in Europe, these practical perspectives did not gain attention in musicological research until the second half of the twentieth century – but that is another story which still has to be written.

References

Bake, Arnold Adriaan. "The Music of India." *The New Oxford History of Music*. Ed. Egon Wellesz. 10 vols. London/New York: Oxford University Press, 1954-90. Vol. 1: *Ancient and Oriental Music* (1957), 195-227.

---. "Indische Musik." *Die Musik in Geschichte und Gegenwart*. Ed. by F. Blume. Kassel/Basel: Bärenreiter, 1957. Vol. 6, col. 1150-85.

Bhatkhande, V. N. *A Comparative Study of some of the Leading Music Systems of the 15th, 16th, 17th & 18th Centuries*. Baroda: Indian Musicological Society, 1972 (written 1930).

---. *A Short Historical Survey of the Music of Upper India*. Baroda: Indian Musicological Society, 1934 (written 1916).

---. *Abhinavaragamanjari*. Hathras: Sangeet Karyalaya, 1915.

Bosanquet, R. H. M. *On the Hindu Division of the Octave, with Some Additions to the Theory of Systems of the Higher Orders*. (1877)

Capwell, Charles. "Marginality and Musicology in Nineteenth-Century Calcutta. The Case of Sourindo Mohun Tagore." *Comparative Musicology and Anthropology of Music*. Ed. Bruno Nettl and Philip Bohlmann. Chicago/London: University of Chicago Press, 1991, 228-43.

Clements, E. *Introduction to the Study of Indian Music*. London: Longmans, 1913.

Danielou, Alain. *Introduction to the Study of Musical Scales*. London: The India Society, 1943, (2)1979 New Delhi.

Day, C. R. *The Music and Musical Instruments of Southern India and the Deccan*. London/New York: Novello, Ewer & Co, 1891 (Reprint: New Delhi 1990, 1996).

Deva, B. Chaitanya. *The Music of India. A Scientific Study*. New Delhi: Munshiram Manoharlal Publishers, 1981.

Ellis, Alexander J. "On the Musical Scales of Various Nations." *Journal of the Royal Society of Arts* 33 (1885): 485-527, 1102-11.

Farrell, Gerry. *Indian Music and the West*. Oxford: Clarendon, 1997.

Fox-Strangways, Arthur H. *The Music of Hindostan*. Oxford: Clarendon, 1914. Reprinted New Delhi 1975.

Geertz, Clifford. *Dichte Beschreibung*. Frankfurt a.M.: Suhrkamp, 1987.

Gosh, Manomohan (ed. & transl.). *The Natyasastra (a Treatise on Ancient Indian Dramaturgy and Histrionics) Ascribed to Bharata-Muni*. Vol. 1 (chapters 1-27). Calcutta: Manisha, 1951, (2)1967.

Gosh, Manomohan (ed. & transl.). *The Natyasastra (a Treatise on Ancient Indian Dramaturgy and Histrionics) Ascribed to Bharata-Muni*. Vol. 2 (chapters 28-36). Calcutta: Asiatic Society, 1961.

Herndon, M., and N. McLeod. *Music as Culture*. Darby, Pa: Norwood, 1981.

Husmann, Heinrich. *Grundlagen der antiken und orientalischen Musikkultur*. Berlin: De Gruyter, 1961.

Jones, William. *On the Musical Modes of the Hindus*. London: n.p., 1792.

---. *Über die Musik der Indier. Eine Abhandlung*. Erfurt: Beyer und Maring, 1802.

Kuckertz, Josef. *Form und Melodiebildung der karnatischen Musik Südindiens im Umkreis der vorderorientalischen und nordindischen Kunstmusik*. 2 vols. Wiesbaden: Hassarowitz, 1970.

Nettl, Bruno. *The Study of Ethnomusicology. Twenty-nine Issues and Concepts*. Urbana etc.: University of Illinois Press, 1983.

Oesch, Hans. *Neues Handbuch der Musikwissenschaft*. Vol. 8: *Außereuropäische Musik*, Part 1, chapter: "Der indische Kulturbereich" (with assistance of Heinz Zimmermann). Laaber: Laaber Verlag, 1984.

Ouseley, Sir William. *Anecdotes of Indian Music*. Calcutta: n.p., 1797.

Paterson, J. D. *On the Grámas or Musical Scales of the Hindus*. Calcutta: n.p., 1875.

Peoples, James, and Garrick Bailey. *Humanity. An Introduction to Cultural Anthropology*. Belmont, CA/London: Wadsworth, (5)2000.

Purohit-Roy, T. "Zur Improvisation indischer Ragas." in: *Colloquium Amicorum. Joseph Schmidt-Görg zum 70. Geburtstag*. Ed. S. Kross and H. Schmidt. Bonn: Beethovenhaus, 1967.

Roy, Rabindralal. "Significant Use of Srutis in North Indian Ragas." *The Journal of the Music Academy* 31 (1960): 89-93.

Stafford, William C. *The Music of India or Hindustan*. N.p.: n.p., n.d. Reprint in Tagore, *Hindu Music*.

Tagore, Sourindo Mohun. *Hindu Music from Various Authors*. Calcutta: privately published, 1875.

---. *Six Principal Ragas. With a Brief View of Hindu Music*. Calcutta: Calcutta Central Press Company, (2)1877. Reprinted Delhi 1982.

---. *The Eight Principle Rasas of the Hindus with Tableaux and Dramatic Pieces Illustrating their Character*. Calcutta: n.p., 1880.

---. *The Dramatic Sentiments of the Aryas*. Calcutta: privately published, 1881.

---. *Hindu Music from Various Authors*. Calcutta: I. C. Bose & Co, 1882 (extended version of 1875).

---. *The Seven Principal Musical Notes of the Hindus with their Presiding Deities*. Calcutta: Stanhope Press, 1892. Reprint 1990; 1995.

---. *Universal History of Music Compiled from Divers Sources Together with Various Original Notes on Hindu Music*. Calcutta: N. G. Goswamy, 1896. Reprint: Delhi: Low Price, 1990, 1999.

Willard, Augustus. *A Treatise on the Music of Hindoostan*. Calcutta: Baptist Mission Press, 1834.

Woodfield, Ian. *Music of the Raj. A Social and Economic History of Music in Late Eighteenth-Century Anglo-Indian Society*. New York: Oxford University Press, 2000.

CHAPTER TEN

Strange Encounters or Succeeding Dialogues? Science, Culture and Modernity in Amitav Ghosh's *The Calcutta Chromosome* and *The Hungry Tide*

FRANK SCHULZE-ENGLER

Is science culture-bound? Ever since Jean-François Lyotard and other postmodern theorists declared the final demise of all "grand narratives" and postulated the so-called incommensurability of cultures, the idea that modernity (including modern science) is a 'Western' construct has undoubtedly enjoyed great popularity in the humanities. Different varieties of postcolonial theory (first and foremost the field of colonial discourse analysis that emerged in the wake of Edward Said's *Orientalism*) have spent a great deal of critical energy on proving the complicity of 'Western knowledge' with colonial bids to dominate 'Europe's Others' (Barker et al.), and many representatives of contemporary postcolonial studies firmly believe that the 'subversion' of Western master discourses lies not only at the heart of their own critical efforts, but also of the material they study.

There is good reason to be skeptical about many of these assumptions. Indeed, I think that many of the classical paradigms of postcolonial theory have by now thoroughly exhausted themselves. While colonial discourse analysis remains a valuable tool for a wide variety of historiographic purposes and for encounters with colonial and anticolonial texts in cultural and literary studies, the idea that 'postcolonial' literatures can endlessly be defined through their antagonistic or subversive relationships with 'Western' master narratives is anything but convincing: much of contemporary literature emerging from formerly colonized parts of the world follows different agendas relating to new social, cultural and political constellations and conflicts. In looking at the half-bizarre, half-utopian articulations of science, modernity, and culture in two novels of one of the best-known contemporary Indian writers, Amitav Ghosh, my primary interest is thus not to expose the conflict between allegedly 'Western' and 'Indian' cultural frameworks and modes of knowledge. Instead, I propose to read Ghosh's texts as explorations of a specifically Indian modernity, and of the multitude of transnational and transcultural connections that link this Indian modernity to modernity at large. While in *The Calcutta Chromosome* (1996) these explorations are still embedded in a 'counter-discursive,' ironic plot focused on the arrogance of Western science in colonial India, in *The Hungry Tide* (2004) they turn toward possible modes of opening up dialogues between modern science and the sociocultural contexts in which they operate.

I will begin with a few remarks on 'modernity,' 'postmodernity', and what might be called 'the location of science'. If from the 1970s onwards, it had seemed that 'modernity' had withered away as a theoretical concept in a vast array of academic disciplines (including important branches of philosophy and the social sciences), and that postmodernism had won the day in much of the humanities, in recent years modernity seems to have returned with a vengeance. Now it is the idea of postmodernity as a total break with modernity (as set out, for example, in Lyotard's *Postmodern Condition*), which seems on its way out. Terminological nonentities such as post-post-modernism have had their day, and once more it is modernity that is at the center of wide-ranging theoretical debates. After what now increasingly looks like a postmodern interlude, modernity thus seems poised to become its own conceptual successor.

The concept of modernity presently debated is, of course, not identical with the concept that was current before the postmodernist intervention. Often enough it is invoked grudgingly or even with open hostility: Fredric Jameson's extended essay on a "singular modernity" sees modernity as an essentially illusory and harmful concept that one should get rid of, but that one needs to battle against for the time being; for Arjun Appadurai modernity has broken free from the last fetters that kept it at bay and is now a "Modernity at Large;" and Zygmunt Baumann's compelling image of a "liquid modernity" carries associations of drenched rather than liberated societies. But of course modernity has also been explored in more positive or at least more ambivalent senses by a wide array of theorists in what has increasingly become a truly global rather than a predominantly Western debate. Globalization theorists such as Ulrich Beck and Anthony Giddens have explored the risks and opportunities produced by the "modernization of modernity" in a "world risk society" and have suggested terms such as "second" or "reflexive" modernity to come to terms with the "consequences of modernity" in our "runaway world."

A key concern in this debate has been the necessity to overcome normative models of modernity associated with the modernization theories of the 1950s and to search for adequate conceptualizations of a globalized and decentered modernity. Modernity is no longer considered an exclusive property (or predicament) of the West; the focus of attention has shifted from an attempt at measuring societies against the yardstick of industrialized societies in Europe and, above all, the USA, to an exploration of a wide variety of modernities practiced in various parts of the world. Increasingly, the personnel of this debate has also changed: Weber, Durkheim, Marx, and Simmel are still being discussed, but today their European perspectives on modernity are debated by theorists of modernity in virtually every corner of the globe. As the Indian sociologist and anthropologist Partha Chatterjee put it succinctly: "One cannot be for or against modernity; one can only devise strategies for coping with it" (Chatterjee 19).

This understanding of a globalized and decentered modernity can no longer be reconciled with notions of modernity as a unitary "Western" entity. As Shmuel Eisenstadt put it in his seminal essay on "multiple modernities:"

> One of the most important implications of the term "multiple modernities" is that modernity and Westernization are not identical; Western patterns of modernity are not the only "authentic" modernities, though they enjoy historical precedence and continue to be a basic reference point for others. (Eisenstadt 2-3)

And further on, he takes up the issue again:

> The undeniable trend at the end of the twentieth century is the growing diversification of the understanding of modernity, of the basic cultural agendas of different modern societies – far beyond the homogenic and hegemonic visions of modernity prevalent in the 1950s. [...] All these developments do indeed attest to the continual development of multiple modernities, or of multiple interpretations of modernity – and, above all, to attempts at "de-Westernization," depriving the West of its monopoly on modernity. (24)

In his contribution to a particularly vigorous debate on the necessity to reconceptualize modernity that has recently emerged in India, Dipesh Chakrabarty has suggested that the most adequate strategy for such a reconceptualization lies in "provincializing Europe," a task that he explicitly distinguishes from a relativist practice of highlighting the alleged 'incommensurability' of cultures:

> The project of provincializing Europe therefore cannot be a project of cultural relativism. It cannot originate from the stance that the reason/ science/universals that help define Europe as the modern are simply "culture-specific" and therefore only belong to the European cultures. For the point is not that Enlightenment rationalism is always unreasonable in itself, but rather a matter of documenting how – through what historical process – its "reason," which was not always self-evident to everyone, has been made to look obvious far beyond the ground where it originated. [...] The idea is to write into the history of modernity the ambivalences, contradictions, the use of force, and the tragedies and ironies that attend it. (Chakrabarty 43)

Where, then, is the location of science in this world of multiple or 'local' modernities? Bruno Latour's rigorous answer to this question would, of course, be "nowhere," as his account of the interplay of science, society, and nature famously suggests that "we have never been modern." Latour's argument is based on the distinction between 'translation' and 'purification,' which he sees as the two basic practices engendered by modernity:

> [T]he word 'modern' designates two sets of entirely different practices which must remain distinct if they are to remain effective, but have recently begun to be confused. The first set of practices, by 'translation', creates mixtures between entirely new types of beings, hybrids of nature and culture. The second, by 'purification', creates two entirely distinct ontological zones: that of human beings on the one hand; that of nonhumans on the other. (Latour 10-1)

According to Latour, the world we are faced with is characterized by a "proliferation of hybrids" (133) and by networks constituting "imbroglios of science, politics, economy, law, religion, technology, fiction" (2). Since these "hybrid networks" continuously undermine the constitutive distinction on which the idea of being 'modern' rests, Latour concludes that we have in fact never been modern.

This wholesale terminological rejection of 'modern' and 'modernity' is counterproductive, I believe, in view of the wide variety of discourses that currently engage in reconfigurations of a decentered, plural, and localized modernity; for the purposes of this paper, I will thus give Latour's apodictic verdict a reformist twist and amend it to "we have never been modern in the manner we thought (or were told)." At the same time, I would like to take up Latour's idea of "hybrid networks" in my readings of *The Calcutta Chromosome* and *The Hungry Tide*, because it is particularly apt for throwing light upon the articulations of science, culture, and modernity in these novels. Latour illustrates this idea of "hybrid networks" that cut across the terrain claimed by the natural sciences, the social sciences, and the humanities with the example of the ozone hole:

> The ozone hole is too social and too narrated to be truly natural; the strategy of industrial firms and heads of state is too full of chemical reactions to be reduced to power and interest; the discourse of the ecosphere is too real and too social to boil down to meaning effects. Is it our fault if the networks *are simultaneously real, like nature, narrated, like discourse, and collective, like society*? (6)

It is only if we acknowledge the existence of these "hybrid networks," Latour argues, that we can hope to understand and influence the world we have created: "we are going to have to slow down, reorient and regulate the proliferation of monsters by representing their existence officially" (12). If, however, we continue to insist on the distinction of the human and the nonhuman and to maintain the separatist logic of the natural sciences, the social sciences, and the humanities, we will be faced with more and more hybrid "monsters" beyond our cognitive (and political) control.

Amitav Ghosh's *The Calcutta Chromosome* (1996), the first of the novels I would now like to turn to, can arguably be read as a 'strange encounter,' ostensibly between an arrogant colonial mode of science and its native 'other,' but on a deeper level between Ghosh's long-standing interest in the exploration of an emerging Indian modernity in the context of a globalized world on the one hand and his ironical subversion of colonial codes of rational superiority with regard to 'the natives' on the other.

The Calcutta Chromosome is set in a not too distant future where the world seems to be governed by mildly benign technocratic, transnational hyperorganizations that regulate all important aspects of life on the planet. Antar, an Egyptian computer expert, works for one of these organizations, the International Water Council, in New York; his work consists of supervising the endless sifting of information that a supercomputer called AVA procures from all corners of the globe. When the identity card of Murugan, a former colleague of his, turns up on his computer screen one day, a delirious plot begins to unfold that takes the reader back to the 1880s in colonial India and the research of the British Nobel Laureate Ronald Ross on the origins of malaria. Murugan had disappeared a few years before after he had traveled to Calcutta to find proof for a mind-boggling theory that had become his life-obsession: Murugan believed that while Ross was undertaking his malaria research in his Calcutta laboratory, a clandestine group of Indian 'counter-scientists' manipulated his research for their own purposes and succeeded in discovering the 'Calcutta Chromosome,' an irregular genetic code that allows for the wholesale transfer of personality traits from one human to the other – and that has turned a small group of initiates into immortals. Murugan, whom everybody thought to be a crank, was right, of course: the clandestine sect of immortal counter-scientists really exists, and at the close of the novel even usurps Antar's computer-generated hyperreality. Whether their final revelation signals the end or a new beginning for Antar remains open.

The 'cultural encounter' staged in the novel is a highly complex one: on the one hand, we encounter a 'Western science' that seems to take its location for granted and conducts its research in India's laboratories with classical colonial disdain for 'the natives,' on the other hand is a clandestine 'counter-science' that despite its religious trappings is anything but 'traditionally Indian.' In an earlier conversation with Antar, Murugan sets out his understanding of this 'counter-science' in the following terms:

> 'Let me put it like this,' Murugan said. 'You know all about matter and antimatter, right? And rooms and anterooms and Christ and Antichrist and so on? Now, let's say there was something like science and counter-science. Think of it in the abstract, wouldn't you say that the first principle of a functioning counter-science would have to be secrecy? The way I see it, it wouldn't just have to be secretive about *what* it did (it couldn't hope to beat the scientists at that game anyway); it would also have to be secretive *in* what it did. It would have to use secrecy as a technique or procedure. It would in principle have to refuse all direct communication, straight off the bat, because to communicate, to put ideas into language, would be to establish a claim to *know* – which is

the first thing a counter-science would dispute.' (Ghosh, *Calcutta Chromosome* 103)

If anyone ever wondered what a poststructuralist natural science might look like, this 'counter-science' seems to have come pretty close; the witty splinter of Derriddean *différance* in anteroom and Antichrist can be read as a pointer, I believe, to the function of this 'counter-science' in the novel: beyond clichéd notions of Indian spirituality or postcolonial fantasies of a 'subaltern science,'[1] it serves mainly to drive forward a plot centered on the deconstruction of the alleged superiority of Western 'rationality,' a project that Ghosh had already delved into in previous novels such as *The Circle of Reason*. One of the strongest features of the novel is thus its systematic transformation of the colonial laboratory from a bulwark of Western intellectual superiority into an uncanny location of Bhabhaesque mimicry. The Indian 'counter-scientists' succeed in their fantastic manipulations of the European researchers not *despite*, but *because of* the racist spirit of supremacy over the 'natives' that informs the European scientists' work: it is only because Indians in a nineteenth-century laboratory can by (colonial) definition be nothing except cleaners, or at best attendants, that they can carry out their own 'counter-research' without being detected. While the Nobel Laureate Ross remains oblivious for the rest of his life to what had really happened in his Calcutta laboratory, another young doctor who visited the laboratory when it was still run by Ross's predecessor gets a glimpse of the uncanny institution that the colonial laboratory has become. When he realizes that it is Mangala, the charwoman, and Lakhaan, the attendant, who really run the place, the laboratory becomes a mirror image of the favorite tropes of orientalist discourse:

> Farley would now gladly have walked away from this place, this so-called laboratory, whose all too familiar instruments seemed to be turned to purposes as perverse as they were unscrutable. Yet he knew that if he left now he would for ever afterwards be tormented by uncertainty and doubt. He had no option but to pursue his enquiry no matter where it led. (144)

Farley's enquiry in fact leads him to a tiny railway station in the middle of nowhere, where he mysteriously disappears, just as so many others who stood in the way of the 'counter-scientists.' While Ghosh delves heavily into the repertoire not only of science fiction, but also of the ghost story genre by providing the immortalists with supernatural powers, it is instructive that the central focus of the ghost story plot is a mysterious railway lantern associated with Lakhaan, Mangala's second-in-command. Once more it is a central symbol of colonial modernity, the railway, that is appropriated by the clandestine sect, and the fact that their opponents are run over by ghost trains – rather than being slain by religious thugs,

---

1   For "postcolonialist" readings of *The Calcutta Chromosome* as a tribute to "subaltern science" see Mathur and Romanik.

for example – clearly shows that even in the most gothic parts of his novel Ghosh is signaling toward a specifically Indian modernity rather than to the notion of a timeless Indian spirituality as an alternative to 'Western reason'. If *The Calcutta Chromosome* is full of strange encounters, then, it is not because "East is East and West is West, and never the twain shall meet," but because Ghosh needs to propel his fantastic plot toward its even more fantastic conclusion at an ever faster rate, and because he is eventually more interested in ironically exposing the manifold links between scientific progress and colonialism than in a sustained exploration of the location of science in an evolving Indian modernity.

Ghosh's novel *The Hungry Tide* (2004) presents an altogether different picture. Once more science is at the center of attention, but this time the focus is not on the colonial laboratory, but on the complex hybrid web constituted by scientific research, nature, culture, and politics. Piya, a young Indian-born biologist who grew up in Seattle, comes to the Sundarbans, a vast mangrove forest area in northeast India stretching into southwest Bangladesh, to study the rare river dolphins found in this unique ecosystem. With the help of Fokir, an illiterate fisherman whose local knowledge and boating skills prove invaluable to her research, and Kanai, a successful middle class educationalist from New Delhi who has come to the small island Lusibari to visit his aunt, she not only discovers important new scientific facts about this severely endangered species of marine mammals, but also learns to understand the complex "hybrid network" of which they form a part.

Large parts of the Sundarbans are heavily protected natural reserves where large numbers of crocodiles and one of the largest populations of wild tigers on the Indian subcontinent are to be found. The area is almost totally under the control of the Forestry Department, which – as Piya realizes soon after her arrival – rules over the local population in the manner of an occupying army. While environmental protection (particularly of the rare tigers) is given the highest priority, the interests of the local population, many of whom are economically marginalized fishermen or agricultural workers, are hardly ever heard in the faraway centers where political decisions are made. A particularly striking example of this "hybrid network" is the conflict between tigers and humans: hundreds of people in the Sundarbans are killed by tigers every year, but these killings have long since become routine, with the political and administrative officials hardly seeming interested in the situation of the local population. When scientists suggest that the tigers may come close to humans because they are looking for drinking water, a large number of freshwater wells are drilled for the tigers, while on many of the islands the local population does not yet have access to clean drinking water. One of the central events in the plot is the violent eviction of settlers (mainly refugees from Bangladesh) from an island that they had unlawfully occupied; like an invading army, the Forestry Department eventually storms the island, kills many of the settlers, and deports the rest. Kanai's uncle, who visits the island just before this violent climax, notes down the despair of Fokir's mother, one of these 'illegal settlers,' in his diary:

> 'Saar,' she said, wiping her face, 'The worst part was not the hunger or the thirst. It was to sit here, helpless, and listen to the policemen making their announcements, hearing them say that our lives, our existence, were worth less than dirt or dust. "This island has to be saved for its trees, it has to be saved for its animals, it is a part of a reserve forest, it belongs to a project to save tigers, which is paid for by people from all around the world." Every day, sitting here, with hunger gnawing at our bellies, we would listen to these words, over and over again. Who are these people, I wondered, who love animals so much that they are willing to kill us for them [...]? (Ghosh, *Hungry Tide* 261-2)

As the plot of the novel unfolds, Piya (and the readers of the text) increasingly become aware that her scientific research forms part of a larger network in which politics, culture, and 'nature' have long since become inextricably intertwined. 'Nature' itself is, of course, no longer simply 'wild,' but part of a politically engineered whole, and even the animals themselves have turned into 'hybrid monsters' whose very existence in a densely populated part of the country forms part of a larger 'hybrid' network.

In a particularly striking scene, villagers illegally slaughter a tiger that has previously killed both people and livestock and has been trapped in a hut during yet another raid. What happens here is clearly not a simple confrontation between man and animal; both the tiger and the villagers' reactions toward it have become monstrous because they are embedded in a mélange of nature, culture, economic interests, science, environmentalism, and politics:

> Directly in front of them, a few hundred meters away, was a small mud-walled structure with a thatched roof. More than a hundred people had gathered around this little hut. Most of them were men and many were armed with sharpened bamboo poles: these they were plunging into the hut again and again. Their faces were contorted in such a way that they seemed to be in the grip of both extreme fear and uncontrollable rage. Many of the women and children in the crowd were shrieking, *Maar! Maar!* Kill! Kill! [...]
>
> Kanai had been translating continuously as Horen was speaking, but at this point Piya stopped him. In a shaking voice, she said, 'Do you mean to tell me that the tiger's still in there?'
>
> 'Yes,' said Kanai, 'that's what he says. It's trapped inside and blinded.'
>
> Piya shook her head as if to wake herself from a nightmare: the scene was so incomprehensible and yet so vivid that it was only now she understood that it was the incapacitated animal that was being attacked with the sharpend staves. [...] There was a sudden surge of people around them and she was pushed up against the man who was stand-

ing next to Fokir. Now, at close quarters, she saw in the dancing light of the flame, that the man's spear-point was stained with blood and that there were bits of black and gold fur stuck between the splinters. It was as if she could see the animal cowering inside the pen, recoiling from the bamboo spears, licking the wounds that had been gouged into its flesh. (291-2; 293-4)

The Hungry Tide does not suggest, of course, that the killing of the tiger is justified; as readers we are made to share Piya's revulsion at this slaughter and probably also her admonition that "you can't take revenge on an animal" (294). As Piya herself comes to understand, however, this killing takes place in a context where 'environmentalism' is administered in an extremely authoritarian manner by a bureaucracy that – in a quasi-colonial manner – takes no interest in the lives of the people living in the protected area, and where 'environmental justice' as yet seems unheard of. In this context, even her own scientific research on the river dolphins becomes part of a peculiar "hybrid network" – but also a possible means of bringing about 'positive change'. What is ultimately staged in *The Hungry Tide*, then, is not a confrontation between 'Western' notions of environmental protection and 'Indian' local realities where environmentalism is simply a luxury; as the novel stresses time and again, environmental protection and sustainable development are vital both for the fragile ecosystem of the Sundarbans and for the survival of the people who live there. Rather, it is a growing insight into the 'location of science' in the complex "hybrid networks" that constitute a specific mode of modernity that has evolved in this part of India. This process gives rise to what I have in a somewhat Habermasian manner called "succeeding dialogues" in the novel between actors with vastly different interests and cultural backgrounds; at the end of the novel, Piya suggests that the huge internationally financed research project that her own pathbreaking dolphin research has catalysed be administered through a local community organization: "I don't want to do the kind of work that places the burden of conservation on those who can least afford it" (397).

Interestingly enough, Piya's insight into the 'hybrid' location of science is echoed in the novel by Kanai's insight into the 'hybrid' location of culture. In going through his uncle's diary, Kanai realizes that the boundary-blurring landscape of the Sundarbans, where water and land are in constant flux and which is inhabited by a unique blend of cultures and peoples, is a 'hybrid' zone. As his uncle puts it:

How could it be otherwise? For this I have seen confirmed many times, that the mudbanks of the tide country are shaped not only by rivers of silt, but also by rivers of language: Bengali, English, Arabic, Hindi, Arakanese and who knows what else? Flowing into one another they create a proliferation of small worlds that hang suspended in the flow. And so it dawned on me: the tide country's faith is something like one of its great mohonas, a meeting not just of many rivers, but a round-about people can use to pass in many directions – from country to country and even between faiths and religions. (247)

To conclude: The two novels discussed in this paper are excellent examples of the complexity involved in "cultural encounters" in a world of decentered modernity. In coming to terms with that complexity, neither 'realist' notions of cultures as self-contained transhistorical entities nor 'deconstructive' programs of endlessly highlighting 'Western' distortions of 'other' cultures are likely to be of much help. What has to be borne in mind, however, is that the discourses of scholarship (including the discourses of science) are never just analyses of these encounters, but always have a performative stake in them as well. It is in this sense that I have tried to explore the potential of Latour's "hybrid systems" for making us aware of the connections between science, culture, and literature – not by collapsing them into each other in some kind of cosmic 'postcolonial hybridity,' but in a much more specific mode of highlighting the complex manner in which they are articulated in Ghosh's texts.

"But these are only fictions," one might assert, "and we all know that there is no world outside the text." Perhaps we ought to remind ourselves from time to time, one might reply, that there is no text outside the world either, and that the discourses of scholarship and those of literature often wrestle with the same demons. And if it is true that we need to face up to the hybrid monsters that – pace Latour – shape the modernities we inhabit, succeeding dialogues in literature (just like succeeding dialogues *with* literature) might just be a promising point to start that engagement.

References

Appadurai, Arjun. *Modernity at Large. Cultural Dimensions of Globalization.* Minneapolis: University of Minnesota Press, 1996.

Barker, Francis, et al. (eds.). *Europe and Its Others: Proceedings of the Essex Conference on the Sociology of Literature, July 1984.* Vol. 1 and 2. Colchester: University of Essex, 1985.

Baumann, Zygmunt. *Liquid Modernity.* Cambridge: Polity Press, 2000.

Beck, Ulrich. *World Risk Society.* Cambridge/Malden, Mass.: Polity Press, 1999.

---. *Global America? The Cultural Consequencs of Globalization.* Liverpool: Liverpool University Press, 2003.

Beck, Ulrich, Anthony Giddens, and Scott Lash. *Reflexive Modernization: Politics, Tradition and Aesthetics in the Modern Social Order.* Oxford: Polity Press, 1994.

Chakrabarty, Dipesh. *Provincializing Europe: Postcolonial Thought and Historical Difference.* Princeton, NJ: Princeton University Press, 2000.

Chatterjee, Partha. *Our Modernity.* Rotterdam/Dakar: South-South Exchange Programme for Research on the History of Development (SEPHIS) and Council for the Development of Social Science Research in Africa (CODESRIA), 1997.

Eisenstadt, Shmuel N. "Multiple Modernities." *Daedalus*, 129.1 (2000): 1-29.

Ghosh, Amitav. *The Circle of Reason*. 1986; London: Granta, 1998.

---. *The Calcutta Chromosome: A Novel of Fevers, Delirium and Discovery*. 1996; London: Picador, 1997.

---. *The Hungry Tide*. 2004; London: HarperCollins, 2005.

Giddens, Anthony. *The Consequences of Modernity*. 1990; Oxford: Polity Press, 1994.

---. *Runaway World: How Globalisation Is Reshaping Our Lives*. London: Profile, 1999.

Jameson, Fredric. *Singular Modernity: Essay on the Ontology of the Present*. London: Verso, 2002.

Latour, Bruno. *We Have Never Been Modern*. Trans. Catherine Porter. 1991; Cambridge, Mass: Harvard UP, 1993.

Lyotard, Jean-François. *The Postmodern Condition. A Report on Knowledge*. Minneapolis: University of Minnesota Press, 1985.

Mathur, Suchitra. "Caught Between the Goddess and the Cyborg: Third-World Women and the Politics of Science in Three Works of Indian Science Fiction." *Journal of Commonwealth Literature*, 39.3 (2004): 119-38.

Romanik, Barbara. "Transforming the Colonial City: Science and the Practice of Dwelling in *the Calcutta Chromosome*." *Mosaic*, 38.3 (2005): 41-57.

Said, Edward. *Orientalism*. 1978; London: Penguin, 1987.

CHAPTER ELEVEN

Wampum as a Cultural Broker in Northeastern America, 1620-60

CLAUDIA SCHNURMANN

Wampum, or zeawant,[1] are small cylindrical beads made from freshwater shells. White wampum is made from sea snails called periwinkles; if the beads are of a black or dark purple color they are made from quahog clams.[2] Wampum is not only pretty to look at and still a fashionable accessory in high demand in the twenty-first century. It also intrigued historians, ethnologists, biologists, and politically interested groups in earlier times as well as it does today. An overwhelming amount of literature exists on this topic. It is equally difficult to resist the alluring temptations of the traditional historiographical literature that deals with the complex aspects raised by the manifold meanings of wampum in North American cultures. The research done on wampum is extensive. Of equal fascination are recent discussions about ownership of so-called wampum belts, wampum on strings combined to form belt-like pieces of art, as an expression and symbol of indigenous identity. Some of the First Nations in Canada as well as Native Americans within the USA are involved in conflicts with the governments of Canada and the US over the question of who has a legal claim to own and to keep special wampum belts.[3]

Although the topic of 'wampum' occupied and still occupies people from different walks of life, scholars only rarely differentiate between the functions given to wampum within different Native American and European societies: with some exceptions, wampum is considered either in its Native American context or within the colonial context of New Netherland/New York, and New England or the Chesapeake colonies. It is hardly ever regarded as an item connecting peoples, as a medium of different cultural attitudes, or as an object that embodies the interdependencies of all peoples involved in its different usages.

---

1 Many spelling variations of zeawant existed, for example "sewant," "seewan," or "sewan," to name but a few.
2 A very important contribution to the extensive literature on wampum is the article by Scozzari.
3 See arguments about the return of wampum belts to Native Americans/First Nations; webpages of the Oneida and Mohawk, etc. http://aboriginallegal.ca/docs/JWG.htm [21.05.2006]; http://www.wampumshop.com/default.asp?page=3 [21.05.2006]; http://www.degiyagoh.net/guswenta_two_row.htm [21.05.2006]; http://www.oneida-nation.net/culture/wampum.html [21.05.2006]; for literature see Foster 111.

This chapter will summarize the disparate and multifaceted research done on the usage of wampum before, during, and shortly after the contact period in northeastern America. This area is defined as the region between the Delaware and Hudson Rivers and Cape Cod. Special attention will be paid to the Algonquian-speaking Native Americans, members of the Iroqouis-speaking Native American nations, and Euro-Americans within colonial North America, i.e., in New England and in New Netherland.

Algonquian and Iroquoian Usage of Wampum before European Interference

Sufficient archaeological evidence exists on the early presence of wampum in Native American societies (Shiel). Specialists differentiate between proto-wampum in the Northeast of North America from circa 200-1510 A.D., and the so-called true wampum in the contact period of the sixteenth century and the first decades of the seventeenth century (Fenton 224-39; Ceci, *Effect of European Contact*). It is important to note that the so-called "true" wampum itself and the term "wampum" with its several variations were used by peoples who belonged to different linguistic families: The term – a shortened version of "wam pumpeage," "wom pomp e ak," or "sewant," (*Webster's Dictionary*) – as well as the beads themselves[4] were created by Algonquian-speaking Native Americans who lived close to the North American salt marshes of the Atlantic Ocean, which are rich in sea shells.

The Algonquians collected sea snails and clams in the shallow waters of the Atlantic. They feasted on the tasty contents of those easy to catch and delicious mollusks or dried them for further trade. Then they turned the protective shells into decorative jewelry to adorn their bodies and dresses (Speck 3-71; Ceci, "Native Wampum" 49). Besides this casual usage of wampum for decoration, the beads slowly acquired other functions for their makers. The tiny, seemingly fragile beads were in high demand with the Iroquois, who belonged to a different language group. As the Iroquois were living in the woodlands, they depended on their cousins, the Algonquians, to supply them with those maritime items. To Iroquois who lived far away from the sea, wampum acquired a special value, whereas it was considered as less valuable by the people living on the Atlantic coast. Together with the Algonquian product – the beads called wampum – Iroquois integrated the term "wampum" into their culture. In addition to beads made from shellfish found on America's Atlantic coast, European beads made of glass, stone, bone, wood, ceramic, and/or beads taken from rosaries were used either as intertribal trade items, as symbols of friendship and peace, for declarations of war and

---

4   "Each dark purple bead was valued at two white beads." See the fine article by Hamell 42.

peace, or simply as gifts.[5] Since the very first Indian-European encounters, Native Americans used European items in ways surprising and sometimes amusing to European observers (Schnurmann, *Europa trifft Amerika* passim).[6] Even the European explanation for wampum, the word 'beads,' still retains its Old World origins because it is an offspring of the Anglo-Saxon verb 'bede' that had made its way into the Christian meaning of the German verb 'beten' or the English verb 'to pray.'[7]

One indigenous story dating back to the sixteenth-century reports that the Iroquois chief and nation builder Hiawatha stole clams from wild ducks and used the shells for rituals. This founding myth of the Iroquois parallels stories of dangerous, monstrous birds decorated with wampum that were killed by brave Iroquois warriors (Fenton 226; Speck). In these traditional narratives wampum is not considered as a manufactured Algonquian product and trade item but is brought to the Iroquois from distant, unknown countries by natural beings capable of traveling long distances and carrying items. In a subtle way these myths 'iroquoized' the foreign Algonquian product: as wampum's profane origin, its commercial and material nature were given up in favor of Iroquois imaginative powers, practical skills, and expertise. As hunters living in a wooded habitat, the Iroquois warriors were quite familiar with birds: real birds like ducks as well as fantasy winged

5   In all the mentioned cases, wampum was considered as a commodity that was given and taken in an exchange also called presentation and acceptation of gifts. This Native American perception of an exchange of goods as an exchange of gifts would survive for many years to come. At the base of this exchange lay the notion that only such things were presentated, given, and taken that carried value for both sides. The more abstract the value connected with an object, the more importance was conveyed by it as it proved the value of the object itself, the person who gave it up, and the value the giver saw in the person who enjoyed the present. This idea, however, could only hold within an exchange of goods by people who cherished the same cultural notions.

6   See, for example, a report by Samuel de Champlain in 1603: "Now after they had made good cheer, the Algonquins, one of the three nations, went out of their lodges, and withdrew by themselves into an open place. Here they arranged all their women and girls side by side, and themselves stood behind, singing all in unison in the manner I have already described. Suddenly all the women and girls proceeded to cast off their mantles of skins, and stripped themselves stark naked, showing their privities, but retaining their ornaments of matachias, which are beads and braided cords made of porcupine quills, dyed of various colours. After they had made an end of their songs, they cried all with one voice, Ho ho, ho; at the same instant all the women and girls covered themselves with their mantles, which were at their feet, and they had a short rest; then all at once beginning again to sing, they let fall their mantles as before […]" (Quinn, *Newfoundland* 4: 397-8). Jacques Cartier wrote: "[…] While making our way along the [north] shore, we caught sight of the Indians on the side of a lagoon and low beach, who were making many fires that smoked. We rowed over to the spot, and finding there was an entrance from the sea into the lagoon, we placed our longboats on one side of the entrance. The savages came over in one of their canoes and brought us some strips of cooked seal, which they placed on bits of wood and then withdrew, making signs to us that they were making us a present of them. We sent two men on shore with hatchets, knives, beads and other wares, at which the Indians showed great pleasure. And at once they came over in a crowd in their canoes to the side where we were, bringing furs and whatever else they possessed, in order to obtain some of our wares […]" (Quinn, *America* 1: 300).

7   See http://www.rosaryworkshop.com/HistoryjournalingBead.htm [04.06.2006]

animals that loomed large in legends and art. Consequently, the stories reacted to and celebrated Iroquoian way of life by ascribing wampum's origin to the skills of sophisticated hunters and warriors who used all the necessary tricks of surprising and killing.

Before Europeans made their problematic appearance in North America, regional or long-distance trade between members of the Algonquin and the Iroquois did not run as smoothly as had other commercial networks between Native American peoples across the continent since the thirteenth and fourteenth centuries. Manufactured beads in the true sense of the meaning 'manu-factum' were only traded across the northeastern American mainland in small numbers. The reasons for this rarity are obvious. One was that long-distance trade had to be conducted on foot or in canoes. The extreme hardship of travel could easily be made even more difficult by just the slightest increase in intertribal Native American conflicts.

The other reason for hampered commercial relations between these Native American nations had to do with the imbalance between supply and demand. Before the arrival of Europeans on the American mainland, the Algonquians living close to the Atlantic Ocean were probably not too interested in items that the Iroquois, the people from the interior woodlands, had to offer in exchange for beads. The exchange of Algonquian wampum for Iroquois products drawn from agricultural and forestry economies seems to have occurred at a very low level during the pre-contact era. Some scholars believe that the European demand for beaver furs increased Algonquian-Iroquois trade to such an extent that the coastal Native American nations, who no longer had access to beaver, bought furs from the Mohawk/Mohican in exchange for wampum, and then sold furs to Europeans in exchange for goods they cherished like European textiles, food, beverages, and metal goods. It seems that Europeans during the first contact period, at the turn of the sixteenth to the seventeenth century, had not yet recognized the importance of wampum as a means to circumvent the Algonquians and trade directly with the Iroquois (Ceci, "Native Wampum" 49).

The coastal producers of wampum kept the majority of those carefully and laboriously crafted beads or strings of beads to themselves and used them to decorate their bodies and to apply them to their dresses. Some of the beads were used for negotiating the everyday internal management of normal relations or alleviating strained ones (matchmaking, medicine, compensation, rehabilitation, and the like), or as gifts to visitors, friends, or former enemies (Speck passim).

With regard to the difficulties in acquiring wampum, the Iroquois esteemed the beads as prime goods, crucial to their cultural ceremonies and for conducting relations with other nations they had fought or wanted to appease. Given the problematic supply channels, the maritime origin of wampum, and the resulting rarity, the landlubber Iroquois invested those precious things with a spiritual value and with symbolic meanings that exceeded the Algonquian perception of wampum as but a useful commodity of everyday life. The Algonquian attitude, however, was understandable because they knew the comparatively humble origin of the hand-made product. Nevertheless, their respect for wampum also grew, and as the seventeenth century proceeded, its cultural, social, and economic value also rose in the perceptions of the Narragansetts, the Pequot, Niantics, and Mohegan of southern New England as well as the Corchaugs, Montaucks, and Shinnecocks who lived on Long Island. All those nations – men as well as women – put an increasing amount of time, energy, and expertise into producing these seemingly fragile but durable gems.

The Iroquois blended the imported beads with their own foundation myths, identity, and self-esteem (Fenton 225). During the sixteenth and at the beginning of the seventeenth century, true wampum (beads of a special size, form, and color) among the Iroquois was rare and its rarity made the few specimens even more valuable and desirable. This mechanism was well known to Europeans who had built their economy on the same correlation of rarity and value in their estimation of precious metals like gold and silver, jewels like diamonds, or pearls (which, incidentally, also originated from maritime fauna). Hurons and Mohawk alike used their few wampum beads, put them on strings and combined them to fashion wampum belts, which were used in politics (as symbols of sovereignty), external affairs, diplomatic relations, and as public records. The founding of the Iroquois confederacy (probably in the sixteenth century) was celebrated with the ceremonial presentation of a sophisticated wampum belt kept by the Onondaga. This archival function of the wampum belt reflects the Onondaga's special position, high prestige, wealth, and strong authority within the confederacy. This idea did not differ from European greed for princely treasures, vaults, and crown jewels (Fenton).[8]

The Hurons, who were Iroquois but not members of the Iroquois confederacy, gave a wampum belt to Samuel de Champlain in 1611[9] and the Mohawk celebrated an agreement with traders from the New Netherland Company in 1617 by ceremoniously presenting them with a wampum belt as a worthy symbol of peace, friendship, and communication. This legal act marked an important change in Dutch-Mohawk relations, and had long-term effects.[10]

As the previous discussion shows, wampum was a trade good loaded with different meanings, functions, and values. The value of wampum depended first on its producers, who knew perfectly well its unspectacular origins and had direct experience with its time-consuming production, and second on people who were

---

8   Regarding the extensive discussion about the founding date of the Iroquois League (Mohawk, Oneida, Onondaga, Cayuga, Seneca) in the fifteenth or sixteenth century (1560-70), see Tooker 418-41.
9   For the Iroquois-speaking Huron and their wampum trade with the Algonquian-speaking Susquehannock, see Heidenreich 368-88. Concerning this event and the use of wampum in Iroquois culture generally, see Trigger, *Natives and Newcomers* 178.
10 Treaty of Tawasentha, 1617. For the wide reaching effect of this treaty for European-Indian relations in general, and for Dutch-Mohawk relations in particular, see Sullivan 96.

far removed from wampum resources and production sites, and therefore charged wampum with a particular symbolic significance.

Enter the Europeans

Starting with Christopher Columbus at the end of the fifteenth century, and well into the sixteenth century, there are many descriptions of Europeans who tried to cheat Native Americans in barter exchanges without knowing about the Native Americans' different cultural attitudes toward the material, form, and color of wampum.[11] While indigenous peoples on the Caribbean Islands and in the Mexico-Texas regions cherished European artifacts made in Italy, Spain, Germany, or the Netherlands, their northern neighbors, the Algonquians and Iroquois, did not consider these Atlantic imports, also trifles to European eyes, as the 'real thing.' They had developed a strong sense for the quality and aesthetics of true American artifacts. Beads of special color shades produced with traditional indigenous drilling tools made from stone or fire hardenend wood were especially valued. The Algonquian sachem Powhatan, who admired the European blue glass beads that Englishman John Smith had shown him in the early days of Virginia, was clearly an exception. As Smith wants to make his readers believe, Powhatan was much smitten by Smith's fantastic explanation that those bright blue beads were made from a very special substance; perhaps taken from a piece of sky:

> Captaine Smith being our interpreter, [...] knowing best the disposition of Powhatan, tould us his intent was but onely to cheate us; yet Captaine Newport thinking to out brave this Salvage in ostentation of greatnesse, and so to bewitch him with his bountie, as to have what he listed, it so hapned [!], that Powhatan having his desire, valued his corne at such a rate, that I thinke it better cheape in Spaine: for we had not foure bushels for that we expected to have twentie hogsheads. This bred some unkindnesse betweene our two Captaines; Newport seeking to please the unsatiable desire of the Salvage, Smith to cause the Salvage to please him; but smothering his distast to avoid the Salvages suspi-

11 See for example Columbus's journal, ed. Cecil Jane. In 1536-37, Alvar Nuñez Cabeza de Vaca wrote about his trip to Texas-Mexico (1527-28) that their Native American counterparts really invested in those exchanges of courtesies by parting from things they valued highly, like arrows: "Half an hour after, they were supported by one hundred other Indian bowmen, who if they were not large, our fears made giants of them. They stopped near us with the first three. It were idle to think that any among us could make defence, for it would have been difficult to find six that could rise from the ground. The assessor and I went out and called to them, and they came to us. We endeavored the best we could to encourage them and secure their favour. We gave them beads and hawk-bells, and each of them gave me an arrow, which is a pledge of friendship. They told us by signs that they would return in the morning and bring us something to eat, as at that time they had nothing." In parting from these items, the making of which required complex handicraft and skills, the Indians demonstrated their willingness for peace and friendship – which the Spaniards noticed but did not value as much as the Indians had assumed (Quinn, *Major Spanish Searches* 2: 28).

tion, glanced in the eyes of Powhatan many trifles, who fixed his humor upon a few blew beades. A long time he importunately desired them, but Smith seemed so much the more to affect them, as being composed of a most rare substance of the coulour of the skyes, and not to be worne but by the greatest kings in the world. This made him halfe madde to be the owner of such strange Jewells: so that ere we departed, for a pound or two of blew beades, he brought over my king for 2. or 300 Bushells of corne; yet parted good friends. The like entertainment we found of Opechankanough king of Pamaunkee, whom also he in like manner fitted (at the like rates) with blew beads, which grew by this meanes, of that estimation, that none durst weare any of them but their great kings, their wives and children [...]. (Smith, *Generall Historie of Virginia* qtd. Barbour 2: 156-7)[12]

Perhaps the value Powhatan assigned to those cheap European imports resulted from Smith's explanation of the quasi-sacred origin of the blue beads. Perhaps the idea of carrying a piece of heaven in his fetish bag was as appealing to the sachem of the Powhatans as the idea of owning a piece of wampum, an element of the sea, and therefore becoming representative of its sublime power.

While European explorers and fortune hunters like Jacques Cartier,[13] Samuel de Champlain,[14] Henry Hudson, and Robert Juet[15] were aware of the existence of wampum in Algonquian societies beginning from the 1530s, to the first decade of the seventeenth century, they were unaware of how high a value wampum held for the Iroquois, and consequently did not exploit the beads' potential in acquiring Iroquois furs. The French Jesuits who in the 1610s sent home letters in which they reported their experience with Algonquians on the Saint Lawrence River did not mention or consider anything that resembled wampum, porcelain, and the like

12 See Lapham for an impressively extensive list of literature.
13 About the use of wampum as ransom, gift, trifle, means of corruption, and peace see, for example, the remarks of Jacques Cartier on his second journey in: Jameson 82; or see "sewan" in http://www.gutenberg.org/dirs/etext00/mohwk10.txt passim [31.08.2007] "Donnacona [...] gave him [the French captain] a present of foure and twenty chaines of Esurgny, for that is the greatest and preciosest riches they have in this world, for they esteeme more of that, then of any gold or silver." He also provided his audience with a gruesome description of the disgusting methods of selecting those mollusks, which the Native Americans of Hochelaga needed to produce wampum. In 1535 Cartier remarked on the use of freshwater shells by the inhabitants of Hochelaga before they were driven away by the Iroquois: "Of them [shells] they make beads, and wear them about their necks, even as we doe chains of gold and silver, accounting it the preciousest thing in the world [...] no care of any other wealth or commodities in this world. For they have no knowledge of it, and that is, because they never travel and go out of their country [...]" (Cartier's second voyage, in: Jameson 60). Cartier expanded the local perspective of some of the inhabitants of Hochelaga when he took (or more probably kidnapped) them to France. Even today, moccasins – decorated with porcupine quills – that once graced the feet of some of the Indians of Hochelaga are part of the exhibits of the Musée de l'Homme in Paris (Allain 1).
14 Report of Samuel de Champlain and François Gravé du Pont on an expedition to the Saint Lawrence River in September 1603, and a visit to the Algonquians and the Montagnais, standing between Algonquians and the Iroquois, in Quinn (ed.). *Newfoundland* 4: 397f.
15 See Meuwese 45.

as worthy of their notice, while they paid much attention to beaver pelts as trading items.[16]

The decision to engage in this trade and combine beaver pelts with wampum was the clever move of the merchants of the New Netherland Company: the change was probably triggered by the experience of 1617 when a wampum belt presented by the Mohawk in a highly charged ceremony greatly impressed the Dutch merchants. By 1620 (and 1622 at the latest) Dutch traders extorted wampum from Algonquian hostages as ransom (Gehring; Meuwese, passim).[17]

Due to Dutch-Mohawk bonding, Dutch demand for fur increased, and in the Dutch perception of business, wampum acquired a new status between 1617 and 1622. Wampum from that period onward sucessfully connected Native Americans and Europeans in an economic and cultural Atlantic system in which all participants could profit from or use natural resources to their specific advantages and thus satisfy their specific demands. Under those circumstances wampum acquired a new function: it was simultaneously used as a commodity in a Native American sense, as a cheap substitute for bullion, a cashless payment in a European sense, and as an object of cultural yearning. Wampum was used particularly by Europeans in the purchase of beaver pelts and thereby helped to support the enterprise "New Netherland."

In the early years of the colony, New Netherland and its settlers were regarded by the Dutch West India Company back home as nothing but a side show. Impressive profits could be made by the Dutch East India Company in the Asian trade while Dutch settlements in the West Indies, i.e., America, were considered long-term and therefore tedious investments (Schnurmann, "'Wherever Profit Leads us'"). The rather more cherished short term quick profits on the American mainland were expected from trade and especially trade in beaver furs. In the rainy, windy and cold but fashion-conscious Netherlands, furs were needed to satisfy the high demand for fancy hats in the Rembrandt style, as those posh pieces were later called. A look at the marvelous paintings in two of Amsterdam's museums, the Rijksmuseum and the Stedelijk Museum, provides people of the twenty-first century with an idea of the prestige that went with those handsome fur hats. The Dutch West India Company recognized the importance of being visibly active in that specific trade branch. The company paid special tribute to the beaver in the official symbol assigned its first and last mainland colony in the Western hemisphere. The 1630 design for a coat of arms for New Netherland reflects the importance of beavers to the colony's economy, existence, and success by highlighting the basis of its riches: the coat of arms depicts beavers and wampum in happy harmony (Jacobs 174).

16 Biard 73: "the savages who have neither copper, iron, hemp, nor manufactured articles of any kind [...] they have no arts." See http: //ia300215.us.archive.org//load_djvu_applet. cgi?file=1/items/jesuits02jesuuoft/jesuits02jesuuoft.djvu [21.09.2007]
17 The term "wampum revolution" was phrased in Salisbury 147-52; 148.

Besides being included in the colony's official symbol, wampum was mentioned in the early correspondence of merchants and administrators in New Amsterdam with the West India Company in the Dutch chambers. Surprisingly neither Oliver Rink's nor Thomas Condon's fine studies on New Netherland pay attention to wampum and its important role in the colony's economy, her trade, and 'foreign relations' (Rink 94-116; Condon).[18] Jaap Jacobs, however, mentions it briefly, but in surprising contrast to his accustomed precision does not do justice to the political and economic impact of wampum on New Netherland activities (Jacobs 174).[19] Let me acknowledge my own oversight in this matter: in my habilitation thesis on Anglo-Dutch communications and networks in the seventeenth-century North Atlantic, I also devoted little attention to wampum and its influence on Anglo-Dutch relations within the North American context (Schnurmann, *Atlantische Welten*).

During the first six years of the Dutch West India Company's control over New Netherland, between 1624 and 1630, the few traders and settlers between the Hudson and the East River sent 42,000 beaver furs to the Netherlands via New Amsterdam. The value of those freights ran up to 330,000 guilders – although it is not clear if this referred to their retail, wholesale, or high street prices.[20] Since the fur animals near the European colonies in the Northeast were soon extinct, all those furs came to *patria* through trade with the Iroquois. Iroquois hunters killed the animals and traded them to Europeans in exchange for the item they wanted most: wampum – the more, the better. The demand for wampum had a positive side effect, as wampum freed the traders from their dependence on crops and the outcome of harvests; the deals were concluded in winter, when the furs were at their best.

Some have argued that the Dutch transferred Old World ideas about the use of cowrie shells from the Indian Ocean and the African slave trade to North America. Cowrie shells were used as money substitutes in Asia and Africa but not yet by the Dutch. Only after the Dutch conquest of Brazil, when the needs of Brazilian sugar cane plantations in the early 1630s became urgent and the Dutch had acquired a stronghold in West Africa, did the Dutch West India Company get involved in the trade with humans, actually buying Africans from other Africans with cowrie shells (Ceci, "Native Wampum" 55).[21] Evidently that happened much later than the Dutch involvement with wampum in New Netherland in the 1610s and 1620s. It does not come as a surprise that Om Pakash in his fine survey of Dutch Asian trade in the early seventeenth century does not mention any cowrie

---

18 Or see Boxer, the doyen of historiography on Dutch expansionism.

19 David Murray also regrets the missing interest in wampum – however, he too steps into the trap of Euro-American arrogance, transferring European notions and ideas to Native American societies, see Murray 121.

20 For precise numbers see Ceci, *Effect* 194, table 9.

21 Johannes M. Postma convincingly describes that the Dutch only in the late 1630s had laid the foundations to enter the slave trade with the capture of Elmina in 1637, see Postma 12f.

as a commodity of interest to the VOC (Pakash; Richter, *Ordeal of the Longhouse* 85; Richter, *Facing East* 45).

There are some hints that the French in Nouvelle France may have developed a sense for the potential of wampum at the same time or even a little bit earlier than the Dutch (Ceci, "Native Wampum," passim). Yet the evidence is rather circumstantial. Perhaps 'wampumpeage,' the word used by Algonquians in close contact with the French, was a combination of the Algonquian word 'wampum' and the French word for payment 'peage.' That might be a hint. However, it is difficult to decide if the Europeans changed an Indian word or if the word linked both cultures, the Algonquian and the French languages.[22]

For some decades Europeans, first in New Netherland and dating from 1627 in Plymouth/New England, supported by Dutch traders like Isaack de Rasières convinced the hesitating New Englanders to participate in the wampum trade as they considered the beads to provide easy access to Indian trade (James 63-80).[23] They would load this American artifact made by Algonquians, this symbol of power, myth, and religious meaning to the Iroquois, with European notions of money, declare it a substitute and a legal tender as well as a trade good. In his journal about the first three decades of Plymouth Plantation, the colony's governor, William Bradford, with hindsight still regarded wampum as a "current commodity," i.e., a trade good to the Narragansetts and Pequot "which grew rich and potent by it." (Bradford 203) In the meantime, de Rasières had already come to the conclusion that wampum could be used as a substitute for money, as cashless payment, "since one can buy with it everything they [the Native Americans] have."[24]

Among the extensive writings on wampum – scholarly as well as popular – one finds irritating comments, remarks, and statements. Of course wampum was not the first American currency, or a currency used by Native Americans. This erroneous judgement is even indirectly echoed by the *Oxford English Dictionary*, which evokes the impression that wampum was "used as money" by the Indians, whereas the more obscure *Nature Bulletin of the Forest Preserve District of Cook County Illinois* rightly questions this idea.[25]

---

22 "Wampum is a contraction from the Algonquian word 'wampumpeage' ([...] pronounced wom pom pe ak) or white shell beads. Historical wampum is small (1/8 inch wide) usually cylindrical, white and purple beads, handpolished, drilled, and strung into strings [...]." http://nativeweb.org/resources/crafts_indigenous_technology/beads_beadwork/ [14.02.2006]

23 On the role of Isaack de Rasières, see Ceci, "Native Wampum" 58.

24 Isaack de Rasières wrote to Samuel Blommaert in 1628: "As an employment in winter they [Indians] make sewan, which is an oblong bead that they make from cockle-shells, which they find on the sea-shore, and they consider it as valuable as we do money here, since one can buy with it everything they have. They string it, and wear it around the neck and hands; they also make bands of it, which the women wear on the forehead under the hair, and the men around the body; and they are as particular about the stringing and sorting as we can be here about pearls [...]" (James, 63-80, quote on 69-70).

25 See the following websites: http://www.askoxford.com/results/?view=dict&freesearch= wampum&branch=13842570&textsearchtype=exact; http://www.newton.dep.anl.gov/natbltn /700-799/nb725.htm [31.08.2007]

Rather, wampum was an artifact, a trade good that provided Europeans with a key to Indian trade. It was a commodity that served different Native American peoples in different ways and yes, it was used as legal tender – but only in European business exchanges because the colonists lacked other acceptable currencies for payments, particularly gold and silver coins (although Spanish pieces of eight, guilders, and taler were also used). However, wampum was not a currency in European-Indian exchange but a kind of cashless payment. The simple fact that wampum did not make it to *patria* and into the Dutch Republic's economy, whereas cowrie from the Indian Ocean did, is a hint that colonists considered it an All-American item not fit for Europe. For them, it was just a useful but unattractive tool to make the Atlantic trade in America work.

How did this trade function? As Europeans tended to regulate things and tried hard to create order when they felt lost in chaos they tried to organize trade within North America the way they were used to. One way to do so was by regulating, standardizing, and controlling the quality of the goods they used as substitutes for cash. Several kinds of monies were simultaneously used by Europeans: rare Dutch, German, English, and Spanish coins, bills of exchange, and trade goods like beaver pelts, tobacco leaves that came from the growing tobacco production in the Chesapeake colonies, Virginia and later Maryland, cocoa beans in the South, and finally shell beads, true wampum, and crude European fakes (McCusker 157).

American shell beads made by Algonquians and European manufactured goods like textiles, metal wares, rifles, and alcohol were the only goods Native Americans cherished and regarded as treasures. Europeans regarded the Indian input to American trade, their locally produced beads, as mere trifles and crude trash that could be transformed into currency or cash according to European will and design. On the other side, those Iroquois who harbored strong desires for Algonquian wampum and European goods (not accidentally they called the Dutch "knife makers") had beaver pelts to offer, something they considered trifles. At first these were easy to get and in abundance, but Europeans nevertheless considered them treasures because from their point of view, the pelts had come a long way.

Before Europeans had come to America, most beavers had led a perfectly happy life there. They had been left mostly unmolested by humans and allowed to concentrate on their dam building. A European sense of fashion and demand for warm hats made of beaver fur changed that for good. First Algonquians, then Iroquois hunted beavers and other hairy mammals, destroyed their environment, and changed their habitat. In the long run Native Americans were forced to withdraw further West, a process that set other Native American nations into motion and created conflicts over hunting grounds where the means to acquire wampum and life style could be found.

Wampum and manufactured goods represented the connection between Europeans and Native Americans. Some have argued against the notion of wampum as an equivalent of a currency – i.e., that it was a form of cashless payment to Europeans and Euro-Americans in their New World. But was it truly a currency? No doubt it was used in exchanges between Europeans in New Netherland/New England, but only on a low value level, on a daily business basis, and only during the first two generations of colonial life when bullion was rare and rates of exchange were set (Van Laer, passim).

Most Europeans used wampum as a payment, bought and sold it but considered it as an inferior currency. For them it was a pragmatic answer to the market's demand in a society that considered itself at the margin of civilization and in close contact with wilderness and brute savages.

Many colonists, no matter if they originated from the Netherlands, from German territories, from France, or from the British Isles, considered wampum a plain, simple, crude item made by savage Indians. It was used in trade with Indians in which the Europeans believed themselves to have the upper hand because wampum was supposedly only a savage trifle adored by godless Indians.

Evidence for the acknowledgment of wampum as a currency even in Europe can be deduced from the so-called Schagen letter, which documents the purchase of Manhattan from the Lenape tribe on 24 May 1626:

> Yesterday the ship the Arms of Amsterdam arrived here. It sailed from New Netherland out of the River Mauritius on the 23d of September. [...] They have purchased the Island Manhattes from the Indians for the value of 60 guilders. It is 11,000 morgens in size [about 22,000 acres] [...]. (Kavenagh 2: 755)[26]

This letter, written on 5 November 1626, is generally taken as proof of the purchase of – indeed of tough European bargaining for – Manhattan, as there is hardly any other evidence of this unique historical real estate transaction. However, the letter leaves some room for misinterpretation. The popular notion that all of Manhattan went just for goods worth sixty guilders, or twenty-four dollars, is somewhat erroneous: more probably, the Lenape did not sell the land itself but only granted its temporary usage to the Dutch.[27] With regard to wampum, the letter is more interesting: the beads which are supposed to have been part of the bargain (as they were in the purchase of Staten Island, see below) must have come from Europe and must have been made of different materials, since it hardly makes any sense to give a product back to its producers. The Algonquians would therefore not have regarded them as real wampum.

Even when Europeans used wampum as a money substitute or talked about places like Gardiners Bay, where wampum was produced by Native Americans, as "the mine" of New Netherland (Secretary van Tienhoven, quoted from Fen-

---

26 For a photographic reproduction of Peter Schagen's famous letter to the directors of the Dutch West India Company, the original of which is held at the Dutch Rijksarchief in Den Haag, see http://www.newnetherlandinstitute.org/nnp/documents/schagen_main.html [31.08.2007]; www.nnp.org/nnp/documents/schaghenletter.html [13.4.2008].

27 http://www.newnetherlandinstitute.org/nnp/documents/60guilder.html [27.08.2008]

ton 227),[28] the colonial government missed one basic effect that for Europeans defined currency: they lacked control of the tender's production, of the amount of wampum in circulation, and of the distribution process. This means that neither the government of New Netherland nor those of the New England colonies had access to all those elements crucial to state controlled bullion. Therefore, the tool that Europeans needed to control the trade with Native Americans was in fact in the hands of the "mintmakers," the Pequots and Narragansetts, who were thus able to turn the table on European arrogance and the perception of European cultural dominance or progress.

The governor of New Netherland was ignorant of the number of wampum producers and their output. It was guessed that between thirty-five and forty-eight beads was the daily output of one producer. Thus, two particularly important principles of monetary regulation could not be fulfilled, either: governmental control over money and the standardization of a currency. Despite those shortcomings, the government of New Netherland as well as that of the New England colonies became infected with the wampum bug. In mutual European arrogance the colonial governments considered wampum as trash that might be exchanged for treasures in the shape of furs. They tried in vain to transfer European control mechanisms to colonial societies and implant European concepts of exchange rates on the wampum producers and the settlers who had their own fish to fry. The result of this governmental weakness and of peoples' strongheadedness was a long list of ordinances, acts, and court decisions designed by colonial governments to organize the hotchpotch of exchange rates, qualities, and commercial behavior. These efforts have been described in detail and need not be repeated here.[29] Only two details should be mentioned in order to prove the regard the government paid to a product of Native American origin. One is provided by Pieter Stuyvesant, who as governor of New Netherland told his employer, the Dutch West India Company, as late as 21 April 1660, "wampum is the source and the mother of the beaver trade, and for goods only, without wampum, we cannot obtain beavers from the savages." (Fernow 8: 470)[30]

Another event provides an idea of the impact wampum had: the attempts of Governor Pieter Minuit to subtly influence the output of beads. In 1626 a group of Native Americans 'sold' an island, later to be called Staten Island in honor of the Dutch States General. Along with other goods, Minuit gave them drilling awls needed for drilling holes into wampum. Minuit regarded that act as a purchase and accordingly considered his input in the deal as payment for property that he was acquiring. Clearly Minuit cherished wrong perceptions of the Native American concepts of property and its transfer with this kind of 'payment'; he never-

28 To demonstrate the impact of Native Americans on the developments and constellations in North America and to get away from their usual representation as victims, Jennings asserts that "Indians were the mintmasters" (93).
29 See the rich information supplied by Jordan.
30 Also see Jordan.

theless hoped that this 'deal' would raise the production of beads in order to meet the rising demand for beavers.[31]

This unruliness of the colonial society on the so-called frontier and the clash of European and Native American interests represented one set of problems; other problems resulted from the Native American origin of the colonial ersatz money, cashless payments. European currencies acquire their value from concepts deeply rooted in Old World ideas of value. Value is created by scarcity, rarity, obstacles to overcome, time and energy invested in prospecting, mining, and working precious materials. As we have seen so far, the thinking that transfers material and collectively agreed abstract value to gold, silver, diamonds, or pearls is not so much different from ideas associated with wampum.

Currency and value are closely related. All parties participating in exchanges and businesses must cherish the same ideas of the abstract value of one item. Otherwise, one side will feel betrayed and the artificially created order will rupture. Europeans perceived themselves as culturally superior. They considered themselves culturally on a much higher level. They believed they could satisfy wild and uncivilized Iroquois savages with knicknacks. Wampum ensured their entry into the Iroquois market for beaver pelts.

This perspective is supported both by contemporary notions and by historiographical research. Most descriptions of the use of wampum are by European witnesses, merchants, fur traders, ministers, or governmental administrators who were deeply interested in their private or public welfare, which depended on the fur trade and its close relation to the wampum trade. Europeans needed wampum to get beaver pelts and arrange minor businesses within their own colony due to a lack of European currencies. Although some of them may have despised their dependency on such a crude, savage, and unsophisticated currency, they knew quite well that much of the raison d'être of New Netherland was based on beaver and that beavers were pulled out of the woods by wampum.

Christian disgust of indigenous commodities is evident in a letter written by Reverend Johannes Megapolensis to the Amsterdam Classis in 1644. By that date the minister of the Dutch Reformed Church had already spent two years in Fort Orange (today Albany/New York) in the heart of Mohawk country. He could neither accept that other cultures had an intrinsic right of existence, nor was he able to see the different concepts of value and exchange. He compared the Native American idea of wampum with the European understanding of money because that was his only way of describing it. Eager to demonstrate his morality and ethics, he compared Mohawk ear jewelry made of wampum with bones. He thereby evoked in the potential reader the image of Native Americans as cruel cannibals. To him, the encounter of civilization with uncultured people was obvious by

---

31 http://www.kstrom.net/isk/art/beads/art_bead.html [04.06.2006] See the treaty explained by Cornelius Melyn: "The natives who were represented by seven named leaders, received for the island, some diffles [duffles], kittles, axes, hoes, wampum, drilling awls, jew's harps [...]" (Francis 60f.).

the Mohawks' disregard of European values expressed by uncontrolled emotions – improper behavior to a staunch Calvinist:

> Their money consists of certain little bones, made of shells or cockles, which are found on the sea-beach; a hole is drilled through the middle of the little bones, and these they string upon thread, or they make of them belts as broad as a hand, or broader, and hang them on their necks, or around their bodies. They have also several holes in their ears, and there they likewise hang some. They value these little bones as highly as Christians do gold, silver and pearls; but they do not like our money, and esteem it no better than iron. I once showed one of their chiefs a rix-dollar; he asked how much it was worth among the Christians; and when I told him, he laughed exceedingly at us, saying we were fools to value a piece of iron so highly; and if he had such money, he would throw it into the river. (Jordan)

Mohawk Reactions and New England's Subjection of the Pequots

A careful analysis of European sources reveals Iroquois concepts of wampum and Iroquois attitudes towards those objects that Europeans assumed the Iroquois regarded as sacred. Of special importance is the slim journal of Harmen Meyndertsz van den Bogaert, who pays tribute to the close commercial relations between Dutch traders and the Mohawk shortly after the Mohawk had driven the Mohican out of the beaver-wampum deals in 1634-35. On one occasion, he "bought a very fat turkey for 2 hands of sewant" (Gehring and Starna 4f.), on another the Mohawk "sold each salmon for one guilder or two hands of sewant" (Gehring and Starna 6). Similarly, van den Bogaert recorded that the Mohawk "said that the French gave them six hands of sewant for one beaver and all sorts of other things in addition" (Gehring and Starna 13). In one instance,

> they [the Mohawk] laid five more beaver skins at my feet, and thereby requested that they would like to have four hands of sewant and four hands of long cloth for each large beaver because 'we have to travel so far with our pelts and when we arrive we often find no cloth, no sewant, no axes, kettles or anything else, and thus we have labored in vain.' (Gehring and Starna 15, 18)

Van den Bogaert also mentions the diplomatic function of wampum: "In the evening the Indians hung up a belt of sewant and some other strung sewant that the chief had brought back from the French Indians as a token of peace that the French Indians were free to come among them" (Gehring and Starna 14). He leaves us in no doubt as to the high value the Mohawk assigned to it by describing how "six and a half fathoms of sewant were stolen from our bags and never recovered" (Gehring and Starna 18), and how one evening, "another 100 fathoms of sewant were distributed to the chiefs and friends of closest blood" (Gehring and Starna 21).

Between the lines van den Bogaert depicts the Mohawk as tough businessmen, who know the market value of their goods as well as their own interests. In fact, both parties engaged in the deals stood their ground. Their behavior also shows that the acquisition of wampum was for them the main goal of trade. Moreover, in the Mohawks' concept wampum did not function as legal tender, cashless payment, or a medium of trade: Iroquois did not sell or buy wampum to use it in other commercial transactions. They did not give it away as part of a bargain the way its producers, the Algonquians, did. Therefore one must differentiate between the three notions of wampum that Iroquois, Algonquians, and Europeans developed. For the Iroquois, wampum had a value that went far beyond its function as a means of cashless payment. Neither did they regard it as cash or as an alternative form of money. The symbolic and economic value Iroquois assigned it influenced their behavior as well as the way they acquired wampum.

The trade in beaver furs had an impact on New Netherland's politics toward their other European neighbors as well as toward the Native Americans upstream. The fight for control over the wampum-beaver supply not only shaped New Netherland's and New England's politics by integrating the different Native American nations into inter-European power constellations in the American Northeast. The Native American nations were actors in these consellations with their very own interests, aims, and methods for reaching their goals. The Mohawk-Mohican wars of the 1620s, which were won by the Mohawk (Sultzman), are only one example of how Native American nations followed their own agendas and considered the Europeans as servants to their interests. It was a question of manpower until Europeans got the upper hand and the Algonquian mintmakers had to surrender to European dominion: in the 1630s New England subdued the Pequot and forced them to pay fees in the form of wampum. More than nine million pieces of wampum thereby entered the New England system, which helped New England's own economic growth without support from storm-ridden England that was headed towards civil war.[32]

We may also recall the bickerings between New Netherland and New England over Long Island in the 1640s, which ended with the Hartford Convention of 1650. The majority of the few historians who paid attention to those early examples of intercolonial affairs considered them as typical colonial conflicts between Europeans over land within an international context (Jacobs, passim; Schnur-

---

32 "The records do indicate that payments between 1634 and 1664 to English colonists amounted [...] to over 21.000 fathoms of wampum – almost 7 million beads [...] beads worth about 5.000 pounds in English currency entered colonial coffers [...] more if double-valued purple beads were included. Thus, a second outcome of the Pequot War was, in effect, the partial underwriting of New England colonization costs by the conquered natives. A third outcome was the creation of a new, English trade triangle [...]" (Ceci, "Native Wampum" 61 and table 1: wampum payments by New England-Long Island Indians, 1634-64, 62). 21.043,4 fathoms equal 6.94 million beads.

mann, passim). This important observation shows that the idea of being independent from European power politics and steering another course than that accepted by the mother countries was not the brain child of the Founding Fathers of 1776, but had been cherished since the middle of the seventeenth century. This European perspective of colonial politics, however, does not tell the whole story. With the conclusion of the Hartford Convention, the Euro-Americans in New Netherland and Connecticut also settled their conflict about the shell resources and the makers of wampum (the mintmakers), especially the Narragansett.[33] The Algonquian word for Long Island, the one bone of contention, was something like 'Sewanhackey,' which means 'place of seawan.' The term itself proves that the Algonquians knew the meaning of Long Island and its potential for their interests, too.[34]

The Effect of Wampum on the American Northeast and the Atlantic Economy

For a correct understanding of wampum it is not really important who discovered its economic potential (the French or the Dutch or the Native Americans themselves) or to answer the question of whether wampum really fits the European definition of a currency. What is important, however, is that for four decades, from the 1620s to the 1660s, wampum was crucial to New Netherland/New England, the European-Indian, and the Indian-European-Indian trade in America's

33 This aspect of the conflict is eloquently described by Louis Jordan.
34 "The significance of the area was brought out during discussions of the realignment of the borders between New Netherland and the British colonies, which took place at the Hartford Convention in September of 1650. The secretary of New Netherland, Cornelis van Tienhoven, wrote several communications on the disputed lands. In a description of the boundaries of New Netherland written on February 22, 1650 van Tienhoven included a discussion of Long Island, in which he stated, 'The greatest part of the Wampum, for which the furs are traded, is manufactured there by the Natives.' [...] In a supplemental letter written less that two weeks later, on March 4, 1650, he further explained the importance of the area: 'I begin then at the most easterly point of Long Island [...] This point is also well adapted to secure the trade of the Indians in Wampum, (the mine of New Netherland,) since in and about the abovementioned sea and the islands therein situated, lie the cockles whereof Wampum is made, from which great profit could be realized by those who would plant a colony or hamlet at the aforesaid Point, for the cultivation of the land, for raising all sorts of cattle, for fishing and the wampum trade [...]." The lawyer Adriaen van der Donck was more emphatic on the importance of Long Island in his diatribe against the province's border concessions to the British. His paper was written in reaction to a provincial resolution of February 16, 1652 in which Long Island was divided into two parts, the British taking the eastern portion up to the westernmost point of Oyster Bay, while the Dutch took the remainder of the island. Concerning this concession of part of Long Island, van der Donck firmly stated that the entirety of the island should be retained by New Netherland, "otherwise the trade will suffer great damage, because the English will retain all the Wampum manufacturers to themselves and we shall be obligated to eat oats out of English hands." (Jordan) Also see http://www.nativeweb.org/resources/crafts_indigenous_technology/beads_ beadwork/ [14.02.2006]

Northeast. To a certain degree wampum survived the political changes from New Netherland to New York first in 1664, then finally in 1674. While the New England colonies gave up wampum as a money substitute rather quickly, the Dutch inhabitants of New York continued to use the formerly little loved sewant for petty trade transactions. It was still so profitable within the colony that one of the most influential merchants of New York, the Frisian-born Frederick Philipse, in 1668 tried to control the wampum circulation by putting European-Caribbean fakes on the market. He imported conches from the Bermudas and employed Native Americans and Europeans alike to manufacture beads with European tools (Ritchie 61 f.).[35] The Iroquois detested this because mass produced beads lacked the aesthetic qualities and therefore the special glow they cherished in wampum.

For Europeans in America, wampum was a substitute for money in a society that lacked a European currency. It connected Europeans and Native Americans. Yet the latter used wampum only as a trade good or as an item much cherished but they did *not* regard it as an instrument of cashless payment. The Algonquians 'sold' wampum as a trade item. The Iroquois 'bought' it. Only the Europeans 'sold' *and* 'bought' it and turned wampum into a currency like beaver pelts and tobacco leaves that temporarily (in times of low cash flow) fulfilled the same purpose.

But there is more to wampum than just the question of whether it was a currency or not. Wampum created more than the classic trade triangle described by historians like William N. Fenton and Lynn Ceci ("Native Wampum" 58). For this trade triangle is more a scholarly concept than a reflection of the commercial reality of the seventeenth century. Wampum certainly was much more important than just a negligible item on the so-called "periphery" of European economies (Ceci, "Native Wampum" 50f.). Besides, there is nothing like a center or a periphery in seventeenth-century Atlantic trade (Schnurmann, *Atlantische Welten*).

Wampum was a tool that helped to create an Atlantic system that expanded in different directions. Today we consider the idea of center and peripheries as outdated. It takes us back to old notions of European exploitations of the Americas and ignores the fact that Native Americans knew of profit, could take the initiative in trade and politics, and did develop and follow their very own political and commercial interests. Wampum combined Europeans in America and Europe, Algonquians and Iroquois into one Atlantic system of cultures, trades, and economics. Surely different concepts of the function, meaning, value and use of wampum existed. But wampum helped to support New Netherland and New England in their difficult beginnings when colonial governments functioned poorly and financial means were even poorer. In a way, New Netherland resembled today's developing countries. Then and now settlers and merchants, in their drive to make a living and even profits, relied on the same means that poor and weak economies lacking powerful statehood still do: they circulate substitute monies in all possible forms. Access to as well as the production, ownership, and distribution of

35 Also see Fernow 8: 114-7.

wampum defined power constellations between Native American nations as well as with and between European colonies. In the beginning of the seventeenth century, due to their control of the production and input of wampum into the Northeastern American markets, the Algonquians profited till they were subdued by Europeans and Iroquois; Mohawk and Europeans prospered on different levels and at different times. The only ones who really suffered and were never happy as clams were the clams, snails, and beavers that lost their lives, pelts or shells.

By the time colonists had achieved a better supply of coined money, the beaver populations in the New Netherland hinterlands had been destroyed and the Mohawk had to rely on other tribes within the Iroquois Confederation to supply the colonists with beavers as the most important method to obtain wampum. When New Netherland changed into New York, and Mohawk-French relations improved in the 1660s (Fenton and Tooker), wampum lost its importance as a cultural broker and esteemed trade item. The fewer beavers that were brought to the market, the more wampum was produced and inflation set in. Supplied with millions of beads since the 1640s[36] the Mohawk, Oneida, and other members of the Iroquois confederacy relied more and more on the traditional use of wampum – wampum belts as an object of diplomacy.[37]

While the Euro-Americans on the East coast of the North American continent for many reasons lost their former interest in wampum, it did not lose its importance in the intercourse and in the relations of nations and peoples of North America's interior. Its instrumentalization as commodity, cultural item, diplomatic messenger, and means of exchange followed the so-called westward expansion in the centuries to come. In the late eighteenth century, the German Moravian missionary David Zeisberger described the use of wampum by the Delaware society in the Ohio Valley (Wellenreuther and Wessel, passim); in the first half of the nineteenth century another German migrant, Johann Jacob Astor, used wampum to build his fur empire, thanks to the successful hunters among the Plains Indians, and last but not least, in the twenty-first century ill-informed tourists in Native American territories within the USA are tempted to buy fake wampum made of plastic (Armado 30).[38]

References

Allain, Mathé. "The Image of the Indians in early French Atlases and Travel Accounts." The Newberry Library 1989, http://www.newberry.org/smith/slidesets/ss13.html [21.05.2006].

36 See Ceci, "Native Wampum" 50; in two Seneca sites more than 350,000 beads and twenty-three wampum belts have been found that dated between 1640 and 1675.

37 Fenton and webpages produced by members of the Six Indian Nations describe the prolific production and use of wampum belts in the later seventeenth century.
See http://www.mohicanpress.com/mo08017.html [24.07.2006]

38 See also http://www.newton.dep.anl.gov/natbltn/700-799/nb725.htm [24.07.2006]

Barbour, Philip (ed.). *The Complete Works of Captain John Smith (1580-1631)*. 3 vols. Chapel Hill/NC: University of North Carolina Press, 1986.

Biard, Pierre. "Canadian Mission. [Missio Canadensia. Epistola ex Porturegali in Acadia, Transmissa ad Praepositum Generalem Societatis Jesu.]." *The Jesuit Relations and Allied Documents. Travels and Explorations of the Jesuit Missionaries in New France, 1610-1791* (Native American Studies H-201). Ed. Reuben Gold Thwaites. Cleveland/OH: Burrows, 1896-1901, vol. 2: 57-123.

Boxer, Charles R. *The Dutch Seaborne Empire, 1600-1800*. London: Hutchinson, 1965.

Bradford, William. *Of Plymouth Plantation 1620-1647*. Ed. Samuel Eliot Morison. New York: Knopf, 2001.

Ceci, Lynn. "Native Wampum as a Peripheral Resource in the Seventeenth-Century World System." Laurence M. Hauptman and James D. Wherry (eds.). *The Pequots in Southern New England. The Fall and Rise of an American Indian Nation*. Norman/Oklahoma: University of Oklahoma Press, 1990. 48-63.

---. *The Effect of European Contact and Trade on the Settlement Pattern of Indians in Coastal New York, 1524-1665*. New York: Garland Publications, 1990.

Condon, Thomas. *New York Beginnings. The Commercial Origins of New Netherland*. New York: New York University Press, 1968.

Fenton, William N., and Elizabeth Tooker. "Mohawk." Bruce Trigger (ed.). *Northeast* (= *Handbook of North American Indians* Ed. William C. Sturtevant, vol. 15). Washington/DC: Smithsonian Institute, 1978. 466-80.

Fenton, William N. *The Great Law and the Longhouse. A Political History of the Iroquois Confederacy*. Norman/Oklahoma: University of Oklahoma Press, 1988.

Fernow, Berthold (ed.). *Records of New Amsterdam from 1653-1674*. 7 vols. New York 1897.

Foster, Michael K. "Another Look at the Function of Wampum in Iroquois-White Councils." Francis Jennings et al (eds.). *The History and Culture of Iroquois Diplomacy. An Interdisciplinary Guide to the Treaties of the Six Nations and their League*. Syracuse/NY: Syracuse University Press, 1985. 99-124.

Francis, Peter. "The Beads that did not Buy Manhattan Island." Alexandra van Dongen (ed.). *'One Man's trash is another Man's treasure.' The Metamorphosis of the European Utensil in the New World / De Metamorfose van het Europese Gebruiksvoorwerp in de Nieuwe Wereld*. Rotterdam: Museum Boymans-van Beuningen, 1995. 53-69.

Gehring, Charles T., and William A. Starna (eds.). *A Journey into Mohawk and Oneida Country 1634-1635. The Journal of Harmen Meyndertsz van den Bogaert*. Syracuse/NY: Syracuse University Press, 1988.

Gehring, Charles. "Annals of New Netherland." http://www.nnp.org/nni/Annals/2000.pdf [30.08.2007]

Hamell, George R. "Wampum. Goed is het te denken, wat wit is, helder, licht. Light, White and Bright Things are Good to Think." Alexandra van Dongen (ed.). *'One Man's Trash is Another Man's Treasure.' The Metamorphosis of the European Utensil in the New World / De Metamorfose van het Europese Gebruiksvoorwerp in de Nieuwe Wereld*. Rotterdam: Museum Boymans-van Beuningen, 1995. 41-51.

Heidenreich, Conrad E., "Huron." Bruce Trigger (ed.). *Northeast* (= *Handbook of North American Indians* Ed. William C. Sturtevant, vol. 15.) Washington/DC: Smithsonian Institute, 1978.

Jacobs, Jaap. *Een Zegenrijk Gewest. Nieuw-Nederland in de Zeventiende Eeuw* (Cultuurgeschiedenis van de Republiek in de zeventiende eeuw 2). Amsterdam: Prometheus, 1999 [English translation: *New Netherland. A Dutch Colony in Seventeenth Century America* (The Atlantic World 3). Leiden: Brill, 2005].

James, Sydney V. (ed.). *Three Visitors to early Plymouth. Letters about the Pilgrim Settlement in New England during Its First seven Years by John Pory, Emmanuel Altham and Isaack de Rasières*. Plymouth/Mass: Plimouth Plantation, 1963.

Jameson, J. Franklin (ed.). *Original Narratives of Early American History.* 18 vols., vol. 8: *Early English and French Voyages 1534-1608*. New York: Charles Scribner's Sons, 1906-17.

Jane, Cecil (ed.). *The Journal of Christopher Columbus (Christoforo Colombo)*. With an appendix by R.A. Skelton. London: Blond, 1969.

Jennings, Francis. *The Invasion of America. Indians, Colonialism, and the Cant of Conquest*. New York: Norton, 1976.

Kavenagh, Keith W. (ed.). *Middle Atlantic Colonies* (= *Foundations of Colonial America*, 3 vols). New York: Chelsea House, 1973.

Lapham, Heather, "More than 'a few blew beads': The Glass and Stone Beads from Jamestown Rediscovery's 1994-1997 Excavations." *The Journal of the Jamestown Rediscovery Center* 1 (2001), http://www.apva.org/resource/jjrc/vol1/hl1into.html [04.06.2006].

McCusker, John J. *Money and Exchange in Europe and America, 1600-1775*. Chapel Hill/NC: University of North Carolina Press, 1978.

Meuwese, Marcus P. *For the Peace and Well-being of the Country. Intercultural Mediators and Dutch-Indian Relations in New Netherland and Dutch Brazil, 1600-1664*. PhD Notre Dame/Indiana 2003, online dissertation: http://etd.nd.edu/ETD-db/theses/available/etd-09272003-005338/ [21.09.2007].

"Money Substitutes in New Netherland and Early New York: Wampum." http://www.coins.nd.edu/ColCoin/ColCoinIntros/NNWampum.html [31.8.2007]. http//www.nativeweb.org/resources/crafts_indigenous_technology/beads_beadwork/ [14.02.2006]

Murray, David. *Indian Giving. Economies of Power in Indian-White Exchanges*. Amherst/Mass: University of Massachussetts Press, 2000.

Pakash, Om (ed.). *The Dutch Factories in India 1617-1623. A Collection of Dutch East India Company Documents Pertaining to India*. New Delhi: Munishiram Manhoharlal, 1984.

Postma, Johannes M. *The Dutch in the Atlantic Slave Trade 1600-1815*. Cambridge: Cambridge University Press, 1990.

Quinn, David B. (ed.). *America from Concept to Discovery. Early Exploration of North America* (= *New American World. A Documentary History of America to 1612*, 5 vols., vol. 1). New York: Arno Press, 1979.

---. (ed.). *Major Spanish Searches in Eastern North America. The Franco-Spanish Clash in Florida. The Beginning of Spanish Florida* (= *New American World. A Documentary History of America to 1612*, 5 vols., vol. 2). New York: Arno Press, 1979.

---. (ed.). *Newfoundland from Fishery to Colony. Northwest Passage Searches* (= *New American World. A Documentary History of America to 1612*, 5 vols., vol. 4). New York: Arno Press, 1979.

Richter, Daniel K. *Facing East from Indian Country. A Native History of early America*. Cambridge/Mass: Harvard University Press, 2001.

---. *The Ordeal of the Longhouse. The peoples of the Iroquois League in the Era of European colonization.* Chapel Hill/NC: University of North Carolina Press, 1992.

Rink, Oliver A. *Holland on the Hudson. An Economic and Social History of Dutch New York.* Ithaca/NY: Cornell University Press, 1989.

Ritchie, Robert C. "Piracy, Trade, and the Law in the Early British Empire." Claudia Schnurmann and Hartmut Lehmann (eds.). *Atlantic Understandings. Essays on European and American History in Honor of Hermann Wellenreuther* (Atlantic Cultural Studies 1). Hamburg/Münster: Lit, 2006. 61-75.

Salisbury, Neal. *Manitou and Providence. Indians, Europeans, and the Making of New England, 1500-1643.* New York: Oxford University Press, 1982.

Schnurmann, Claudia. "'Wherever Profit Leads us, to every Sea and Shore...' The VOC, the WIC, and Dutch methods of globalization in the seventeenth century." *Renaissance Studies* 17.3 (2003): 474-93.

---. *Atlantische Welten. Engländer und Niederländer in der amerikanisch-atlantischen Welt 1648-1713* (Wirtschafts- und sozialhistorische Studien 9). Köln: Böhlau, 1998.

---. *Europa trifft Amerika. Atlantische Wirtschaft in der Frühen Neuzeit 1492-1783.* Frankfurt/Main: Fischer, 1998.

Scozzari, Lois. "The significance of Wampum to Seventeenth Century Indians in New England," in: *The Connecticut Review.* http://www.hartford-hwp.com/archives/41/037.html [24.07.2006].

Shiel, John. *More about Wampum. The Second Coastal Archaeology Reader: 1900 to the Present.* (Readings in Long Island Archaeology and Ethnohistory 5) Lexington/Mass.; Ginn Custom Publications/Stony Brook, N.Y: Suffolk County Archaeological Association, 1982.

Speck, Frank G. *The Functions of Wampum Among the Eastern Algonkian* (Memoirs of the American Anthropological Association 6,1). Lancaster/PA: American Anthropological Association, 1919.

Sullivan, James (ed.). *The History of New York State.* Online edition, book I, chapter III, part VII, http://www.usgennet.org/usa/ny/state/his/ [30.08.2007].

Sultzman, Lee. "Mahican History." http://www.dickshovel.com/Mahican.html [24.07.2006].

Tooker, Elizabeth. "The League of the Iroquois: its History, Politics, and Ritual." Bruce Trigger (ed.). *Northeast* (= *Handbook of North American Indians* Ed. William C. Sturtevant, vol. 15). Washington/DC: Smithsonian Institute, 1978.

Trigger, Bruce G. *Natives and Newcomers. Canada's 'Heroic Age' Reconsidered.* Kingston: McGill-Queen's University Press, 1985.

Van Laer, Arnold Johan Ferdinand (ed.). *Minutes of the Court of Albany, Rensselaerswyck and Schenectady, 1668-1685.* 3 vols. Albany/NY: The University of the State of New York, 1926-32.

Wakida-Kusunoki, Armado T. "Quahogs in eastern North America: Part 1, Biology, Ecology, and Historical Uses." *Marine Fisheries Review* 64.2 (2002): 1-55.

Webster's Revised Unabridged Dictionary (1913), http://dict.die.net/sewant/ [28.03.2006].

Wellenreuther, Hermann, and Carola Wessel (eds.). *The Moravian Mission Diaries of David Zeisberger, 1772-1781.* University Park/PA: Pennsylvania State University Press, 2005.

CHAPTER TWELVE

Melville, Deep Time, and the World in Ruins. Or, Digging toward Eternity

BRUCE HARVEY

The *mundus subterraneus* becomes a realm of fantasy, but also of empirical inquiry, which becomes conscious of its headstrong inquisitiveness with a shiver [...]. [There is yet an] unwritten history of the invisible, as the reservoir rather than the futility of reason [...].

Hans Blumenberg, *The Legitimacy of the Modern Age*

Natural history [...] was based on a thoroughly spatialized conception of Time and provided the paradigm for anthropology as the science of cultural evolution [...]. [I]ts theories and methods, inspired by geology, comparative anatomy, and related scientific disciplines, were taxonomic rather than genetic-processual. Most importantly, by allowing Time to be resorbed by the tabular space of classification, nineteenth-century anthropology sanctioned an ideological process by which relations between the West and its Other, between anthropology and its object, were conceived not only as difference, but as distance in space *and* Time.

Johannes Fabian, *Time and the Other*

The activity of the mind [...] will therefore no longer consist in drawing things together [as it did in the Renaissance], in setting out on a quest for everything that might reveal some sort of kinship, attraction, or secretly shared nature within them, but, on the contrary, in discriminating, that is, in establishing their identities, then the inevitability of the connections with all the successive degrees of a series.

Michel Foucault, *The Order of Things*

Herman Melville envisaged otherness more intensely than most authors of the nineteenth century. Early and late, his writings testify to that which exceeds or escapes definition, calculation, or cataloguing. Marquesan cannibals in *Typee* (1846), the intransigent white whale of *Moby-Dick* (1850), the resentful scrivener

in "Bartleby" (1853): in each case, Melville regards otherness as resisting interpretation and placement within a knowledge grid. His characters' vagaries – essential rather than accidental variances – put them beyond the controlling habit of
Enlightenment and post-Enlightenment tabular deposition that Foucault and Fabian find almost eerily attractive in its raw efficiency.

Melville's fiction celebrates not being a "sort" or a type. What makes his characters *sui generis* cannot only be explained, however, by his distinctive artistry.
Each also rebuffs us with an inherent impenetrability. Why should such otherness
– which cannot be fathomed – nonetheless trouble or call to us; why should the
anonymous narrator of "Bartleby" care about Bartleby, or why should Ahab be
so vexed by the white whale's inscrutability, by its permeable layers of flesh and
yet impermeable intent? Otherness, it seems, is never just negligible; it is never,
simply, *over there*. To be sure, racist and nationalist ideologies only succeed by
sequestering native others into discontinuous temporal or socio-spatial locales, a
practice that averts the off-chance of actual recognition. It works by substituting
numbers in place of being, by imposing types (caricatures as a mock average) instead of engaging an idiosyncratic presence, and by resorting to abstract accounting rather than a more existential taking account of. In this essay, however, the
term "otherness" assumes that the other is to be held, as it were, face-to-face.
Moreover, it stresses that such otherness, especially for Melville, whether prefig-
ured in an alien whale or an alienated postal worker, carries a pressing weight,
obliging us to intuit the other's deeply hidden or opaque interiority. Melville, in
brief, has no patience for the Enlightenment/post-Enlightenment conceit of airy
statistics; he rightly empathizes with a monadic intensity and gravitas that cannot be dismissed by tabulation, comparative measurement, or stereotypical placement.

The last paragraph mixes a vocabulary of interpersonal othering with one of
physical weight and density. For, what emerged in the late eighteenth and nineteenth centuries, for the first time, was an array of disciplines, sciences, and industries – archaeology, geology, and anthropology; the aesthetic theory of the sublime; coal mining and railway and canal and bridge construction – that made visible what lay below the earth's surface or exploited, metaphorically, the imaginary
of deep and weighty spaces. It was not the mere faddishness of Egyptology in its
American heyday that led Melville to equate, otherwise incongruously, the puny
otherness of Bartleby in his demise – he has been imprisoned in "the Tombs" of
New York City for vagrancy, and dies there – to the stolid density of pyramid-
like mass: "The surrounding walls [of the prison], of amazing thickness, kept off
all sounds behind them. The Egyptian character of the masonry weighed upon me
with its gloom [...]. [I felt I was within the] heart of the eternal pyramids [...]"
(44). Rather, Melville's point is that if Bartleby recedes into insignificance when
incarcerated within such menacing massiveness, he also bears, within his small-
ness, the somber weight of his locale.

Melville excels at rendering otherness, as a weighty elsewhere, into concrete images. He reflects his immediate literary milieu – the New England Transcendentalist or Romantic Movement, roughly 1830-1865 – and many of the motifs studied here could find resonance with Ralph Waldo Emerson, Henry David Thoreau, and their U.S. literary peers. In this essay, however, Melville's digging deep into otherness exhibits a larger, nonnationalist cultural-intellectual history pertaining to the metaphorics of depth. The survey of that history will help answer the question, acutely raised by Andrea Zittlau, a respondent to the conference talk occasion of this essay, in respect to our habits of othering: how do we "look up" above or "beyond" surface and depth even as we, heirs to Enlightenment rationalism, take stock of both? Zittlau asks us to query the temptation either to too easily substitute surface marks – physiognomies and tattoos, for instance – for complex interiors or, obversely, to overzealously expose the Other for our own satisfaction.

Historicizing the Metaphorics of Depth:
The Post-Renaissance Desacralization of Verticality

The question of depth in the nineteenth century cannot be separated from that of time. Melville, throughout his oeuvre, broods on archaic time that reaches beyond human scale. His interest emerges from a nineteenth-century sensibility attuned to archaeological revelations, protoevolutionary speculation, and discoveries made about the earth's geological strata, which together opened the prospect of what we now call "deep time," a term coined by the U.S. natural history journalist John McPhee, in his book *Basin and Range* (1981), to designate the vast backward stretch of time evidenced by (and required to tally) geological and evolutionary processes. Melville grounds his fiction in an existentially felt, geophysically heavy, and inestimably aged, resistantly-other world. He thereby engages the uncanny nature of time: that in its passage it loses immediacy and yet also accrues weight in its built-up pastness. Time's palpable otherness becomes increasingly present even as it becomes further removed or estranged from us.

To think of otherness, in its essence, requires us to ponder a weightiness in a locale always elsewhere. For otherness presents not just an ethnographical or philosophical problem (in the sense of "how do we know the other?") but also one involving a specific scientific-technological spatial/temporal asymmetry (in regard to how two different cognitive locales – *here/there* – can relate). I will suggest that this quandary of relating the here/there arose, in the long arc of intellectual and cultural history from the pre-Renaissance to post-Romantic eras, in the context of various sciences or technologies or imaginaries of depth in the nineteenth century. History will be incomplete if we treat the issue of otherness either as only a rarefied philosophical problem of contestation and accommodation (from Hegel through Emmanuel Levinas and Jean-Luc Nancy) or as simply anthropology's disciplinary *raison d'être* (to bring the cultural other into understanding).[1] Hans Blumenberg, in the first epigraph above, notes the powerful frisson "reason" gets from contemplating the hidden or buried, and my argument unpacks what Blumenberg, in passing, highlights as truth's "reservoir," linking the latter to particular industrial-scientific-literary themes coalescing around metaphors of depth. The nineteenth-century world picture, which we inherit, cannot be understood if we disregard those metaphors: they are foundational rather than epiphenomenal.

The itinerary of that historiographic narrative for the purposes of this essay quickly goes from the Medieval-Renaissance concept of nature as a divinely authorized hierarchy, the Great Chain of Being, to the post-Newtonian worldview of nature as self-sustaining and knowable through purely intellectual – what I call ocular or "horizontal" – classifications. At the same time that the world model became emptied of a metaphysical verticality, stretching from Heaven to Hell, the earth itself became radically reconceived: it became a domain of hidden truths to be uncovered and a resource, downwardly measurable, to be industrially exploited. The Romantic and Modern sensibility takes shape, we may surmise, to counter the loss of metaphysical verticality as well as its weighty empirical replacement. It is a sensibility hauntingly fixated on the underground, the subterranean, and the foundational, in multiple and overlapping discourses, from the urban topographical (the marvels of subearth engineering, from bridge piles to sewer systems), to the archeological and geological (the idea of deep time itself), on to the philosophical (the aesthetics of the sublime and its existential negation).

Let's consider how the cosmos and earth were seen before the great-grandfather of Melville's great-grandfather's great-grandfather was born, that is, via the commonplace of the Great Chain of Being. The Medieval-Renaissance scheme, Aristotelian in origin and revised to fit Christian theodicy, ranked each life form according to its degree of excellence. From God's perfect being, the ladder descended, through humankind to noble but nonrational creatures (lions, for instance), and then further downward to ignoble ones (reptiles), to end with vegetables, rocks, and finally at the lowest strata of being, Satan and his kingdom of dark negation (Fig. 1).

There was, of course, curiosity about the planet's interior unrelated to the mythic geography of an underworld Hades or Hell, exemplified, for instance, in Athanasius Kircher's *Mundus Subterraneus* (1665) (Fig. 2), which depicted the earth's bowels as cavities or rivers of interconnected water channels and volcanic lava (Fitting, *Subterranean Worlds* 15). But before the early Industrial Revolution's deep cutting for coal, sinking of mine shafts, or railroad tunneling, only fancy could surmise what lay beneath the surface.

---

1   Emmanuel Levinas and Jean-Luc Nancy are most interesting to the cultural historian, in fact, when they illuminate their theories of the Other in terms of material palpability. See especially Levinas's discussion of the "face" in the essay "Meaning and Sense," in *Basic Philosophical Writings* (52-64); or Nancy's collection, *A Finite Thinking*.

Fig. 1: The Great Chain of Being from Didacus Valadés, *Rhetorica Christiana* (1579). © British Library Board. All Rights Reserved. Picture No. 1022251.091.

Between the Renaissance and the eighteenth century, the Great Chain of Being gradually lost its authority. Its collapse into an antiquated, nonvital theological system is a story that can only be told in long hindsight; for certainly few work-a-day churchmen of the eighteenth century would have had trouble integrating Renaissance theodicy with the Deist argument-by-design, which nonetheless removed God's supervening virtue to outside of nature entirely. With that caveat of historical perspective, two epistemic shifts may be seen as heralding the system's demise.

First, with the transitional texts of Francis Bacon, in particular *Novum Organum* (1620), the prospect of hidden depths as a source of valid intrigue began to gain acceptance. Bacon used metaphors of mining – the prototype of geological exploration – to emphasize the discovery of "truth." The Neo-Platonic and Christian traditions had cordoned off below-ness as the realm of taboo and error; Bacon, drawing upon, even as he demystifies, hermetic, Adamic lore (that the earth was given for human use, alchemically or otherwise), entices us to tunnel down into truth, which although secreted willingly yields its treasures:

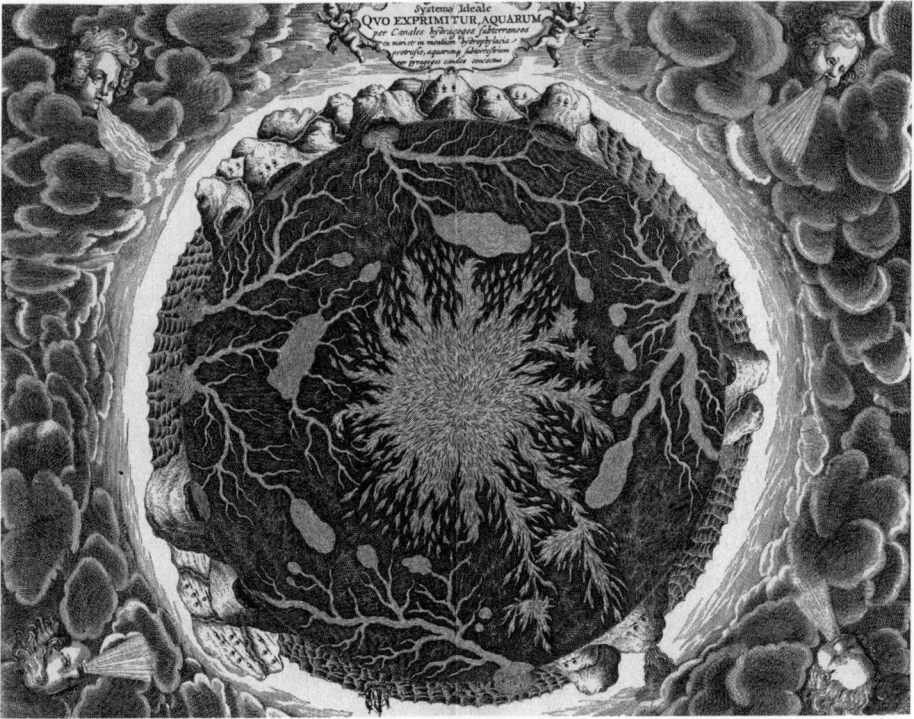

Fig. 2: Drawing for Athanasius Kircher's *Mundus Subterraneus* (1665).

> There is therefore much ground for hoping that there are still laid up in the womb of nature many secrets of excellent use, having no affinity or parallelism with any thing that is now known, but lying entirely out of the beat of the imagination, which have not yet been found out. They too no doubt will some time or other, in the course and revolution of many ages, come to light of themselves, just as the others' did […]. (100)

Bacon still judges the revelatory urge to be passive rather than dynamic or predictive. We do not out of hubris seek to advance in and possess knowledge; knowledge simply waits to "come to light," as if, through its own agency, it reciprocated our desire to unearth it. The second epistemic shift came a century later, when Enlightenment naturalists from Carl Linnaeus to Georges Cuvier developed comparative, visual schemata to articulate Nature, what Foucault (in this chapter's third epigraph) highlights as taxonomic "successive degrees in a series." Nature's species and subspecies became systematically aligned not by theological hierarchy but by horizontal gradations and ocular grids.

Neither rationalist impulse – to investigate the earth's secrets or to lay out nature's patterns sequentially – developed in a self-contained intellectual-cultural trajectory. Rather, during the early Enlightenment and after, both impulses fused together in ways that confounded simple distinctions between the empirical and metaphysical; only when the notions of geological, evolutionary, and cosmological theory combined in the second half of the nineteenth century was a new paradigm of purely secularized deep time secured. Efforts to square the Mosaic account of Creation with progressing scientific observation became increasingly rickety; the most renowned attempt was Thomas Burnet's eloquent *Sacred Theory of the Earth* (1684), which remained influential up to the beginning of the nineteenth century (Gould 29-60 and Rossi 33-41). Exactly the torsion of Burnet's baroque efforts to explain, for instance, the Creator's intent in lodging odd bones deeply within the ground, which bore little resemblance to those of living creatures, remystified the earth even as it became the subject of rational inquiry. Thus Paolo Rossi writes that, through the end of the Renaissance and the better part of the Enlightenment, fossils came "to be seen as stones and natural objects stranger than other stones or objects existing in nature" (4). The Baconian sensibility blurred a generic interest in nature releasing its secrets, otherwise dimly tabooed as God's privacy, with that of a more specific protoindustrial, practical concern in what might actually be serviceable within the 'womb' of the planet. The genius of the earth and human ingenuity would conspire to bring forth wonders; but if ingenuity, practically applied, would demystify the realms of nature, rumination on fossils and, as Rossi points out, on non-Mosaic accounts of human history, emphasized how much opacity, resisting intellectual penetration, remained.

My latter phrasing implies, however, that reason (as if it were a standalone mental faculty) always seeks to maximize its own domain. Blumenberg's point about the "invisible" being reason's "reservoir" is rather that reason requires a continual substratum of obscurity for it to be adequately motivated. Reason, it seems, always yearns for an ample hidden-ness. We can illustrate that dependency by examining two of the most well-known paintings of Charles Willson Peale, one of the most famous artists of the U.S. Early Nationalist era. Peale, a close friend of Thomas Jefferson, opened the first natural history museum in the U.S., in Philadelphia, and commemorated his contribution to American science by his 1822 work *The Artist in His Museum* (Fig. 3). In it, Peale invites us past the curtain to see nature's marvels housed in a grid of display cabinets: here, because we can barely discern the actual specimens, is an almost abstract lateral series of measurable distinctions, coordinated by reason's power, so aptly suggested by the visual dominance of Peale's forehead and his austere expression. Nature or natural history, in the absence of the hierarchy of the Great Chain of Being, lays itself out flatly along the categorized surfaces of the left receding wall and the back wall of the museum. Here, there is only objectification, not an other to be countenanced, as if the sublimity of the unknown – the hidden – withers under the gaze of Peale's will-to-clarity.

Peale presents himself as the consummate Enlightenment naturalist-scientist, whose august desire is merely to bring into full visual tabulation the flora and fauna of Nature. The painting's compositional eccentricity, though, belies the will-to-clarity it otherwise manifests. Note, first, the partially drawn curtain, revealing an orderly display of bird species, immobilized in their boxes by the taxidermist's craft, and yet also distinctly not revealing the reconstructed skeleton

Fig. 3: Charles Willson Peale, "The Artist in His Museum" (1822). Courtesy of the
Pennsylvania Academy of the Fine Arts, Philadelphia. Gift of Mrs. Sarah Harrison
(The Joseph Harrison, Jr., Collection).

Fig. 4: Charles Willson Peale, "The Exhumation of the Mastodon" (1805-08). Courtesy of the Collections of the Maryland Historical Society.

of a mastodon. The mastodon is indeed left as a "reservoir," as what Blumenberg refers to as rationality's tease, of "empirical inquiry, which becomes conscious of its headstrong inquisitiveness with a shiver" (see first epigraph). The mastodon, in this sense, functions as a mere naturalist object; but it also, insofar as the woman's gaze of petite astonishment is directed toward its ambiguated space, offers us a visage simultaneously present (to the museum's visitors) and not present (to us, as viewers of the painting). The skeleton, in brief, is and is not disclosed, at once a demystified and not-demystified "other." So, too, the representational design is something of a quirky bifocal tour-de-force. For, even as the museum embodies measured tabulation and an encyclopedic comprehensivity, it also, pictorially, recedes into an indefinite endpoint: the two foci, the abyss of the endpoint and Peale's forehead (his intellection), suggest at once a command over and concession to, as Blumenberg puts it, the "unwritten history of the invisible."

We have only to look at Peale's earlier painting, depicting the actual unearthing of the mastodon bones, to recognize that the Enlightenment directive to systematic visual clarity depends on a zone of unclarity, a necessary penumbra of shadow. In *The Exhumation of the Mastodon* (1806-08) (Fig. 4), Peale (the well-dressed figure, with unscrolled sketch in hand) gestures toward the mastodon about to be unburied in the same fashion as in his self-portrait/museum painting.

Similarly, as in the museum painting, Peale would have us link representational efficacy (the sketch), the rational faculty (Peale's mentality), and the empirical object itself (the bones being uncovered from the dredged pit). Here, however, the enticement of that triad depends entirely on what, finally, eludes our gaze: the not-manifest objects of the dredged-up skeletal remains of the mastodon. Here is Enlightenment illumination, and yet also an emphatic residual secretiveness (a secretiveness reinforced all the more in the two paintings' chronology, as the skeleton still remains largely hidden in the later painting of 1822).[2]

Excavating Depth in the Nineteenth Century

Peale's *The Exhumation of the Mastodon* shows day workers employed in the task of excavation. The effect, though, is odd: for what we must assume is strenuous and grimy muscular labor Peale subordinates to the pure power – indeed, the heroism – of representation itself, that is, the efficacy and accuracy of the unfurled drawing.[3] Male prowess as shown here (or, more singularly, by the upright figure in *The Artist in His Museum*) has been sublimated to the Enlightenment gaze-as-will, but not entirely. In that regard, Peale's *The Exhumation of the Mastodon* marks a transition into the nineteenth-century era of what might be called a masculinist and quasi-imperialist fad for excavating and disclosing depths and interiors. By the middle of that century the subterranean took on palpability, and a gender dynamic within cultural discourse, fundamentally different from either the restraint of the Enlightenment penetrating gaze or the earlier theology of a descent from divine excellence.

Rosalind Williams, a historian of science and technology, remarks that in a multitude of developing nineteenth-century fields and industrial practices (geology, archaeology, and paleontology; deep mining; railroad tunneling and bridge construction) subterranean exploration "was seen as a modern version of the mythological quest to find truth in the hidden regions of the underworld" (23). To which, importantly, we should add the techno-phallicism of the enterprise, the surcharge of marshaling labor.

The inaugurating excavatory exposé was likely at the hands of Napoleon Bonaparte's legion of scientists who, during the French campaign in Egypt, scoured the Egyptian countryside for buried monuments and discovered the Rosetta Stone which, unearthed in 1799, was translated in 1822 by the French scholar Jean-François Champollion. The ensuing archaeological fetish with all-things-Egyptian

---

2 My discussion here is informed by Lacan's notion of the stain and gaze in the visual/interpersonal field, a not-quite placeable returning gaze from the Other that negates the looker's drive toward sovereign and scopic mastery. See Lacan, *Four Fundamental Concepts of Psychoanalysis* (67-105).

3 For a fascinating discussion of Peale's paintings in a larger context of the politics of labor, see Laura Rigal's essay "Peale's Mammoth" in *American Iconography* (18-38).

led, in the U.S. context, to the adoption of Egyptian architectural designs (the Washington Monument obelisk is an example, started in 1848, and finished in 1884) and to public accolades for such scholarly volumes as George R. Gliddon's *Ancient Egypt. Her Monuments, Hieroglyphics, Archeology, and Other Subjects Connected with Hieroglyphic Literature* (1847). Gliddon's works, along with John Lloyd Stephens's immensely popular *Incidents of Travel in Central America, Chiapas and Yucatan* (1844), which reported on the ruins of Copan and other sites in the depths of the Mesoamerican jungle, allowed armchair tourists to exult in the masculinist exploits of archaeological adventurers.[4] What "higher excitement" could there be, Stephens reports in the latter volume, "than to go through that country with a strong force, time, and means at command, to lay bare the whole region in which so many ruined cities are now buried" (2:107).

Stephens's zeal to expose ruins and open interiors of ancient holy sites can be politicized as another example of his century's Orientalist depredations. The contours of Orientalism as a practice of othering are well enough known not to require being reviewed here, but it should be emphasized that the allure of such othering invariably requires the dramatic juxtaposition of contemporary force (either mental or physical) against a deeply secreted time (represented by arcane languages and texts, ancient "inscrutable" cultural habits and beliefs, and alternative histories putting into question Biblical chronology). Unintentionally, Stephens puns in the above quote: given adequate Western "time" – its efficient deployment – the antique and exotic haunts of time ("ruined cities") may be denuded and exposed to view. In the Western tradition, the reservoir of other time simply cannot be left alone. Similar to the conflation of cultural and temporal othering in Stephens's text, Edgar A. Poe in his fabulistic *Narrative of Arthur Gordon Pym of Nantucket* (1838) fuses, towards the climax of the story, a discovery of an ancient formation of odd chasms – "one of the most singular-looking places imaginable" – and a group of autochthonous "savages" (1164). Stephens's and Poe's texts suggest that in the middle of the nineteenth century the motifs of cultural or racial othering, deep time, and the sublime merged together and were resonant largely because of their shared or analogous vocabularies.

Melville, Strata, and the World in Ruins

In a late chapter of *Moby-Dick*, Melville, spinning an analogy, compares the loss of spiritual heritage to orphanhood: "Where is the foundling's father hidden? Our souls are like those orphans whose unwedded mothers die in bearing them: the secret of our paternity lies in their grave, and we must there to learn it" (492). Melville's enduring ache for all things lost, at sea and elsewhere, derives from

---

4 The best analysis of the literary effects of the Egyptology fad in the period is Irwin, *American Hieroglyphics*.

both emotional privation (his father died when he was eleven) and from his meta-physically anguished sense of irrecoverable sublime origins. And thus, invariably, he balances a strong impulse to divulge the buried or hidden against his recognition that access to such hallowed regions is always blocked, which in turn leads to his suspicion that, in the absence of felt plenitude, all else is merely a ruse of surfaces.

The natural world for Melville, therefore, often appears as one of ruins, shards, or fragments. The prospect that all is surface vexed him, and in his fiction he continuously notes the deceits and superfluity of surfaces as much as surfaces being promissory of a hidden depth to be exposed. Surfaces are at once the necessary avenue to what is below and a thick layer that impedes access to a sub-terra incognito. Paradoxically, moreover, the detritus of time piles up, surface-upon-surface, with accumulated strata acquiring a delusive, fallen weight, an excremental barrier to primordial or Edenic time.

Three passages – respectively, naturalistic, ethnographic, and historio-meta-physical – can serve to highlight Melville's preoccupation with weighty layers or the tension between surface and depth. The first comes from the travel sketch "The Encantadas or Enchanted Isles," published in 1854. The sketches were based on Melville's brief visit to the Galapagos Islands as a young man. Charles Darwin had also voyaged to the Encantadas, on the ship *The Beagle*, taking scrupulous notes of finch beak variety in his 1838 narrative of his trip (Fig. 5).

Darwin, his observations not yet coalescing into his theory of evolutionary descent, ordered Nature's specimens into a visual table; Melville, surveying Nature, sees a world emptied of value and composed of mass only:

> Take five-and-twenty heaps of cinders dumped here and there in an outside city lot; imagine some of them magnified into mountains, and the vacant lot the sea; and you will have a fit idea of the general aspect of the Encantadas [...]. It is to be doubted whether any spot of earth can, in desolateness, furnish a parallel to this group [...]. (Melville, "Encantadas" 126)

Darwin's drawing, contrasted with Melville's roughly contemporary verbal sketch, may iconically present the end line of Enlightenment tabular narrative, as it exhibits a species' horizontal differentiation that just over a decade later would become *historicized* as evidence for evolutionary theory.[5]

The sense of a decrepit, overly thick surface carries over into Melville's more anthropological texts. In *Typee*, his semi-autobiographical novel of a renegade sailor's encounter with Polynesian cannibals published in 1846, the natives' bodies seem incarcerated in their own weightiness and inexorable decay:

---

5   Two excellent essays juxtaposing Melville and Darwin in respect to their youthful voyages to the Galapagos Islands are Franklin, "The Island Worlds of Darwin and Melville"; and Howarth, "Earth Islands: Darwin and Melville in the Galapagos." See, also, Wilson, "Melville, Darwin, and the Great Chain of Being."

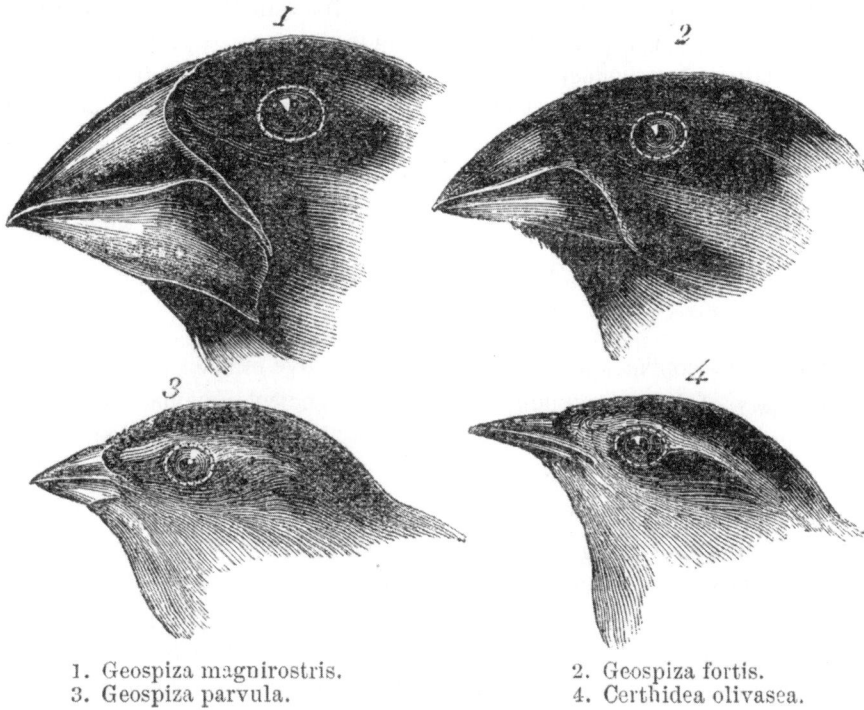

1. Geospiza magnirostris.
2. Geospiza fortis.
3. Geospiza parvula.
4. Certhidea olivasea.

Fig. 5: Drawing of finches, for Charles Darwin's *The Voyage of the Beagle* (1838).

[On] four or five hideous old wretches […] time and tattooing seemed to have obliterated every trace of humanity […]. [The] bodies of these men were of a uniform dull green color – the hue which the tattooing gradually assumes as the individual advances in age […]. Their flesh, in parts, hung down upon them in huge folds, like the overlapping plaits on the flank of a rhinoceros […]. These repulsive-looking creatures appeared to have lost the use of their lower limbs altogether; sitting upon the floor cross-legged in a state of torpor. (Melville, *Typee* 93-3)

The Eurocentric perspective is not entirely Melville's (in the larger context of the novel, the first-person narrator is treated ironically), and yet the anxiety of impenetrability is. The script of unintelligible tattoo markings – a fleshy, stratified surface, grotesque in its density – denies all hermeneutical exploration. Otherness here entails maximal surface weight; what these natives lack, collectively, are faces that gaze back – they are indeed faceless in respect to their "humanity."

The third passage, from an unpublished private journal, recounts Melville's visit to an Egyptian pyramid. Here, paradoxically, there is an alienating surface whose blank "vastness" is inseparable from a "cunning and awful" depth, unfathomable in its purely other all-too-heavy interiority:

A feeling of awe & terror came over me. Dread of the Arabs. Offering to lead me into a side-hole. The Dust. Long arched way, -- then down as in a coal shaft [...]. I shudder at [the] idea of ancient Egyptians. It was in these pyramids that was conceived the idea of Jehovah. Terrible mixture of the cunning and awful. Moses learned in all the lore of Egyptians [...]. As with the ocean, you learn as much of its vastness by the first five minutes glance as you would in a month, so with the pyramid. Its simplicity confounds you [...]. It refuses to be studied or comprehended. It still looms in my imagination, dim & indefinite [...]. A dead calm of masonry. (Melville, *Journals* 75-8)

Temporality here conflates immediate surface (the "five minutes glance") and the nonimmediacy of remote antiquity (the "idea of ancient Egyptians"). Melville, given some of his key words – "awe," "terror," "dim," and "indefinite" – clearly has been tutored by the aesthetic theories of the sublime of Edmund Burke or Immanuel Kant.[6] But more salient here is Melville's paralysis over the notion of a faceless deity ("conceived the idea of Jehovah") and by extension the faceless *weight* of history, an other or "it" that refuses to reciprocate the subject's gaze or "glance."

So, to sum up thus far, Melville simultaneously intuits the world as lacking in depth *and* as being all-too-weighty. We could attribute this to Melville's existential dread, but I want to propose that the paradox of surface and depth, and his paranoia in the face of hermeneutical blankness, is also closely aligned with the technological sciences of the early-to-mid nineteenth century that offered the imagination, whether novelistic or philosophical, *for the first time*, the very possibility of hidden subterranean strata. Melville's anxiety was exacerbated by nineteenth-century geology, which opened up a temporal corridor into an indefinite past. In that context, the most significant image in the previous passage is not the massive pyramid, but rather the "side-hole," tunneling "down as in a coal shaft."

The Scotsman James Hutton, in 1795, published his *Theory of the Earth* (Fig. 6). In it he proposed that land mass change – from erosion, for example – took place uniformly throughout time. He radically departed from the more conventional "catastrophist" theory that proposed that the earth took shape from a series of cataclysms, such as the Biblical deluge. Hutton's notions revealed that geological effects accumulated slowly only after many long epochs. His ideas were conveyed to the general public through such volumes as Charles Lyell's masterful *The Principles of Geology* (1830-3). Lyell's summation offered the dim vista of endless strata upon strata of anterior time, which could not be calibrated by traditional scales of, say, Biblical-Mosaic genealogy.

In contrast to the Great Chain of Being, which ascends into perfect being, the geological model of strata (as depicted in Fig. 6) descends into sheer blankness. Rosalind Williams aptly comments that Lyell's bottomless illustrations are

6 A respectable, brief introduction to the history of the sublime as an aesthetic-philosophical category, with particular attention to Burke and Kant, is Shaw, *The Sublime*.

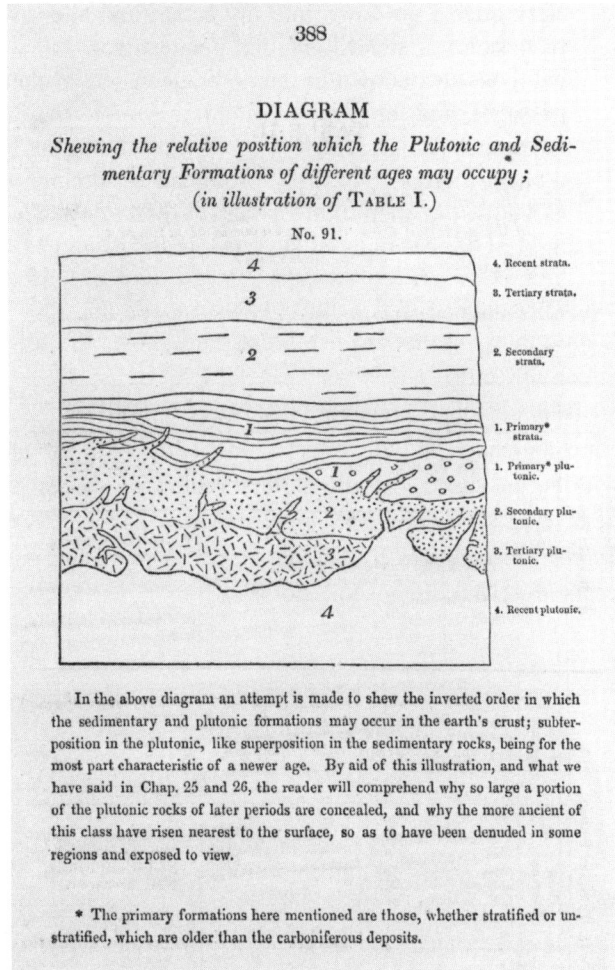

a visual correlative of his "conviction [that] there was no beginning point in the history of the earth" (31).

The paradox of the empirical uncovering of strata should now be clear: even as sacred history was replaced by the evidence of the rocks, the geological images of stratification or a succession of limits ultimately suggested a limitless, open-ended sublimity, a horror vacui. Two examples can indicate how easily geological analogy slipped into Melville's psychological and metaphysical concerns. In *Pierre: or, The Ambiguities* (1852), as a measure of his protagonist's despair, Melville refers to the earth's history as being "surface stratified on surface," below which there is only "vacancy" (Melville, *Pierre* 285). Geological discoveries made Melville intensely aware of time's immensity as a barrier to Edenic plenitude. In this scene from his 1856 short story "I and My Chimney," the unnamed narrator fetishizes a massive chimney rooted in his house's cellar in terms of a metaphoric geological dig into the antediluvian past:

Very often I go down into my cellar, and attentively survey that vast square of masonry. I stand long, and ponder over, and wonder at it. It has a druidical look, away down in the umbrageous cellar there whose numerous vaulted passages, and far glens of gloom, resemble the dark, damp depths of primeval woods [...]. I set to work, digging round the foundation, especially at the corners thereof, obscurely prompted by dreams of striking upon some old, earthen-worn memorial of that by-gone day, when, into all this gloom, the light of heaven entered [...]. (Melville, "I and My Chimney" 357)

Such musings exhibit a metaphysical nostalgia and are kindred to all post-Romantic thinking that at once seeks, and knows the folly of seeking, a foundational core of truth.

It is striking, however, that more empirical-technologically oriented texts, from the same period, reflect kindred longings for the hidden and are obsessed with buried spaces that are at once sublimely suggestive and geologically a matter of layered surfaces. Take, for instance, a passage from the popular volume, *The Subterranean World* by George Hartwig, published in 1871 (Fig. 7), only fifteen years after Melville's short story:

Fig. 7: Drawing for George Hartwig, *The Subterranean World* (1871). The University of Michigan Library, Making of America, http://moa.umdl.umich.edu

A large mine displays unquestionably some of the most interesting scenes of human activity. The restless industry pervading its subterranean caves and galleries impresses the visitor with feelings of wonder akin to those which he experiences when he first sets foot on a man-of-war; and if he feels giddy in seeing the sailor climb the loftiest masts, the sight of the yawning abyss into which the miner undauntingly descends seems terrible to this unaccustomed eye; and as he penetrates further and further into the recesses of this unknown world, his sensations are not rendered more agreeable.

The intricate passages branching out into a mysterious distance; the vaults and high halls faintly illumined here and there by a glimmering lamp; the dark forms emerging every now and then from some obscure recess, and then again, plunging into night, like demon shades [...] all [these sensations] combine to produce an impression which can seldom be made by any scenes above ground. (246)

Hartwig's excitement is one of a tourist of nether realms. Urban historians have chronicled the public's curiosity with edifices built underground, whether sewer systems or transportation tubes or subsurface cities and dwellings imagined in science fiction. The allure of constructing technological or alternative living-space havens *within* the earth, in particular, led to the fantastic novels of Jules Verne – *Journey to the Center of the Earth* (1864) and *Twenty Thousand Leagues Under the Sea* (1869), the latter of which presents us with a mobile "hollow earth" core in Nemo's submarine (see Williams 99 and Pike 155-64). In our own era, we replicate this absorption in vast enclosed spaces through other means, such as all those standardized scenes of science-fiction immensity depicting the interiors of gigantic starships: even in the hollows of machines with hard edges, it appears, we yearn for the earthly sublime.[7] We desire to subdue the interior of the earth, or the silent reaches of space, in the interests of the bourgeoise.

Melville and the Eco-feminist Cavity of Otherness

At what point does Hartwig's phantasmagoria of men-below-the-earth oblige us to transcode the terminology of industrial, subterranean might into a sublimity more explicitly registering matters of gender? What are we to make of men working within the space of, as it were, mother earth, which nonetheless is re-appropriated as a "man-of-war" ship? Melville, who knew firsthand the hazards of naval life, and pointedly alluded to male rape in his novel *White-Jacket* (1850) in the chapter, "A Peep thru a Port-Hole at the subterranean Parts of a Man-of-War,"

---

7   For serviceable surveys of the urban and cultural thematics of the subterranean, see Fitting, *Subterranean Worlds*; Williams, *Notes on the Underground*; and Pike, *Subterranean Cities*.

was uncannily sensitive to regimes that pressured otherwise polymorphous delights into distorted forms of aggression.[8]

To fully explore the latter theme would push this essay into different zones of inquiry and require a more extensive psychoanalytical excursion into Melville's paranoia over carceral spaces as well as a much more expansive query of how gender inflects the excavatory, technological sublime than can be given here. Nonetheless, it is easy to see Melville as being intrigued by the possibility of cavernous spaces that just *are*, which require no hyperboles of hermeneutic deep-diving or narratives of suffocating anxiety.

In the same year that Moby-*Dick* came out, 1851, Louis Agassiz, an immigrant Swiss who taught zoology at Harvard, published his *Principles of Zoology*. Agassiz glibly takes confidence in surfaces re-surfaced:

> It is evident that there is a manifest progress in the succession of beings on the surface of the earth [...]. The Creator['s] [...] aim, in forming the earth, in allowing it to undergo the successive changes which Geology has pointed out, and in creating successively all the different types of animals which have passed away, was to introduce Man upon the surface of the Globe [...]. (qtd. Wilson 134)

For Agassiz, there is only succession, a "manifest progress" of continual lateral replacements; there is no hidden depth, no otherness. Ishmael's discourse in *Moby-Dick*, by contrast, recognizes depths that are deep because they are absolutely other to ourselves:

> But far beneath this wondrous world upon the surface, another and still stranger world met our eyes as we gazed over the side. For, suspended in those watery vaults, floated the forms of the nursing mothers of the whales, and those that by their enormous girth seemed shortly to become mothers [...]. One of [...] [the] little [whale] infants, that from certain queer tokens seemed hardly a day old, might have measured some fourteen feet in length, and some six feet in girth. He was a little frisky; though as yet his body seemed scarce yet recovered from that irksome position it had so lately occupied in the maternal reticule; where, tail to head, and all ready for the final spring, the unborn whale lies bent like a Tartar's bow. The delicate side-fins, and the palms of his flukes, still freshly retained the plaited crumpled appearance of a baby's ears newly arrived from foreign parts. (Melville, *Moby-Dick* 387-8)

Here Melville adopts what we may call an eco-feminist release from his masculinist, hermeneutical urge, and conceives the weight and depth of otherness as a cavity of being – a "watery vault" – that need not and cannot *be placed*.

---

8   For the best discussion of Melville's anxieties about carceral spaces, see Casarino, *Modernity at Sea* (32-42).

Melville was strongly drawn to depth's irresistible call. His urge is, of course, a manifestation of what we call the "Romantic" sensibility, which is always attuned to where a limit edges into unlimited or indefinite dimensions. In addition, though, as with perhaps all of the images in Melville that fantasize unearthing a buried space, there is an eco-Oedipal aspect. Such might seem rather at odds with the metaphysical and scientific lineages I've been charting in this essay. In fact, however, Melville's ambition is to cut through inauthentic, deracinated modes of being and to find a home, emergent from the soil, beneath all surface detritus. The desire for autochthony, for indigenous being: is it not a desire to exist in the cavities of the earth, to find a *there* that becomes a *here* where there are no orphans?[9]

It is likely that fuller exposition of the metaphorical history of deep geological spaces or temporality would require a rigorous feminist-psychoanalytical approach conjoined with a fresh archival understanding of scientific epistemic shifts.[10] So, too, such an exposition would need to have folded within it the story of the transition from a pre-Modern to an entrepreneurial-global attitude. What perhaps in the long arc is of most interest is that the Baconian mystery of the depths as intellectual treasure continued to prevail when the depths also meant merely materials to be extracted from the bowels of the earth, bringing the local and isolated into the surface fold, the enveloping global spread of capitalism. The history of the sublime-as-depth in its full techno-industrial, metaphoric, and gender parameters has yet to be written.

One unsettling irony of that history would be that the tradition of the sublime could have provided a profound counter-narrative to racism – its fixations on exteriors, whether physiognomies or skin pigment – and to all those scientific and quasi-scientific efforts to measure the inessential as the essential. Melville, in exemplary fashion, having peered into the depths, had scorn for the *shallowness* of race discriminations. Unfortunately, the Romantic allure of depth, especially in the latter half of the nineteenth century, also led to the exoticizing of the Orient and Africa as realms of the unknown, of benighted darkness and strange taboos. Romanticism's capacity for progressive critique thus became compromised, and in that sense it may be that Melville's metaphysics are wondrously – and yet to the shame of other discourses conflating geographies of the inward and outward – idiosyncratic.

9   My argument that Melville should be interpreted in global/geological, nonnationalist terms parallels the movement, developing over the last decade in American Studies, to reorient the field to a more planetary perspective. See, especially, Buell, *Writing for an Endangered World*, and Dimock and Buell, eds., *Shades of the Planet*.

10 Melville's anguished longing for a luminous, earthly, internal hollow resonates with the psychoanalytical gloss Jean-Joseph Goux provides on holy sanctuaries in his *Symbolic Economies*: "Distilled in the emptiness of the sanctuary is the acceptance of the law of the dead (invisible, unrepresentable) father as a necessary condition for nonincestuous desire for the female *hollow*. The imageless temple is, on one hand, the Father's vault, but it is also the void of femininity, now tolerable and even desirable: the woman's cavity" (147).

References

Bacon, Francis. "Novum Organum." *Works*. Ed. James Spedding, Robert Leslie Ellis, and Douglas Devon Heath. 14 vols. London: Longmans Green, 1875.

Blumenberg, Hans. *The Legitimacy of the Modern Age*. Translated Robert M. Wallace. Cambridge, MA: MIT Press, 1985.

Buell, Lawrence. *Writing for an Endangered World. Literature, Culture, and the Environment in the U.S. and Beyond*. Cambridge, MA: Harvard University Press, 2001.

Casarino, Cesare. *Modernity at Sea. Melville, Marx, Conrad in Crisis*. Minneapolis: University of Minneapolis Press, 2002.

Darwin, Charles. *The Voyage of the Beagle*. 1838. Reprint, intro. Steve Jones. New York: Random House, 2001.

Dimock, Wai Chee, and Buell, Lawrence (eds.). *Shades of the Planet: American Literature as World Literature*. Princeton: Princeton University Press, 2007.

Fabian, Johannes. *Time and the Other. How Anthropology Makes Its Object*. New York: Columbia University Press, 1983.

Fitting, Peter. *Subterranean Worlds. A Critical Anthology*. Middletown, CT: Wesleyan University Press, 2004.

Foucault, Michel. *The Order of Things. An Archaeology of the Human Sciences*. New York: Random House, 1970.

Franklin, H. Bruce. "The Island Worlds of Darwin and Melville." *The Centennial Review* 11 (1967): 353-70.

Gliddon, George R. *Ancient Egypt. Her Monuments, Hieroglyphics, History, Archeology, and Other Subjects Connected with Hieroglyphic Literature*. New York: Wm. Taylor & Co., 1847.

Gould, Stephen Jay. *Time's Arrow, Time's Cycle. Myth and Metaphor in the Discovery of Geological Time*. Cambridge, MA: Harvard University Press, 1987.

Goux, Jean-Joseph. *Symbolic Economies. After Marx and Freud*. Translated Jennifer Curtiss Gage. Ithaca: Cornell University Press, 1990.

Hartwig, George. *The Subterranean World*. London: Longmans, Green, and Co. 1871.

Howarth, William. "Earth Islands: Darwin and Meville in the Galapagos." *Iowa Review* 30.3 (2000): 95-113.

Hutton, James. *Theory of the Earth*. 1788. Whitefish, MT: Kessinger Publishing, 2004.

Irwin, John T. *American Hieroglyphics. The Symbol of the Egyptian Hieroglyphics in the American Renaissance*. Baltimore: John Hopkins University Press, 1983.

Kircher, Athanasisus. *Mundus Subterraneus [...]*. Amsterdam: Janssonius & Wyerstrat, 1664-5.

Levinas, Emmanuel. *Basic Philosophical Writings*. Ed. Adriaan T. Peperzak, Simon Critchley, and Robert Bernasconi. Bloomington: Indiana University Press, 1996.

Lacan, Jacques. *The Four Fundamental Concepts of Psychoanalysis. The Seminar of Jacques Lacan, Book 11*. Ed. Jacques-Alain Miller. Translated Alan Sheridan. New York: Norton, 1981.

Lyell, Charles. *The Principles of Geology*. Vol. 3. London: Murray, 1833.

McPhee, John. *Basin and Range*. New York: Farrar, Straus and Giroux, 1981.

Melville, Herman. *Journals*. Ed. Howard C. Horsford, with Lynn Horth. Evanston, Ill., and Chicago: Northwestern University Press and the Newberry Library, 1989.

---. *Moby-Dick*. 1851. Ed. Harrison Hayford, Hershel Parker, and G. Thomas Tanselle. Evanston, Ill., and Chicago: Northwestern University Press and the Newberry Library, 1988.

---. *The Piazza Tales and Other Prose Pieces, 1839-1860*. Ed. Harrison Hayford, Alma A. MacDougall, and G. Thomas Tanselle. Evanston, Ill., and Chicago: Northwestern University Press and the Newberry Library, 1987.

---. *Pierre: or, The Ambiguities*. 1852. Ed. Harrison Hayford, Hershel Parker, and G. Thomas Tanselle. Evanston, Ill., and Chicago: Northwestern University Press and the Newberry Library, 1968.

---. *Typee. A Peep at Polynesian Life*. 1846. Ed. Harrison Hayford, Hershel Parker, and G. Thomas Tanselle. Evanston, Ill., and Chicago: Northwestern University Press and the Newberry Library, 1968.

---. *White-Jacket; or, the World in a Man-of-War*. 1850. New York: New American Library, 1979.

Miller, David C. (ed.). *American Iconology. New Approaches to Nineteenth-Century Art and Literature*. New Haven: Yale University Press, 1993.

Nancy, Jean-Luc. Simon Sparks ed. *A Finite Thinking*. Stanford: Stanford University Press, 2003.

Pike, David L. *Subterranean Cities. The World Beneath Paris and London*, 1800-1945. Itaca: Cornell University Press, 2005.

Poe, Edgar Allan. *Poetry and Tales*. New York: Library of America, 1984.

Rossi, Paolo. *The Dark Abyss of Time: The History of the Earth and the History of Nations from Hooke to Vico*. Translated Lydia G. Cochrane. Chicago: University of Chicago Press, 1984.

Shaw, Philip. *The Sublime*. New York: Routledge, 2006.

Stephens, John Lloyd. *Incidents of Travel in Central America, Chiapas and Yucatan*. 2 vols. 1841. Dover Publications, 1969.

Valades, Didaco. *Rhetorica christiana ad concionandi, et orandi usum accommodata*. Perugia: P. Petrutium, 1579.

Williams, Rosalind. *Notes on the Underground. An Essay on Technology, Society, and the Imagination*. Cambridge, MA: MIT Press, 2008.

Wilson, Eric. "Melville, Darwin, and the Great Chain of Being." *Studies in American Fiction* 28.2 (2000): 131-50.

Contributor Biographies

Stefan Altekamp teaches Classical Archaeology at the Humboldt-Universität zu Berlin (Germany). His major publications are books and editions on Greek architectural ornaments, Italian colonial archaeology in Libya, posthumanistic classical archaeology (with Mathias Hofter and Michael Krumme), the contemporary significance of archaeology (with Knut Ebeling), notions of the underworld in classical antiquity (with Kathrin Schade), and classical archaeology and national socialism. He is currently working on a new book called *Rekonstruktion. Monumentale Inszenierungen der Archäologie* (Reconstruction. Monumental Stagings of Archaeology).

Dominik Collet studied history and the history of art in Göttingen, Bamberg, Norwich, and Madrid, earning his PhD at Hamburg University. His book *Die Welt in der Stube* (The World at Home, 2007) investigates early modern museums as a site of cross-cultural encounter and examines the impact of exotic artifacts on the history of science. He is now a lecturer in Early Modern History at Göttingen University. His interests lie in the fields of the cultural history of colonial encounter, comparative environmental history, and the relationship between art and science in early modern Europe.

Johannes Fabian is Professor Emeritus of Cultural Anthropology at Amsterdam University (Netherlands). Among his many books are *Time and the Other. How Anthropology Makes Its Object* (1983), *Power and Performance* (1990), *Language and Colonial Power* (1991), *Remembering the Present* (1996), and *Out of Our Minds. Reason and Madness in the Exploration of Central Africa* (2000). Most recently, Fabian has completed two books, a collection of essays called *Memory Against Culture. Arguments and Reminders* and a monograph, *Ethnography as Commentary. Writing from the Virtual Archive* (both published in 2008).

Bruce A. Harvey is Associate Professor of English and Director of the Humanities Program at Florida International University, Miami (USA). He received his Ph.D from Stanford University. In *American Geographics. U.S. National Narratives and the Representation of the Non-European World, 1830-1865* (2001) and a number of articles, he has explored U.S. selfhood and national identity in relation to global geographical contexts. His research interests also include pre-Civil War American literature and culture, literary and culture theory, and cross-cultural contact zones (current focus: Polynesia). He is now completing a cultural studies book project, entitled *The Muse of Melancholy in the New World. Essays on Location, Mourning, and Cultural History*.

Sünne Juterczenka is a Historian and currently holds a post doctoral research fellowship at the Graduate Center for the Study of Culture at the Justus-Liebig-Universität in Gießen (Germany). As a postdoctoral fellow at the graduate school "Cultural Contact and the Discourses of Scholarship" at Rostock University, she developed a research project on the media representation of eighteenth-century geographical discovery. She received her Ph.D from the University in Göttingen, where she was also a doctoral fellow at the former Max Planck Institute of History. Her doctoral thesis was published in 2008: *Über Gott und die Welt. Endzeitvisionen, Reformdebatten und die europäische Quäkermission in der Frühen Neuzeit*.

Lars-Christian Koch is Head of the Department of Ethnomusicology and the Berlin Phonogramm Archiv at the Museum of Ethnology in Berlin (Germany), and Professor for Ethnomusicology at the University of Cologne. He has conducted field work in Gujarat, Calcutta, Santiniketan, and Kolkata (India), as well as in Seoul (South Korea). His research focuses on the theory and practice of North Indian raga music, organology (with special focus on instrument manufacturing), Buddhist music, aesthetics of music in intercultural perspective, music and medicine, media and ethnomusicology, popular music and urban culture, historical recordings, and music archaeology. His major publications include *Zur Bedeutung der Rasa-Lehre für die zeitgenössische nordindische Kunstmusik. Mit einem Vergleich mit der Affektenlehre des 17. und 18. Jahrhunderts* (1995).

Susanne Lachenicht is a post doctoral researcher and lecturer in history at Hamburg University (Germany) and a research assistent at the Laboratoire FRA.M.ESPA DIASPORAS (CRNS – UMR 5136) Université de Toulouse 2 – Le Mirail (France). She has been a visiting fellow at All Souls College, Oxford, and a research fellow at the Herzog-August-Bibliothek, Wolfenbüttel. Her publications include: (as editor) *Religious refugees in Europe, Asia, and Northamerica, 16th-21st centuries* (2007) and *Information und Propaganda. Die Presse deutscher Jakobiner im Elsaß, 1791-1800* (2004) Her latest monograph is due to appear in 2009: *Hugenotten in Europa und Nordamerika. Immigrationspolitik und Integrationsprozesse in der Frühen Neuzeit (1548-1787)*.

Gesa Mackenthun teaches American Studies at Rostock University, Germany. Her research centers on the analysis of colonial discourse in the Americas and postcolonial theory. Her publications include *Fictions of the Black Atlantic in American Foundational Literature* (2004), *Metaphors of Dispossession. American Beginnings and the Translation of Empire, 1492-1637* (1997), and (coedited with

Bernhard Klein) *Sea Changes. Historicizing the Ocean* (2004). Since fall 2006 she has chaired the interdisciplinary doctoral program on "Cultural Encounters and the Discourses of Scholarship," and she is currently working on a project on nineteenth-century American travel writing and scientific discourse called "The Conquest of Antiquity."

Susanne Mühleisen is Professor of English Linguistics at the University of Bayreuth (Germany). Her main reserach interests are sociolinguistics, Creole Studies, intercultural pragmatics, and English word formation. She is the author of *Creole Discourse. Exploring Prestige Formation and Change Across Caribbean English-lexicon Creoles* (2002), and editor of *Politeness and Face in Caribbean Creoles* (2005).

Andreas Nehring is Professor of Religious and Mission studies at the Friedrich-Alexander Universität in Erlangen (Germany). Between 1993 and 1996 he held a lectureship in religious science at the Gurukul Lutheran Theological College and Research Institute in Chennai (Madras, India) as well as guest professorships at the Union Biblical Seminary in Pune and the United Theological College in Bangalore (India). He is the author of *Rissho Kosei Kai. Eine neubuddhistische Religion in Japan* (1993), *Fundamentalism and Secularism* (1994), and *Orientalismus und Mission* (2003). He is currently working on a project on postcolonialism and religion.

Samuel Rubenson is Professor of Church history at Lund University (Sweden). He was born in Addis Ababa, Ethiopia and studied theology, history, Arabic and the languages and literature of the Christian Orient in Lund and Tübingen. He received his doctoral degree in theology from Lund University. His research has focused on the Oriental churches and on early monasticism, and he has lectured extensively in Europe and the Middle East, where he also lived in Cairo and in Jerusalem. He has published widely on the rise of monasticism, the appropriation of Graeco-Roman culture by the early Christians, and medieval as well as modern aspects of the history of the Coptic Church and of Ethiopia, and is the coeditor of *Acta Aethiopica*.

Claudia Schnurmann is Professor of North American and Atlantic history at Hamburg University (Germany). Her major publications include *Kommerz und Klüngel. Der Kölner Englandhandel im 16. Jahrhundert* (1991) and *Atlantische Welten. Engländer und Niederländer im Amerikanisch-Atlantischen Raum 1648-1713* (1998), which was awarded the OAH Foreign Language Book Prize as the best study worldwide on American History in 2001. She also wrote a book about the economic encounter between Europe and America: *Europa trifft Amerika. Atlantische Wirtschaft 1492-1776* (1998). Her fields of research include the history of North America, the Caribbean, and Western Europe, early modern cultural history, nineteenth-century US history with special emphasis on Methodist families in Ohio and Indiana, California history and ego-documents, land and landscapes as well as German-Atlantic networks.

Frank Schulze-Engler is Professor of New Anglophone Literatures and Cultures at the Johann Wolfgang Goethe-Universität in Frankfurt am Main (Germany). His publications include his doctoral thesis on East African literature, *Intellektuelle wider Willen: Schriftsteller, Literatur und Gesellschaft in Ostafrika 1960-1980* (1992), coedited volumes of essays on *African Literatures in the Eighties* (1993), *Postcolonial Theory and the Emergence of a Global Society* (1998) and *Crab Tracks: Progress and Process in Teaching the New Literatures in English* (2002), as well as numerous essays on African, Indian, and Caribbean literature, comparative perspectives on the new literatures in English, postcolonial theory, transculturality and the cultural dimensions of globalization. A monograph on *Experiences of Globalized Modernity in African, Asian and Caribbean Literatures in English* is in preparation.

Benedikt Stuchtey is Deputy Director of the German Historical Institute in London (U.K.), and a Lecturer at Konstanz University (Germany). His research interests are the theory and history of historiography, Western European (esp. British, French, and German) imperialism from the eighteenth to the twentieth centuries, the history of science, and family history. His major publications include *W.E.H. Lecky (1838-1903). Historisches Denken und politisches Urteilen eines Anglo-Irischen Gelehrten (1997)*. He has also edited a volume on *Science Across the European Empires, 1800-1950* (2005), and coedited three volumes: *Across Cultural Borders. Historiography in Global Perspective* (2002), *Writing World History, 1800-2000* (2003), and *British and German Historiography (1750-1950). Traditions, Perceptions, and Transfers* (2000). He is currently preparing for publication a major study on the history of European colonial expansion and its critics from the eighteenth to the twentieth centuries, and embarking on a new project on the history of child adoption in the twentieth century.